(Mor

The Family, Politics and Social Theory

'8

0710205228

The Family, Politics and Social Theory

D.H.J. Morgan

Department of Sociology
University of Manchester

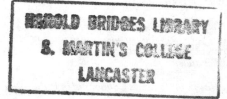

ROUTLEDGE & KEGAN PAUL
London, Boston, Melbourne and Henley

First published in 1985
by Routledge & Kegan Paul plc

14 Leicester Square, London WC2H 7PH, England

9 Park Street, Boston, Mass. 02108, USA

464 St Kilda Road, Melbourne,
Victoria 3004, Australia and

Broadway House, Newtown Road,
Henley on Thames, Oxon RG9 1EN, England

Set in 10 on 12 point Century
and printed in Great Britain
by Butler & Tanner,
The Selwood Printing Works, Frome, Somerset BA11 1NF

© *D.H.J. Morgan 1985*

Library of Congress Cataloging in Publication Data

Morgan, D. H. J.

The family, politics, and social theory.
Bibliography: p.
Includes index.
1. Family.   2. Sociology.   I. Title.
HQ728.M573   1985   306.8'5   84-27570

British Library CIP data also available

ISBN 0-7100-9943-6 (cloth)
  0-7102-0522-8 (pb)

Contents

Acknowledgments

Any list of acknowledgments must be an arbitrary affair. I know that I have obtained useful suggestions, references and even more helpful encouragement from the following at various times during the development of this present project: Claire Bacha, Bob Chester, Susan Edwards, Ann Fillmore, Ronald Frankenberg, Janet Finch, Iris Gillespie, C. Margaret Hall, Chris Harris, Frances Hepworth, Diana Leonard, Nod Miller, Valdo Pons, Kate Purcell, Robert Rapoport, Shirley Rheubottom and Liz Stanley. Equally, I am aware of many other conversations, discussions and influences from colleagues, friends and students both within the University of Manchester and the wider sociological community. The usual apologies, both to those whose names have been excluded from the above list and to those whose names have been included.

A special acknowledgment to Janice Hammond who typed the manuscript so speedily and efficiently; to Janet for her friendship and encouragement during the final stages of this book; to Jacqui and Julian who constantly reminded me not to take myself, or sociology, too seriously.

Introduction

It is now some nine years since the publication of my first book, *Social Theory and the Family* (Morgan, 1975). During the intervening period I have been gratified by many friendly suggestions, criticisms and comments. Recently it has been suggested that the book be revised, in order to take account of the many developments that have taken place in the field since the book was written. While I recognised the force of this argument, I was unhappy about the suggestion of a simple updating for several reasons. In the first place, *Social Theory and the Family* did not claim to be a 'survey of the field' but an argument, using a selective number of issues, around the confrontation between certain orthodox sociological treatments of the family and certain more heterodox approaches coming for the most part from outside sociology. Consequently while some of the sources cited would now seem to be dated, what should be important is the usefulness or otherwise of that argument. Any further writing should be a development or reworking of the argument rather than a simple updating of the sources used. In the second place, the changes that have taken place in the field have been so great and so widespread that a piecemeal textual revision would seem to be out of the question. Finally, any book is very much a product of a person's autobiography and times, both of which are subject to change. An attempt simply to revise or update a book may obscure or distort such changes.

Outside of the changes that have taken place in the field, the author and the wider social context, I have become aware of certain defects in *Social Theory and the Family*. My treatment of 'women as a social class' is probably the least satisfactory in the book and not simply because of the datedness of the material used. Close to the time of publication, Juliet Mitchell's *Psychoanalysis and Feminism* (Mitchell, 1975) came out and the 'domestic labour debate' got fully under way. Some of these developments I ought to have predicted or given more recognition. But a more important criticism might be made of my overall stance, one which, while sympathetic, tended to relativise and 'sociologise' the feminist critique and experience, rather than appreciate the full importance of this critique for my own practice and writing. My stance was somewhat too detached, a product no doubt of my own gender. I now consider that it is probably impossible, and certainly impolitic, for a male academic to write about feminism although it is essential for that academic to be aware of the continued feminist critique and research and to make himself aware of the implications of that for his own practices in all aspects of his life. Feminism as a movement cannot become, at least at the present time, a topic for male investigation although the central themes and concerns of feminist theory must have consequences for a male sociologist who would claim some sympathy with the Women's Movement (Morgan, 1981).

It is hoped, therefore, that this whole book – the issues chosen for investigation and the way of approach – reflects the impact of feminism on my thinking in the intervening years. While I include some specific treatment of certain issues raised by Marxism and feminism in Chapter 10, I do not feel it necessary to provide a comprehensive discussion of the feminist literature that has appeared since 1975. Very full and adequate accounts already exist (Barrett, 1980; Oakley, 1981) and will no doubt continue to be produced.

Another defect of the original book lay in my concluding chapter. Poster, in a brief footnote reference to my book (Poster, 1978, p. 207), notes that I do 'not attempt a theory of the family'. While I specifically eschewed the project of providing a theory of the family, instead providing a loosely linked checklist of points to be considered in family analysis, I was aware that I had done little more than provide a critical account of some contrasting theories. I still feel that the aim of providing a 'theory of the family' presumes too much; however, there is a need to develop a somewhat more integrated discussion than was provided in the concluding chapter of *Social Theory* and I attempt this in my conclusion to the current book.

Of the other chapters in the original book I am reasonably content with the one on functionalism. There is little of the kind of functionalism outlined in that chapter to be found any more (to such an extent that it might prove necessary to rehabilitate some of the more positive features in the Parsonian account (Harris, 1983) although some aspects of it may be seen to have been incorporated within systems theory. Since these theories are important, particularly in terms of their consequences for therapeutic interventions into the family, I deal with them in Chapter 7. More interestingly, some of the problems associated with Parsonian functionalism re-emerge in Marxist accounts of the family, and many of the criticisms directed towards the former can also be directed at the latter.

The chapter on 'kinship' (probably the one most often singled out for appreciation) similarly seems to stand and I would not wish to make any substantial alterations to it. Some of the issues, however, re-emerge in different parts of the present text. The chapter, 'The Modern Family: A Success Story?' dealt with a rather specific issue and while the claim continues to be made, but with less frequency, the older concern about the 'decline of the family' seems to have displaced it. In a sense the whole of my first section here may be said to deal with some of these questions.

I feel that the section on R.D. Laing in the earlier book, while being very much of its time, is still useful particularly in its attempt to rework the Laingian material into a sociological framework. But much of this has, subsequently, been treated in literature deriving from family and marital therapy and some versions of systems theory, and there seems little need for any further extended treatment of Laing's work as a whole. More detailed studies, in fact, already exist (Collier, 1977; Sedgwick, 1982). I quite liked my own chapter on 'Sex and Capitalism', particularly in some of the rather scattered hints about the possibilities of a sociology of sexuality. But, as Diana Leonard pointed out in a review, I was not sufficiently aware of the diversities of sexualities or, more accurately, failed to place this at the centre of my analysis. I am also rather unhappy about a certain archness of tone that creeps into this chapter, possibly reflecting some personal uncertainties. In any event, there does not seem to be much need for further treatment of Reich *et al.* although there is some discussion of sexualities in Chapter 2.

But the main grounds for preparing a completely new book are chiefly in terms of the changes that have taken place since 1975. The enormous growth of feminist literature and theorising is the most obvious one. The British Sociological Association held a conference dealing with gender issues in 1974; a second conference on the subject took place in 1982. Between those times there were many debates about theory – domestic labour and patriarchy, for example – re-examinations of the inter-relationships between class and gender, gender and the family, the state, education, sexuality and so on. Few areas of socio-logical work, including the actual practices of sociologists in their various institutions, remained untouched by these develop-ments although in some cases the actual effect may still be small, a fact sometimes enhanced by the possible ghettoisation of 'Women's Studies' (Stacey, 1981). Clearly, the subject of the family has been profoundly affected by these developments although it is still possible, as I shall show, for certain kinds of family theorising to continue as if nothing had happened.

Probably the second major change in the field has been the rapid growth in the development of historical studies of the family (Anderson, 1980). I discuss some aspects of this development in Chapter 8. In many cases, of course, this growth in the historical study of the family has been shaped by concerns deriving from the Women's Movement.

In recent years much theorising in Britain has been influenced by European theoretical developments – Marxist, pheno-menological, structuralist, hermeneutic, etc. Perhaps as a reaction against structural-functionalism and various modes of positivistic research, developments in the United States have received much less emphasis, particularly in the study of the family. Nevertheless, it can be argued that, for example, the versions of systems theorising that are currently available deserve at least as much attention as, say, Althusserian Marxism. Moreover, such theories have an influence beyond the areas of academic discourse in the practice of marital and family therapy and hence require our critical attention. The areas of therapy themselves both represent an important area of professional, and sometimes state, intervention into marriage and the family, and also a more syncretic set of theories about relationships within and, to a lesser extent, outside the family.

This point about the growth of family therapy may be generalised in order to remind us that sociology theories do not develop autonomously in academic ghettos but arise in response to various developments in other sectors of society. Here I should note the development of a more explicit politicisation of the family. In a sense it may be argued that the family is always involved in politics; yet the growth of public political pronouncements about the family and the growth of official and quasi-official interventions into the family have been particularly striking in recent years. These developments are themselves related to the inter-relations between the crises in Western capitalism and the Welfare State. In this book, I have attempted to treat this problem, focusing upon one particular example of state intervention in the family and placing that intervention in a widening set of analytical circles.

If there have been changes in the field and in the social and political context in which the field has developed, there have also been changes in my own life. My marriage came to an end, relatively amicably, my children have grown into adolescence and early adulthood, I have experienced marital therapy, at the receiving end. I have gained several new friends and have learned the value of friendship. What all this adds up to is difficult to assess without deeper self-analysis. In general, these personal and political experiences have deepened my scepticism about the institutions of marriage and the family but also about the searches for 'alternatives'. I am more than ever convinced that what is needed is a change in focus, in the way in which we look at and conceptualise the 'family'. Politically, this is as likely to mean focusing our attention on non-familial relationships as on the family itself.

ON FAMILY THEORY AND THEORISING

'Family theory', writes Berardo, 'has become a fully-fledged and respectable area of specialisation' (Berardo, 1980, p. 728). This statement occurs in the course of a decade preview, introducing a review of the previous decade's work in family research and theory. What is meant by 'family theory' is indicated in the next paper which traces the growth of such theories in the 1970s (Holman and Burr, 1980, pp. 729–41). Somewhat unrigorously,

Introduction

the authors divide theories into three categories: major theoretical approaches; minor theoretical approaches; and peripheral approaches. In the first category we find included interactionist, exchange and systems theories; in the second there is mention of conflict, developmental and behavioural theories, ecosystems and phenomenology. Peripheral theories include the 'generally abandoned' structural-functionalism, psychoanalytical and learning theories. Feminism and Marxism do not, it seems, get a look in even as peripheral approaches. (Conflict theory refers to writers such as Sprey, Duke and Turner; elsewhere Sprey makes the point that a conflict framework is not necessarily Marxian (Sprey, 1979, p. 130).)

Although the next paper (Scanzoni and Fox, 1980, pp. 743–56) refers to the 'virtual torrent of sex-role studies', it would be difficult to find any indication in this review of the 1970s of the growth of the feminist movement and its extended influence in all areas of study. The brief episode when the *Journal of Marriage and The Family* (*JMF*) was apparently taken over for a couple of issues by feminists seems to have been expunged from the editorial memory (*JMF*, 1971).

What this omission does highlight is a radical difference in the understanding of the word 'theory'. For Holman and Burr, and for most of the contributors to the *JMF Retrospective*, theory is a rigorous, scientific exercise. Theoretical developments involve formalisation and refinement, the identification of control and test factors, the identification of logical connections between parts, and so on (Holman and Burr, 1980, p. 735). Feminist theorising, on the other hand, does not look like this. It tends to be devoid of the kind of systematisation favoured in the *JMF* survey, indeed regarding such theorising with some suspicion. It tends to see the touchstone of theory in terms of its links with experience and with its ability to bring about change. It tends not to go in for the kind of meta-theorising typified by the Holman and Burr article. In short, it would appear that two different kinds of theoretical game are being played and the refusal of the one to admit the other is paralleled by the other's unwillingness to play by the patriarchally established rules.

Elsewhere in the *JMF* survey, things seem to be much the same. Such familiar topics as pre-marital sex (still!), mate-selection, parent-child relations, marital quality, family power, racial and cultural variations and kinship continue to appear.

Newer topics included violence in the family, 'non-traditional family forms', 'same-sex intimate relationships' and marital and family therapy. The latter topic clearly reflects the explosive development of this kind of therapy in the United States but some of the other, newer topics might owe their presence to the more widely diffused critique developed within the Women's Liberation Movement. This, however, is not acknowledged or entertained as a possibility and it is only a paper on cross-societal family research that sees the impact of the Women's Movement on the emphasis on changing sex-roles (Osmond, 1980, pp. 995–1016).

To develop this argument about the two contrasting understandings as to what is meant by 'theory' a little further, I shall consider two particular texts. The first is Burr's *Theory Construction and the Sociology of the Family* (Burr, 1973) and the second is a collection edited by Thorne and Yalom, *Rethinking the Family*, which is subtitled 'Some Feminist Questions' (Thorne and Yalom, 1982). I do not claim that these two texts exhaust the range of possible activities that might come under the label of 'theorising'; they should serve, however, to illustrate the point that theorising is not necessarily a unified activity and that the label refers to a variety of quite different games.

An example of the kind of theorising particularly favoured in the *JMF Review* is Burr's *Theory Construction and the Sociology of the Family*. His Preface gives a clear indication of the author's understanding of the nature of sociological enquiry and theorising. Referring to the work of Homans, Simon, Zetterberg, Stinchcombe, Dubin and Blalock and the resulting 'progress in the methodology of theorizing', Burr writes:

> The result is that not only has a need been created to reformulate earlier theoretical formulations to clarify, systematize, and integrate them, but we now have the methodological tools to do it. (Burr, 1973, p. vii)

This contains some of the key words – 'clarify, systematize and integrate' – together with a model of social sciences as a cumulative, progressing and integrated discipline. He goes on to list the long-term goals of his theoretical project which range from identifying 'theoretical propositions that seem to be useful in understanding processes in the social institution of the family' to developing 'computer simulations with some of the theoretical models' (*ibid.*). These key words and orientations are re-emphasised and reaffirmed throughout the book.

An early chapter deals with the nature of deductive theory. The basic ingredients of such a theory are: '*variables, propositions* that identify *relationships, explanation* that is provided by logically *deducing* and the principle of *ceteris paribus. . . .*' (*ibid.*, p. 22, his emphasis). A theoretical proposition 'has to be sufficiently abstract and general that it is possible to explain more specific phenomena through the process of deduction' (*ibid.*, p. 30). Theory represents, therefore, a set of relationships between abstract propositions linked, sometimes through sets of propositions of a lower order of generality, to particular hypotheses. The main body of the book deals with a set of familiar issues in the sociology of the family – marital satisfaction, mate-selection, pre-marital sexual relationships, kinship and power – in each case identifying some of the central concepts, pointing out ambiguities where these exist, attempting to establish propositions and linking these, where possible, to more general propositions about social behaviour and using these sets of propositions to generate hypotheses. These hypotheses are then examined in the light of the existing research. The aim is not so much to reject or accept certain hypotheses but to demonstrate the theoretically established links between variables and to highlight those areas where gaps exist in the research, or where there is a particular lack of conceptual clarity. The emphasis throughout is on the provisional nature of his 'findings' and on the need for a concerted and cumulative scholarly assault on the issues thrown in sharp relief by his approach.

It has been noted that the *JMF* survey did not include feminist theory among its list of theoretical contributions. The collection edited by Thorne and Yalom returns the compliment and few, if any, of the theorists seen as central by the *JMF* appear in their pages. Yet, both would claim to be engaged in theoretical enterprises in connection with the family.

The editor, Barrie Thorne, sets out, in an admirably concise summary form, five themes central to the feminist rethinking of the family:

1 The challenge to prevailing assumptions about the family, particularly to the ideology of 'the monolithic family', beliefs

in the naturalness of the family and functionalist or role-
theory approaches to the family, particularly those which
reify the family.

2 The attempt to 'reclaim the family . . . for social and historical
analysis'. This involves a decomposition of the family
into 'underlying structures of sex and gender, and of
generation'.

3 Following from this theoretical 'decomposition' is the
recognition that different family members do not necessarily
experience and understand the family in different ways.

4 Questions about family 'boundaries' are rendered
problematic.

5 Finally, there is an ambivalence or tension between values
of individualism and equality on the one hand, and those of
nurturance and collectivity on the other (Thorne, 1982,
pp. 2–3).

The collection of papers that follows is extremely various and
this variety, some might say eclecticism, is one of the main
contrasts between this mode of theorising and the mode advocated by Burr. There are papers by historians and anthropologists, disciplines scarcely recognised by Burr and others who
tend to favour mainstream sociology and social psychology.
Other disciplines represented in this collection are philosophy,
literature and law. There are papers on 'The Fantasy of the
Perfect Mother', on 'Maternal Thinking', on 'Why Men Resist'
and on 'Family and Class in Contemporary America'. A central
concern running through several of the papers is to do with
ideology and with the ideological construction of family and
gender. It should perhaps be noted that this particular collection
differs in some respects from other collections of papers which
would also claim the label feminist, for example Friedman and
Sarah's *On the Problem of Men* (Friedman and Sarah, 1982). For
example, the Thorne and Yalom collection includes papers by
men and deals with points of difference or contention within
the feminist movement, for example over the use of the word
'patriarchy' or approaches to motherhood. Nevertheless, the
contrast between this collection and the approach advocated by
Burr and others remains striking.

There are a variety of fairly obvious differences between the
two approaches. The approach of Burr and others like him aims

for conceptual rigour, replicability and precision; in contrast, the feminist approach is more eclectic, much 'looser' in style and approach. The former would see the word 'scientific' as signifying worthwhile goals to strive for and models to emulate; the latter would tend to treat the word somewhat more sceptically. For the former, 'experience' may be a potential source of bias or difficulty; for the latter 'experience' is close to the heart of the enterprise. These and other differences between the two approaches are either obvious or could reasonably be extrapolated from the two texts. But there are some other differences which are worth exploring in a little more detail.

1 Burr and his 'school' tend to favour a somewhat pre-Kuhnian model of scientific progress: slow, painstaking but essentially cumulative. A sentence at the end of the book illustrates this tone perfectly:

> It has taken decades of work by extremely able scholars to make the progress that has been made. The point here is that the job that remains is *very very* large. (Burr, 1973, p. 270, his emphasis)

While there are obviously scholarly differences and debates – several of them are outlined in the main body of his book – there is an underlying unity behind these differences. A possible implication of this approach is that voices at odds with this model may be placed outside the scientific community, denounced as 'ideological', 'political' or 'strident'. More recently, Burr has taken the argument a stage further by arguing that studies of the family within different disciplines have progressed so far that it is possible to speak of the birth of a new discipline, 'Famology' (Burr and Leigh, 1983).

The model of social science and the social science community which emerges from the Thorne and Yalom collection (and other feminist or critical writings) if it emerges at all, is much more untidy. There would appear to be much less concern with scientific credentials, the boundaries of the community of practitioners would seem to be much fuzzier and, while no doubt there would be some agreement that progress is possible and has been achieved, the growth of the discipline(s) would be seen in much more dialectical terms, in terms of conflict, disagreement and ideological struggle.

2 In the volume by Burr there is little attempt to define the key terms which appear throughout its pages such as 'marriage', 'family', 'parenthood' and 'kinship'. In a work which aims for some kind of conceptual rigour this taken-for-granted quality would seem to be a little odd. Presumably there is an assumption that everybody, at least everybody within the assumed scientific community, knows what these words mean, that they are part of their shared understandings. An example of this taking of implicit everyday understandings occurs where Burr is explaining the nature of categorical variables: 'An example of this type of variable is sex. Sex has two categories of male and female, and people fall into one category or the other.' (Burr, 1973, p. 9.) Everyday language, practice and understandings would no doubt agree with Burr. But might not one measure of a scientific orientation be an unwillingness to take even apparently basic and obvious distinctions for granted?

In contrast, the Thorne and Yalom volume takes as topics for investigation what Burr and others use as given resources. Their aim, through the use of historical, anthropological and sociological analysis, is to deconstruct terms such as 'marriage' and the 'family'. A feminist orientation, as Dorothy Smith and others have maintained, almost necessarily entails the adoption of a sceptical orientation towards a male-dominated social science within which women have been marginalised for so long. This may sometimes lead to the use of other taken-for-granted terms: 'patriarchy' in some works (but not in Thorne and Yalom) or possibly even 'gender' (Matthews, 1982; Morgan, 1985).

3 Most of the propositions or axioms in Burr's study do not in fact refer to society or societies but to individuals. Homans-type propositions about the relationship between interaction and sentiments or similar propositions about the relationships between norms and behaviour imply a strong kind of methodological individualism, one which is, however, for the most part unexamined. In terms of prevailing disciplinary boundaries, the theory is social-psychological rather than sociological. History, on the other hand, would appear to be some kind of a problem or the source of difficulties in the analysis. While there are individualistic forms of analysis present in the Thorne and Yalom volume (I shall be examining Goode's paper in a little

more detail later), the overall emphasis would seem to be at the societal, comparative or historical level while, in some cases at least, seeking to avoid the dangers of an excessively holistic approach through a reference to experience.

4 The key difference between the two orientations is, of course, in their treatment of gender. Detailed examination of this topic will be deferred until Chapter 10. It is possible, in Burr's study, to find some scattered references to gender, especially in his chapter on marital satisfaction. The point is, however, that gender differentiation does not form a significant point of departure in any of his explorations into family theorising. It is not entirely certain whether this weakness is inherent in this kind of approach or whether it is something peculiar to Burr's own work. Certainly a distinguished founding father discovered gender to be an important variable in the analysis of marriage and suicide rates (see Morgan, 1982) and even if we were to ignore Durkheim, a near associate of Burr, F. Ivan Nye, has produced an interesting study of family roles which does take gender as a major axis for analysis (Nye *et al.*, 1976). Gender, of course, forms a main consideration (along with age) in the process of deconstructing the 'family' advocated in the Thorne and Yalom volume.

It should be clear that this has not been an exhaustive account of the available modes of theorising within the study of the family. Other modes will emerge in subsequent chapters. The aim has been to present, in sharp contrast, two highly divergent claims to theoretical thinking. It should also be clear to the reader that my own preferences are for the second mode, what I have referred to here as 'feminist' but which I should like to expand to 'critical'. This is not to say that the first approach, almost unknown in current British work on the family, should be rejected out of hand. Anything that demands of its practitioners clarity of definition and a careful explication of hypothesised relationships, and that sociological enquiry should move beyond the merely descriptive, and which emphasises that the task is often difficult and frustrating, cannot simply be dismissed as trivial or reactionary. What, then, are the grounds for my preference for the more critical approach to theorising?

Ultimately, such a choice must rest upon value judgments: moral, political and perhaps even aesthetic. Perhaps *especially* aesthetic. However, I should also like to argue that the critical mode of theorising is to be preferred, firstly, in that potentially at least it does take account of a much wider range of factors. The works cited by Burr and which are often included in the *Journal of Marriage and the Family* tends towards a narrowness of focus, based largely on a methodological individualism and a strong tendency towards quantification. Indeed, an analysis of papers submitted to and published by the *JMF* discovered that papers were more likely to be published if they used complex statistics, while papers that used no statistics at all were rarely submitted and, if submitted, least likely to be accepted (Miller, 1980, pp. 1032–4). Historical, anthropological or psychoanalytical work (to name three areas that remain popular within critical theorising) tend to be ignored or marginalised. The *JMF*, for example, would seem to favour the more quantified forms of historical scholarship. Critical and feminist approaches would seem to be more capable of achieving the promise outlined in Mills's *The Sociological Imagination*, the imaginative linking of biography and history (Mills, 1959).

In the second place, again potentially at least, critical theorising does appear to be more skilful at forging the tools of its own criticism and so stands at some distance from some of the more optimistic models of cumulative and steady scientific achievement found within the more positivist kinds of theorising. For one thing, critical theorising is more likely to be actively cognizant of the role of the theorist or the investigator in the problem under investigation. For another, the unwillingness to take the everyday terms and practices for granted can be, and often is, turned on to the critical projects themselves, and consequently there is a constant strain towards 'depassing', historicising and relativising. Of course, plenty of examples may be provided of critical rigidity from within the critical 'school' (especially from within some versions of Marxism) but it would appear that an approach that is not clearly or unambiguously wedded to a somewhat narrow version of scientific progress does have greater opportunities for self-criticism even if these opportunities are not always taken.

But are these two orientations so irreconcilable? A paper by Goode (1982) in the Thorne and Yalom volume entitled 'Why Men Resist' suggests that some meeting points are possible. This paper does not, in my opinion, stand alone. Burr *et al.*

Introduction

(1979) include a chapter on phenomenological approaches to the family in a collected volume of papers about family theories (McLain and Weigert, 1979) and several of the papers in a collection edited by Cromwell and Olson on power in the family include critical or phenomenological references or orientations (Cromwell and Olson, 1975). The book by Nye has already been mentioned as a text which has considerable critical potential while being very close in style to the Burr approach (Nye *et al.*, 1976). Nevertheless, the Goode paper should serve as an apt illustration.

This paper addresses itself to the question of why men resist what the author rather optimistically assumes to be an irreversible trend towards equality between the sexes. Goode argues that the question as to why men resist is not as simple or obvious as some feminist writers might suggest, and seeks to place his analysis in a wider context of 'the sociology of subordinates'. Here we have a set of fairly general principles being used to explain and to examine a particular instance. Generally, his argument may be seen as an elaboration of Simmel's point about the superordinate being more able to forget his dominance than the subordinate her subservience. A variety of questions are raised and suggestions made, for example:

6. Men view even small losses of deference, advantages, or opportunities as large threats. Their own gains, or their maintenance of old advantages are not noticed as much.
(Goode, 1982, p. 137)

Goode would be the first to maintain that what we have are a set of issues to be explored, hypotheses and linkages to be tested. He also recognises that men are not exactly the same as other superordinates and that differences as well as similarities must be explored; he is not dealing therefore with reified sets of timeless propositions. Indeed, the essay as a whole shows a recognition of history and the possibility of change. His essay is a political as well as a theoretical contribution.

This is not a plea for some simple-minded amalgam or synthesis of these or any other two radically different paradigms. It would probably be best to admit that what we have here are, indeed, radically different orientations, and that for most of the time we shall be called upon to make some kind of a choice between them. However, Goode's paper does

14

represent an interesting, if rare, example of a work open to the potentialities within each orientation. Generally, however, it shall be argued that such alternative paradigms exist not to be fused or amalgamated in some grand synthesis but to provide points of criticism and questioning. While this present book will attempt to remain faithful to a critical sociology, it will also realise that the very promise of such an approach lies in its reflexivity and constant self-questioning and that the source of such questioning can sometimes come from very different paradigms and approaches, even such an approach as that advocated by Burr.

OUTLINE

The present book is divided into two parts. Part I is more directly concerned with the current 'debate' on marriage and the family. I start with a consideration of the Home Office/ DHSS publication, *Marriage Matters* (Working Party on Marriage Guidance, 1979), a text which serves as both an impressive example of the way in which private marital problems may become constructed as public issues and, through an exploration of some of the wider ramifications, as an illustration of a more general theoretical concern, namely the examination of the family as an institution uniquely located between the private and the public, between the micro and the macro, the personality and the society and between process and structure. *Marriage Matters* is explicitly about marital counselling, its changing nature and the need for greater research and coordination. I therefore consider, in the second chapter, some of the themes and contradictions within marital counselling. The very fact of *Marriage Matters* (and subsequent discussions and publications), however, also points us in another direction, namely towards a consideration of the involvement of the state in marital and family affairs. Chapter 3, therefore, considers some issues in the complex overlaps and interplays between state, politics, ideology and the family. Chapter 4, in the light of discussions in the previous two chapters, returns to *Marriage Matters*, this time seeking to examine it for exclusions and absences, particularly the absence of considerations of class and gender inequalities.

Introduction

The concluding chapter of Part I examines in some more detail the social construction of the 'problem of divorce'.

In the course of considering *Marriage Matters* and its various ramifications and implications I came across some wider questions of sociological theory, of ways in which we understand and analyse the family and its place in society. Part II is entitled 'Themes', and examines a variety of ways of treating the family. I prefer the looser term 'themes' to the more academically respectable 'paradigms', partly because I find the delineation of paradigmatic boundaries a somewhat problematic operation, and more because the approaches I have outlined represent quite different kinds of methods which may often cut across different paradigms. In the first place, for example, I consider the work of the Rapoports, a style which seeks to be comprehensive, eclectic, empirical and policy orientated. Chapter 6 serves, therefore, as a link to what has gone before. In the next chapter, I move into a very different world, that of various forms of systems theorising in the study of the family. Chapter 8 considers the rapidly expanding field of family history. Here I do not attempt to cover all the issues raised but instead focus on the particular contributions that historical analysis may make to family theory. The historical approach does, of course, include people working within a variety of paradigms. Chapter 9 attempts to examine studies located within what might very loosely be called the 'phenomenological school'. The final chapter considers approaches derived from various critical schools, notably those located within a Marxist and/or feminist tradition and my conclusion will attempt to draw some of these family themes together.

The use of the term 'family theme' has two related meanings, one specific and one general. The specific meaning derives from the usage by Hess and Handel (Hess and Handel, 1950, pp. 11–13, 268–73). Here they are talking about shared feelings and understandings between family members that serve in various ways to define that family experience to its members, to define who and what we are. They represent kinds of stories that family members tell to and about each other. At the same time, and this is perhaps not fully recognised by the authors, the construction of the family theme is an outcome of the intervention of the analyst and therapist and hence, necessarily, is not simply a private or internal

16

matter. More generally, I use the term to indicate various bundles of issues, each more or less distinct themselves, but each more or less obviously to do with the family. These might be better described as family issues although the deliberate use of the term 'family themes' is a reminder that my aim should be to point to links between what is experienced and understood within 'families' and the way in which these 'families' are shaped by wider social and historical circumstances.

A NOTE ON METHOD

How I came to write this book the way that I have is a matter of personal and intellectual autobiography. While I have attempted to be faithful to the developments within the field since the publication of *Social Theory and the Family* this book does not claim to provide a comprehensive literature survey. I have attempted to adopt the approach of a social anthropologist, not the kind who attempts to cover the whole of a culture under a set of appropriate institutional headings, but rather the kind who examines social dramas, moving out from these dramas to considerations of wider history and social structure. Authors, government and quasi-official publications, etc. stand in the place of 'good informants'; I hope that I have taken these informants seriously although not simply at face value. I shall attempt to draw the reader's attention to these questions of 'method' at those points in the text where they most directly arise. At this point I shall say simply that I consider reading to be 'real research', to be empirical research which raises many of the problems encountered by the field worker who encounters, more directly, individual actors and social situations.

Part I
ISSUES

If there has been something of a growth in the interest in the family in Britain in recent years this growth has little to do with developments within the academic discipline of sociology. A glance through the articles accepted for *Sociology*, the journal of the British Sociological Association, should underline this point. The stimulus to family studies, broadly conceived, would appear to come from two sources: the continuing development of feminist-inspired scholarship, both within and outside sociology, and the growth of more policy-orientated studies represented, most recently, by the work of the Study Commission on the Family. The more specific feminist or feminist-inspired studies will be considered in Chapter 10. In this first part, I shall concentrate on the more policy-orientated studies, focussing on one such intervention, the publication of *Marriage Matters*.

The apparently narrow focus in Part I is justified on two grounds. In the first place, I intend this part to serve as an extended case study of the issues which should be at the heart of family analysis: the intersections of the private and the public, the intimate and the political, the interpersonal and the structural. In the second place, I hope to show that theory is not some kind of rarified luxury at the opposite pole from the immediate and the practical, but that in all kinds of ways, directly and indirectly, it is built into the ways in which people attempt to confront everyday concerns and practical issues. I also hope to show, in the second part of this book, how theory can hold up these concerns and issues to critical scrutiny.

1 *Marriage Matters*

In 1975 a Working Party was set up by the Home Office in consultation with the DHSS. Its terms of reference were:

> To assemble information relating to marital problems and the provision of helping services as regards:
>
> (a) the existing range of relevant activities and liaison between the individuals and bodies concerned;
> (b) the use being made of marriage counselling;
> (c) coordination of knowledge and treatment methods;
> (d) training;
> (e) research
>
> and to produce a consultative document containing suggestions for any improvement in relation to these matters. (Working Party on Marriage Guidance, 1979, para. 1)

The report of this Working Party was produced in 1979 under the title *Marriage Matters*. A one-day conference on the report was held in London in April 1980, chaired by Judge Jean Graham Hall and addressed by Robert Morley of the Family Welfare Association, Lord McGregor and Sir George Young, Minister of State at the DHSS. A transcript of this conference was produced towards the end of 1980.

The Appendix to *Marriage Matters* lists twenty-two persons as members of the Working Party, six of whom are listed as serving at earlier stages. Of these twenty-two members, five (including the chairman and two secretaries at different times) were connected to the Home Office and the Probationary Service;

21

five were connected with the Social Services Division of the DHSS; five were connected with various aspects of marital counselling and guidance (including the National Marriage Guidance Council and the Catholic Marriage Advisory Council); and four had some medical or psychoanalytical responsibilities. Men slightly outnumbered women on the Working Party as a whole. In the list of bodies that served as witnesses, there was a high representation from social work agencies or the social services and from medical bodies. Medical authorities dominated the list of independent witnesses. A similar spread of witnesses, but concentrated in the marriage guidance, medical and legal fields, can be gathered from the list of participants to the conference which also included several clergy, some academics and three members of the House of Lords.

Something of the flavour of the report can also be gained from the sources consulted and cited in its pages. There are several references to official reports such as the Finer Report on one-parent families and the Denning Report on procedure in Matrimonial Causes. There are, as might reasonably be expected, several references to reports or publications by the National Marriage Guidance Council (NMGC), and similar bodies and books published by or about the Tavistock Institute also stand out. In contrast there are relatively few works by sociologists cited: these include Gorer, a brief reference to Goldthorpe *et al.*, the Rapoports, McGregor and Jacques.

To cite these sources is not to imply any conspiracy theory. The Working Party did not have the time or resources to commission a survey or study of its own and it can be assumed that existing networks were used and mobilised in order to seek out witnesses and source material. But it is important to note that this way of proceeding did have the effect of editing out some of the more discrepant views on marriage and divorce which might have been available. Such views would include not only those from members of the feminist movement but also, at the other extreme, fundamentalist religious views.

Marriage Matters is not, it must be stressed, a particularly conservative document, and certainly not a Conservative document. Indeed, the general tone of the report may be described as humane and liberal, concerned with the pain sometimes brought about by divorce and marital disharmony, but not concerned in any simple or direct way to support a traditional model of Christian marriage. This sense was certainly reinforced by attending the 1980 Conference: if feminist views appeared to be placed at the margin so too did the view of one clergyman who objected to the failure of the Working Party to consider the Christian sense of marriage (*Marriage Matters*, 1980, p. 38).

Much can be gained from a study of the style of the report, indicated in the following quotation:

> We have come to the view, which we think is shared by many informed people in the educational and caring services, that the part which marital disharmony plays in the creation of social problems is a frequently neglected cause of personal and social distress. Similarly we consider that, in marital relationships, the potential for the development of the couple and their children is too often overlooked in the current climate. We hope that this document will enable these views to be more widely investigated. (Working Party, *op. cit.*, para. 10)

This paragraph indicates the general sense of humane concern which informs the document as a whole; the references to 'personal and social distress' and to 'potential for development' indicate this. Yet we can also see a particular definition or understanding of marriage being presented here, one which emphasises interpersonal relationships and growth, a therapeutic, possibly medical model of marriage. Of particular significance is the opening sentence which, it might be imagined, constitutes standard official discourse. The 'We', while clearly referring to the collective membership of the committee, both indicates a consensus or a striving for consensus and, as becomes apparent, a membership of a wider community of 'informed persons in the educational and caring services'. There is more than a hint here of the informed, objective professional as against the relatively uninformed or more subjective lay-person. It is other people's pain, other people's marriages and divorces we are concerned with, not our own experiences of love or betrayal or separation. This theme will be considered in more detail in a later chapter but it is something that must inevitably pervade much of the discussion around this document.

Issues

These considerations of style become more relevant when we examine some of the specific themes of the report. Here I shall outline some of the main themes leaving until later chapters a more detailed treatment.

(i) THE DEFINITION OF MARRIAGE

In the first place, marriage is defined in terms of cohabitation rather than in terms of a formally defined legal or religious status:

> We decided to interpret the word 'marital' as including any cohabitating relationship between a man and a woman, and the evidence showed that almost all organisations offering a counselling service interpreted the word similarly. (Working Party, *op. cit.*, para. 3)

This understanding is in line with more recent, although not uncontested, legal understandings (Polak, 1975; Samuels, 1976), yet whether it adequately represents the more complex patterns of meaning that exist elsewhere in society remains open to question. As we have seen, the report had to confine its sources of evidence within a relatively narrow professional range; it is likely that some sections of the population, while accepting 'cohabitation' particularly as a temporary pre-marital status, might still operate with notions of 'proper' weddings and being 'properly married' (Leonard Barker, 1978; Leonard, 1980). The issue of definitions will be taken up again in Part II of this volume; here it is enough to note that the definition offered is in accordance with the general 'liberal' approach of the report as a whole.

This definition of marriage as 'any cohabiting relationship between a man and woman' clearly excludes homosexual couples from its field of reference. It also excludes any reference to relationships involving more than two individuals, patterns of complex marriage or communal arrangements, for example. While this is probably in accordance with general understandings of the word 'marital' (and it is likely that many members of these 'alternative' arrangements would also reject the label 'marital' and notions of conventional heterosexual coupledom (Plummer, 1978)), the definition does have an excluding effect. Since the concern of the report is with 'relation-

24

ships' and since these interpersonal relationships are seen as a source of growth and maturity, the exclusion of possibilities other than the heterosexual couples does imply, if not state, some kind of hierarchy of human relationships. However liberal-minded the general tone of the report, it still continues to give a privileged place to heterosexual marriage.

This formal definition of marriage is in accordance with the report's general understanding of the substantive content of marital relationships. The analysis in the report hinges on a set of oppositions, roughly ranked along some kind of time continuum from the past to the present. Thus marriage, in the view of the report, has shifted from being an institution to a relationship. Here the word 'institution' is used in a sense somewhat different from the general sociological understanding of the word as almost any more or less stable clustering of roles, behaviour and expectations. A more specialised formal understanding is adopted: an institution here is something which has all kinds of formal, legal or quasi-legal underpinnings and circumscriptions, chiefly from the Church and state. To treat marriage as an 'institution' implies that the main points of reference for what constitutes appropriate marital statuses and roles comes from outside and 'above'; to call it a 'relationship' implies that the main points of reference come from within, from the parties themselves. That this variation of the move from 'status' to 'contract' has some paradoxical features (i.e. professionals stating what constitutes the 'relationship') is a point that will be taken up later.

This shift from institution to relationship, charted in the report, has important qualitative consequences. Marriage has become a 'source of personal well-being and happiness' (Working Party, 1979, para. 1.4). These shifting expectations for the marital relationship are related to rising affluence and standards of living; the very forces which contribute to these rising standards of living, however, also serve to give marriage an important set of new functions in terms of primary relationships:

> In so far as marriage affords a supportive environment within which the emotional development and growth of the individual is fostered, it can contribute to adaption and help to compensate for the loss of a more communally defined identity. (*ibid.*, para. 2.27)

25

The view of marriage that is being presented, therefore, is very much a view of marital counsellors; the key words are 'growth', 'close', 'personal'. Sexuality plays a key part in this close interpersonal relationship.

There are one or two other aspects of this definition – in its substantive rather than formal aspect – which are worthy of comment. In the first place, the report appears to accept the argument that marriages, as they have moved from institution to relationship, have become more egalitarian and companionate. This is seen as a corollary of the fact that marriages are based upon the personal choice of the spouses and have increasing expectations in terms of personal growth. In the second place, it would appear that this model of marriage is increasingly widespread; the only important source of possible variation considered in the report is in terms of different ethnic groups. In the third place, the particular understanding of marriage adopted here also entails the recognition of the need for divorce and separation in some cases. It is part of the general liberal orientation of the authors of the report that divorce is seen as being necessarily related to their particular understanding of the changing nature of marriage. However, in spite of these rising divorce rates, marriage is seen as a statistically normal goal, part of the normal expectations of adolescent men and women (*ibid.*, para. 2.22).

The report adopts the now familiar argument that rising divorce rates do not necessarily indicate a repudiation or essential weakening of the institution of marriage (Morgan, 1975, Ch. 3).

(ii) THE NATURE OF MARITAL PROBLEMS

The central concern of *Marriage Matters* is with marital disharmony and marriage breakdown. In common with several recent publications and in keeping with the general liberal tone of the report, the emphasis is not on the morality of divorce or separation or simply on the consequences of marital breakdown for the partners or children but more on the multiple 'personal and social distress' occasioned by such crises. The authors of the report operate with a notion of a benevolent state that has, over the years, come to be concerned with the well-being of its members. This concern is threatened on a 'large scale' by marital disharmony. The problem, therefore, is understood not so much in terms of divorce as such but in terms of the multiplicity of problems that accompany marital disharmony and divorce and the cost of all these individual problems added together. There are the problems of one-parent families, legal aid, the recognised and unrecognised costs in terms of calls upon medical services, and so on. This 'massive level of domestic change' presents a particular challenge to all the agencies that come into contact with marital problems and their consequences: not just marriage guidance counsellors but also GPs, social workers, the legal profession, the police, and so on. The business of constructing a social problem will be examined in more detail in a later chapter but it may be noted here that what is involved is a shift in focus: from seeing divorce (taking this to be the key, although not the sole, indication of marital disharmony) as a concern of a number of individuals and their children, to seeing it as some kind of nodal point connecting a whole set of diverse institutions and spheres of life. The 'problem of divorce', therefore, is not simply a problem of scale but also a problem in terms of the range of ramifications.

On the question of causation, the report tends to lack precision. To a large extent, as has already been indicated, the rising rate of divorce and marital disharmony can be seen as a necessary corollary of marriage's move from institution to relationship. Put simply, an emphasis on freedom of choice in relation to whom one might marry also implies a freedom of choice in the matter of getting unmarried. There are also loose references to the turbulence of our times (*ibid.,* para. 2.21 – a somewhat out of context reference to a work by Emery and Trist), while the advice columnists consulted by the Working Party gave emphasis to the unreal expectations that many parties bring to a marriage (*ibid.,* para. 2.23). In general, divorce and marital disharmony seem to be accepted as facts of life, consequences of the times in which we live and the central issue is that of finding ways of coping with the levels of distress brought about by these facts.

Again, the approach to marital problems is in keeping with the general liberal tone of the report, a desire to solve personal and societal problems rather than to make judgements or to offer punitive sanctions. Yet, just as in the case of the definition of 'marital', we also find the subtle underlining of a particular

27

version of marriage. Just as marriage is seen as the central relationship in our society, providing opportunities for personal growth and fulfilment, so too 'marital disharmony' is seen in interpersonal dynamics and in terms of the psychic costs accompanying such disharmony. The notion of the heterosexual dyad as a key relationship in our society is reaffirmed, even when considering the costs and contradictions involved in such a relationship. This centrality is reaffirmed by the treatment of marital disharmony as a nodal 'connecting' problem; the move is from marital disharmony to personal distress to costs to the economy rather than, say, the quite reasonable assumption that things might flow in the opposite direction, i.e. from economy to relationship.

(iii) THE NATURE OF THE PROFESSIONALS

Throughout the report there are references to the 'caring professions' and to 'caring agencies'. More specifically, it can be seen that the report adopts a 'medical' model of marriage, a theme to be explored at greater length in the next chapter. One indication of the use of this model is to be found in the following passage, where the report considers the value of research obtained by actual practitioners in the course of their work:

> There is a resemblance here to the understanding between the clinician and the patient whose condition he is studying. Many investigations are permitted by the individuals investigated only because, as patients, they are assured of treatment. The medical model offers another analogy; the head or senior member of a 'firm' in hospital will often be involved in research while at the same time he has responsibility for patients and for teaching. (*ibid.*, para. 8.8)

Elsewhere, in the same chapter (para. 8.12), the report notes that the Working Party considered using the term 'clinical studies' to refer to one kind of research that ought to be encouraged but decided against the term 'because of its medical connotations' in favour of the more neutral sounding 'case studies'. I suspect the term was abandoned with some regret; certainly the tone of the report reflects a familiarity with medical practice at all levels throughout its text and appendices.

The term 'medical model' is used here in two overlapping senses. In the first place there are, as we have seen, constant references to different sections of the medical profession. The fact that the only Appendix to be reproduced in full comes from the Royal College of General Practitioners is a fact of some significance, reflecting not simply the fact that individuals often turn to their GPs for marital advice in the first instance but also, it might be suspected, the general attractiveness of the doctor-patient relationship and the general prestige of medicine, at least in the eyes of the members of the Working Party. In the second place, it would appear that the Working Party sees some kind of analogy between the doctor-patient relationship and the professional-client relationship reflected in marital counselling. This is not to say that marital disharmony is regarded as a 'disease' but rather a reflection of the belief that marital problems belong to that category of problems which are best treated by dispassionate, professional (or trained amateur) advice. The concern is with improving the quality and co-ordination of the advice that is offered and the research upon which it is based.

This medical model also appears in another dimension. Just as we have witnessed a shift in the nature of marriage from institution to relationship, so has there been a shift from marriage guidance (with the emphasis on repairing a marriage) to marital counselling, with a stress, where appropriate, on helping individuals to part with dignity. Counselling is held to be more 'non-directive'. The shift in reference group, it might be said, is from priest or minister to doctor or therapist. I have encountered more than one marriage guidance counsellor who wishes that the name of the NMGC be changed to something more explicitly aligned with 'relationship counselling'.

It has been seen how, in this report, marital breakdown is treated as a connecting phenomenon, that is a phenomenon that can, with a shift in viewpoint, be seen at a nodal point of a set of hitherto unconnected institutions and processes. This shift in point of view is paralleled by the emphasis in the report on coordination. The report is aimed largely at a whole range of practitioners and members of the caring professions and caring agencies who are involved, in some way or another, with marital breakdown or conflict and its aftermath. As we have seen, these include not simply marriage guidance counsellors but also GPs, social workers, solicitors, and so on. As well as a general need for better training and the development of new counselling skills, emphasis is put on the need for greater coordination between these agencies.

The way in which the report treats solicitors is instructive. It notes that: 'As a professional group, solicitors probably have the most experience of marriages at the point of breakdown.' (*ibid.*, para. 7.15.) And yet the report also notes the fact that the solicitor is more likely to be involved on behalf of only one of the two separating partners. There is, therefore, a contradiction between the normal traditions and expectations of members of the legal profession and the coordinated counselling approach advocated by the report. It therefore recommends that solicitors receive some training in counselling skills. The sense being conveyed, therefore, is of a unity of concern. Even the tradition-ally combative elements within the legal profession may be modified in terms of the medical, counselling model.

A variation, and in part an implied criticism of this approach, comes in Robert Morley's address to the Marriage Matters 1980 Conference. Morley, on the whole, is disappointed by the rela-tively muted treatment of conflict in *Marriage Matters*. (He is Director of the Family Welfare Association.) Speaking of the role of the courts he says:

> It might be of better service to the divorcing couple and their children, if in addition to providing them with opportunities to talk through their sadness and anxiety, we also gave them a secure arena where their anger could be discharged, thus enabling the couple to free themselves from each other as marital partners. (Marriage Matters, 1980, p. 8)

Referring to the film *Kramer v Kramer* he says:

> Having discharged all this bitterness they then come together in quite a different way to settle how the child's custody is to be arranged, and a much more amicable process appears to have got going. (*ibid.*)

The differences here seem to be only superficial. Anger and conflict are here seen as being potentially therapeutic – indicated by the use of the word 'discharge' – and hence the same medical or therapeutic model is still very much present.

The penultimate chapter of the report deals with research.

The emphasis here is firstly on the need for a close link between research and practice and for action research. Sociology, in under three pages, is linked with epidemiological studies. There is a reference to a need for 'more coherent and complete statistics about marriage and its breakdown' (Working Party, 1979, para. 8.21), in short, better statistics rather than, say, a critical account of the production of marital statistics or of the categories used. The more detailed reference to epidemiology shows, once again, the underlying medical model. Finally, this section asks for a systematic monitoring of relevant social legislation. Other studies called for come under the general heading of 'organisational studies'.

The link between this kind of research and the medical model should be clear. It is not simply in the use of the term 'epidemiological' and its bracketing with the word 'sociological'. It is in the stress on linking research and practice (we have noted how the parallel with medical research has been made) and the overall positivistic orientation. Research provides a set of tools and understandings which practitioners in the field can use to help them towards a better practice of their skills. A kind of practical circle is created, from practice to research and back to practice. The opportunity for a critical evaluation of professional practice, such as might be provided by historical or more phenomenologically informed studies, is not considered. The medical model remains supreme.

The final piece of the puzzle is fitted in the last chapter, listing various administrative proposals. The need for coordination is reiterated and reference is made to the role of central government. This is not the call for a 'Minister of Marriage' which was referred to in some press accounts of the report. But the report did recommend that the job of coordinating the various practices of different sections of the caring professions and of research with these practices should be the responsibility of a Minister of the Crown. They discuss the relative merits of the Home Secretary and the Secretary of State for the Social Services. In addition to this recommendation was one for the establishment of 'a small expert Central Development Unit for Marital Work' (*ibid.*, para. 10). Science, professionalism and the state are thereby brought together.

In one sense, *Marriage Matters* was very much a product of its time. Possibly, its tone now seems much too muted or gentle in the harsher climate of the 1980s. Calls for greater government intervention (and presumably for greater deployment of resources) might receive less sympathetic attention in a context guided by monetarist policies. More profoundly, perhaps the emphasis on relationships and non-directive counselling might come to be challenged in a general critique of a narcissistic culture (Rapoport and Rapoport, 1982, p. 493). There has probably been a shift towards a greater emphasis on the needs of the children (Pringle, 1974), something which receives only passing treatment in *Marriage Matters*. This omission is tacitly recognised in a latter volume with the title *Family Matters*. This represents the proceedings of a symposium on 'priority for the family' (held at the Royal Society of Medicine) and focuses its attention on the needs of children (Franklin, 1983).

Yet the growth of policy-orientated studies of the family and marriage has continued and is likely to continue for some years to come. In Britain this has been reflected in the various publications of the Study Commission on the Family and the collection edited by Rapoport, Fogarty and Rapoport called *Families in Britain* (1982). This is a collection edited on behalf of a body called The British Committee on Family Research (whose directors include Jack Dominian, John Pinder and Michael Young as well as the three authors already mentioned) which was also responsible for the establishment of the Study Commission. While these publications deal with a much wider range of issues than *Marriage Matters*, there is a certain continuity in terms of tone and overall orientation. In these more recent publications there is the same liberal recognition of diversity (in this case of family forms and experiences) while at the same time they betray a striving for consensus and 'the middle ground'. There is, indeed, a possible contradiction between this recognition of diversity and the emerging emphasis on the need, if not for explicit family policy, at least for some kind of 'family impact statement'. Since the work of the Rapoports is so closely associated with this more recent development in policy-orientated studies, I defer a discussion of these issues to Chapter 6.

2 The medicalisation of marriage

Our books, magazines and television dramas all announce the healing and prophylactic power of parental love and the toxicity that follows closely on its absence. (J. Kagan in Rossi *et al.*, 1978)

INTRODUCTION

In the last chapter it was argued that *Marriage Matters* represented an example of a wider process, namely the adoption of a medical model in relation to the institutions of marriage and the family. In this chapter this theme will be examined more critically and in more detail. In the first place it will be necessary to explicate a little further what is meant by the terms 'medical model' and 'medicalisation'. In the second place one feature of this medical model, the 'counselling model', will be examined with particular reference to recommended texts for marriage guidance counselling. Finally, I shall ask questions about how this model developed, referring in particular to the writings of Foucault, Donzelot and Lasch.

Let us begin by noting an apparent paradox. At one level, the increasing specialised nature of medical practice has been the occasion for critical comment and analysis. For example, Jewson has traced the 'disappearance of the sick-man', out-lining a shift in medical cosmologies over the period 1770 to 1870 from 'Bedside Medicine' through 'Hospital Medicine' to 'Laboratory Medicine' (Jewson, 1976). In general terms this overall shift could be characterised as a 'shift away from a person orientated toward an object orientated category' (*ibid.*, p. 232). In more popular terms this has been characterised in terms of a decline in the treatment of the 'whole person'; in political terms this has been seen as a reification of sickness and disease, mystifying the professional and scientific roles and thereby obscuring some of the structured inequalities in health needs and care.

At another level, however, the title of this chapter seems to imply something of an opposing trend, the growing encroachment of medical ideas, models and practices over areas of life previously excluded from such analysis. The growth of the concept of mental illness and mental health is of course the most striking example, although the increasing use of the word 'therapy' – occupational therapy, marital therapy, etc. – may provide further illustrations. Here the argument is often that the incursion of medical models has served to detach mental and interpersonal processes from wider societal and ethical considerations.

It can be seen that this contrast between two hypothesised trends, the dwindling of the areas of focus of medical practitioners and the encroachment of medical models on to a wider area of life is only a superficial paradox. A large part of the discrepancy can be resolved simply by referring to specialisation; the medical model has grown in terms of the number of areas of life that can be subsumed under it, while, within this growth, there has been increasing specialisation. Thus, psychiatry becomes largely separated from medicine while still adopting something of the original model.

It remains to outline, with a little more precision, what is entailed in this idea of the medical model as it applies to marriage. It is being suggested here that this is more than simply a matter of the fact that people with marital problems (and for the purposes of discussion I shall tend to focus on marital problems as an instance of a wider class of family problems) will often consult their GP, at least in the first instance. Conversely, it is likely that family doctors may still, in some instances, read off family problems from consultations about other, physical matters. *Marriage Matters* makes a lot of this point, that GPs are often inevitably involved in marital counselling and, consequently, need to be advised and informed as to how to proceed and to provide appropriate advice. The medical model, however, is more than this.

1 In the first place, the medical model implies that there exists some class of problems called 'marital problems', that is a class of problems related to the marital relationship in some strong sense and which can, therefore, be relatively isolated for examination and treatment. Marital problems are seen as

problems to do with the complex pattern of emotional, inter-personal and sexual relationships that constitute marriage as the term is normally understood. Marital problems, at least in some versions of the model, are held to be, if not primary, at least of key importance, often underlying other problems of interpersonal relationships. Further, 'marital problems' can often be said to 'underlie' other problems – e.g. financial problems – the latter being some kind of symptomatic expression of the former.

To treat a class of problems called 'marital problems' is to recognise or endorse the centrality of a particular definition of marriage within society as a whole. To refer to marital problems is to enter into some kind of tacit agreement or negotiated understanding between patient/client and professional/therapist about the importance and centrality of this relation-ship. There is, therefore, some kind of agreed understanding about the expectations that partners bring, or should bring, to marriage and about the expectations that therapists/counsellors have of their client's expectations.

2 Secondly, the application of the medical model to marriage implies that there exists a body of professional or otherwise appropriately trained individuals to whom couples with problems defined as 'marital' may turn. The relationship between these professionals and the marital problems is one of reciprocity; the professionals do not simply 'treat' the problems, responding to the initiatives of the client/patient, but are also responsible for defining, at least in part, the problems as 'marital' in the first place. This may occur directly, where a client/patient approaches professionals, perhaps through a variety of possible channels, in relation to some other 'problem' (impotence, a troublesome child or so on) and has that problem reclassified as a marital one; or, indirectly, where the profes-sionals play a part in the definition of marital problems through advice columns, the media and so on.

These professionals (or rigorously selected and trained volunteers in the case of the NMGC) possess the familiar characteristics, ideal typically, ascribed to all professionals, such as concern for the needs of the client(s) and affective neutrality. This last feature is of particular importance, contrasting the emotional turmoils and spirals of the clients' immediate familial relationships with the objective and detached stance of the professional. The professional is like the sympathetic ear of a stranger rather than the friend or relative who may have some kind of real or assumed commitment to particular parties in the dispute. Particular features of trust and confidentiality are also involved as is the fact that the counselling or therapeutic relationship is not normally one of *mutual* disclosure: the patient/client speaks, the practitioner listens. In some cases, this sense of medical quasi-professionalism is enhanced by the location of the counselling session in a medical setting at a hospital or some other building or place associated with, say, the National Health Service.

3 Another often cited feature of professionalism is the existence of a body of specialised knowledge and theory. The practice of marital guidance is informed by a variety of psychological and psychoanalytical theories and by theories and knowledge that have evolved through practice and recorded accounts of that practice. The professional warrant is, so to speak, grounded in this accumulated and inter-related body of theory and reported practice. One consequence of this is the ability, already noted, to redefine symptoms as being symptoms of 'marital problems', to recognise 'evasions' and 'rationalisations', etc. on the part of the patient/client.

4 The sense of professionalism is also heightened by the reference to other professionals for support, guidance and advice and by the fact that the major reference group defining 'correct' procedure is other similarly located practitioners. The use of regular case conferences, training sessions and refresher courses is one of the mechanisms by which this is achieved. That such regular interaction performs important emotional and supportive functions as well as more practical functions, such as exchange of information and updating of knowledge, is recognised by the practitioners themselves and may be seen as being of particular relevance given the problems of involvement and tension often entailed by all forms of counselling. Such regular meetings also help the development of a more coherent professional world-view or ideology, even where – as is clearly the case here – several different and competing theoretical traditions may be involved.

Thus, when we refer to the adoption of a medical model in marital counselling we have in mind the creation of a particular set of problems labelled as 'marital' and the existence of a body of trained persons of professional or quasi-professional status who exist to 'treat' these problems, guided by a cumulative body of universalistic knowledge, the norms of affective neutrality and peer-group control and guidance. This medical model is clearly an ideal type and there are some possible deviations from the model.

In the first place the notion of 'cure' or a solution to the marital problem may be problematic. This has become particularly true as marriage guidance has shifted its emphasis from saving marriages to providing a whole range of guidance, possibly including help for parties wishing to part with the minimum of pain and anguish. Of course, not all physical ailments can be said to have 'cures' either (and the understanding of 'cures' in mechanistic terms is something that has been increasingly challenged) but it can be said that marital counsellors do not, in the eyes of the lay public at least, appear to be searching for 'cures' to marital conflicts in the same way as certain sections of the medical profession may be said to be searching for 'cures' for cancer. A successful outcome to a marital counselling session may be stated in more diffuse terms such as 'getting on better', 'understanding self/partner better', 'feeling happier in oneself' and so on.

In the second place it may be noted that I have been using the terms 'therapy' and 'counselling' almost interchangeably. It is clear, however, that there is at least a difference of emphasis between the two terms. Therapy is much closer to the medical model, has a more clearly defined body of knowledge and theory and is often carried out in a medical setting. Counselling has a more general referent, is often carried out by trained volunteers and is more likely to involve notions of understanding rather than cure. Therapy may be said to be the extension of the medical model into areas of life hitherto defined as non-medical; counselling may be seen to be the formalisation of practices which often take place anyway, say between a tutor and a student, a doctor and a patient or within Citizens Advice Bureaux.

THE GROWTH OF FAMILY AND MARITAL THERAPY

The growth of theory and practice in the area of marital and family therapy has been most striking, especially in the last ten years. Gurman and Kniskern (1981, p. xiii) provide the following figures of membership of the American Association for Marital and Family Therapy:

1970	973
1975	3373
1979	7565

Clearly, the establishment of such an association is itself a significant pointer, an essential stage in the growth and evolution of a profession (see also Gurman, 1973). So too is the growth of journals – such as the *British Journal of Family Therapy* which started in 1979 – and the publication of large collections of readings which bear witness, not only to the phenomenal growth of such a movement, but also to the increasing diversity of schools and orientations that may be subsumed under the general rubric. It is important to note also that this is not simply a development in ways of treating family or marital 'disorders' but in ways of theorising and thinking about the family.

Julia Lawrence refers to 'the historical fact that family therapy was developed in medical practice' (Family Welfare Association, 1973, p. 3) and the medical influence has not diminished over the years. The term 'medicalisation' has been objected to by some marital and family therapists and clearly, if the word is taken to mean some narrow definition which would include hospitalisation and medication, then the objection is well taken. But in a broader sense, in the sense indicated at the beginning of this chapter, the growth of family/marital therapy can be seen as an important stage in the medicalisation of those institutions, that is the placing of those institutions in a framework of medical discourse. Evidence for this is not difficult to find. The titles of books and articles themselves often leave us in no doubt as to the orientations of the authors. For example:

Treating the Troubled Family (Ackerman, 1966)

The Skilled Helper (Egan, 1975)

Brief Casework with a Marital Problem
(Guthrie and Mattinson, 1971)
Family Therapy: The Treatment of Natural Systems
(Walrond-Skinner, 1976)

That the use of terms with medical associations in these titles is more than simply metaphorical is indicated in the backgrounds of the authors who contribute to collections of papers or who sit on the editorial boards of journals such as *Family Process* and the *Journal of Family Therapy*. In three collections of papers on family or marital therapy (Ackerman, 1970; Carter and McGoldrick, 1980; Gurman and Kniskern, 1981) authors with a medical or psychiatric background or with a 'medical', professional address predominate, although sociologists have a somewhat better representation in the earlier Ackerman volume. The editorial board of the first issue of the *Journal of Family Therapy* shows strong representation from the Tavistock Institute, the Bethlem and Maudsley Institutes and the Hospital for Sick Children.

It may be that such evidence is just circumstantial, that the origins or backgrounds of the authors tell us little about their actual orientations. However, the tone and orientation of most of the writings, the language used and the assumptions made hardly detract from this overall impression of the medicalisation of marriage. Take, for example, this sentence:

In the case reported here, my colleagues were impressed by the unconscious agreement between the partners to maintain mutual misperceptions as a defence against the recognition of their underlying problems. (Woodhouse in Introduction to Bannister and Pincus, 1971, p. 5)

Here it is not simply a question of the terms used – 'cases', 'therapy', etc. – but of the general approach which, even while it recognises the necessary involvement of the therapists, maintains a stance which is external and where there is confusion, disturbance and mystification on one side, and clarity, health and insight on the other. Further evidence of the way in which the language reveals a medical orientation is to be found in the Introduction to Gurman and Kniskern's collection where they outline the extensive guidelines drawn up for their contributors. These include: 'The Healthy or Well-Functioning

Marriage or Family', 'The Pathological or Dysfunctional Marriage or Family', 'The Assessment of System Dysfunction' and 'Treatment Applicability' (Gurman and Kniskern, 1981, pp. xv–xvi).

Perhaps a more detailed examination of this medical orientation can be provided. Ackerman, in his Introduction to his collection *Family Process* (Ackerman, 1970, pp. 11–12) examines some of the challenges that are presented to the family therapist. Firstly, there is the task of the delineation of 'the core conflicts of the family and the family defences'. Where there is conflict there are the tasks of helping the family to achieve a clearer recognition of the conflict and its sources, to bring it to a level where it can be tackled and to move away from scapegoating. While these goals would seem to be worthwhile they do presume a straightforward therapist/patient model, with the patient this time being the whole family. This becomes more apparent in the tentative list that Ackerman provides of 'family defences'. These include:

(4) Compensation: escape, diversion, drugs, alcohol, vacation and sexual escapades.
(6) Reorganisation of complementarity of family roles by means of:

   (a) reversal of parental and sexual roles, reversal of parent-child roles
   (b) repeopling of the family: removing or adding persons to the family unit

etc.

What is apparent here is not simply a straightforward thera-peutic stance on the part of the family analyst but a fairly conventional model of family roles and household structure. Once a label has been applied, any form of behaviour may be seen as a confirmation of that label and this occurs as much in the treatment of family 'pathology' as in individual 'pathology' (Smith, D.E., 1978). More recent texts may show somewhat more ambiguity, a greater sense of a tension between a recog-nition of the diversity of human relationships and the weight of the medical model. Framo, for example, is aware of the limitations of the word 'pathology' in this connection, yet feels able to provide a list of some of the ideal principles of healthy or normal functioning in marriage and family (Framo, 1981, pp. 139–40).

It is important here to emphasise two further points. In the first place, it is not argued that family therapy is useless, misguided or even dangerous. It can be all of these just as it can also often be of benefit to family members. If we take Kovel's simple, but open-ended, approach to neurosis – 'the loss of the ability to make choices' – as a guide then there is little one could object to in any therapy that aimed to tackle such conditions (Kovel, 1978, p. 34). But Kovel goes on to point out that the therapeutic movement has much wider ramifications:

> Therapies have an ideology, a certain view of the human world, a theory of neurosis and health, a set of practices, a training programme, membership qualifications, training centres and so forth. (*ibid.*, p. 71)

Secondly, it would be wrong to present too unified a model of family/marital therapy. A detailed examination of the family/ marital therapy movement would reveal not simply a unified movement fed by different streams but all kinds of differences, even conflicts. Thus there is a contrast between the more strictly Freudian tradition represented by Pincus and the Tavistock Centre which is more theoretically unified, more cautious in terms of talking about treatment, and which perhaps has a slightly melancholy, pessimistic view of the human family condition and the more optimistic traditions represented by the American therapies, where Freud is mentioned but in practice assumes second place to more contemporary accounts of inter-personal communication, such as those of Bateson. Cutting across this distinction over the centrality or otherwise of Freud is another concerning the use of 'history' (the term here meaning the use of the patient's past and the past of his/her parents and family of origin). Still further differences can be seen in the assessment of the therapists' own role and the importance of directedness in the therapeutic interview; the contrast here being between the notion of the trained listener with the more directive approach adopted elsewhere. Still further differences can be seen in questions such as the length of therapy, whether there should be one analyst or more, the size of the group being treated and whether it should be treated at home or in a clinic.

Nevertheless, behind all this diversity, some points of unity can be seen. The central emphasis is viewed, quite simply, as a shift in emphasis from the treatment of the individual to the treatment of the group, or the set of transactions between at least two people. In most cases it is the relationships, the structural properties – in other words the space between individuals – that is stressed. This is seen by many people within the movement as a paradigmatic shift which has intellectual consequences beyond the consulting room (see Chapter 7). Such therapists adopt broader intellectual horizons: Skynner sees links with Shamanism and Eastern modes of thought (Skynner, 1981, p. 73) while the names of Alan Watts and Buber appear in some other texts and articles.

MARRIAGE GUIDANCE

This is not the place to present a detailed history of marriage guidance in this country, but simply to note some of the main changes that have taken place in its functioning over the years of the existence of the NMGC. In the first place, all commentators as well as the NMGC's own literature, trace a development from marriage *guidance* to marriage *counselling*. The 'guidance' model implied the acceptance of a fairly traditional understanding of marriage, often within a Christian framework, as a yardstick and an attempt to guide couples over marital 'difficulties' in terms of this understanding. There was an implied congruence between the preservation, wherever possible, of an individual marriage and the preservation of marriage as an institution. The 'counselling' model, on the other hand, implies a greater willingness to listen to the partners themselves, to seek to discover their own wishes and expectations for the marriage and, where appropriate, to help partners to separate with 'dignity'. There is also a recognition of the needs of couples who are not formally married, perhaps even including homosexual couples. The stress, therefore, is in terms of relationships in the strong sense of the word.

The work of the NMGC and similar bodies has been seen as one of the streams that has fed into the wider marital and family therapy movement (Broderick and Schrader, 1981). The two are clearly linked; more recently, it may be assumed, the NMGC has received guidance itself from the growing literature on counselling and therapy and this has entered into its training programmes. Works by Skynner, Satir, Rogers, Pincus, Klein, Haley, Walrond-Skinner, Minuchin and Berne appear on the reading list for counsellors. Sexuality is given considerable emphasis in these lists; in the general list of recommended books there is a list of several books under the label of 'sexual techniques', including Alex Comfort's *Joy of Sex* and Nancy Friday's *My Secret Garden*, and similar references appear in the list of recommended texts for counsellors. it is clear that there is considerable room for variation within the NMGC and that much of the advice will be of a more immediately practical kind, on legal or financial matters for example. Nevertheless, the counsellor training reading list does indicate some steps towards the medicalisation of marriage, however much this effect may be muted in actual counselling sessions; the absence of more sociological or historical references from the reading list is striking. Other organisations may also indicate similar trends. The Family Welfare Association, for example, is described as:

> A voluntary association with a long tradition of using intensive casework based on psychodynamic theory and with a particular interest in working with marriage and families.
> (J. Lawrence in Family Welfare Association 1974, p. 2)

A STUDY OF THE LITERATURE

What follows does not claim to be a complete literature survey and it is certainly not an account of *practice*. It is based upon a non-random sample of books recommended to potential marriage guidance counsellors (the basis being availability rather than any more scientific criteria) plus an examination of the three previously mentioned collections of papers on marital and family therapy. One or two other recent books and collections were consulted.

(a) Definitions of marriage

How is marriage defined in these texts? In the overwhelming majority of cases definitions were not supplied; the convention-ally understood definition of marriage as a legally recognised relationship between an adult male and an adult woman was taken for granted. Several writers recognise some form of 'living together' and argue that these couples could be analysed within the same framework. I could find no reference to gay couples or more complex 'marital' arrangements. In general, therefore, the living together of a man and a woman seemed to be the defining characteristic and the concern for therapeutic intervention.

(b) Understandings of marriage

Perhaps more important than the actual definitions of marriage provided in these texts is the general understanding of the nature of marriage, in other words, the more strictly qualitative dimensions of family living. A central premise of almost all of these texts is that marriage is a 'relationship', in the strong sense of the word (Morgan, 1982). In other words it is more than a legal contract or an institution defined in terms of its reproductive, economic or other assumed functions. Courtenay, following Balint, argues that we are dealing with not one partner or the other but with the space between the two, and this is echoed in many other places (Courtenay, 1968). Each is subject and object to each other (Pincus, 1976). This strong relational property of marriage is, of course, a central premise of any kind of therapeutic intervention.

The sources of this relationship are variously described. To some the source would appear to be biological or nearly so (Hinchcliffe *et al.*, 1978, p. 2; Whitaker and Keith, 1981, p. 193). Others take a more strictly Freudian view seeing marriage as a 'happy re-creation of early family lives' (Klein and Riviere, 1962, p. 74). Other authors, while possibly not dissenting from a biological or Freudian approach, at least in part would also seek to outline some features of the social context. Monger, for example, recognises the changing social context of marriage and sees marital problems as the 'price to pay' for the growing emancipation of both the husband and wife (Monger, 1971). Kaslow considers a variety of sociological explanations for growing divorce rates: individualism, trends towards the equality of the sexes, growing acceptability and affluence (Kaslow, 1981, p. 667). It is not entirely true, therefore, to suggest that marital therapists are unaware of the wider social context in which they practice.

One taken-for-granted assumption that runs through many of the accounts is the trend towards egalitarian marriage, perhaps an essential adjunct to its increasing relational properties. English and Pearson (1947) define it as a partnership and Rayner sees marriage as increasingly egalitarian, based upon romantic love (Rayner, 1971). As already indicated, Monger and Kaslow also recognise the assumptions about the trend towards a growing egalitarian marriage.

Clearly, all the authors recognise marriage as an important and central institution although this importance is seen in terms of the partners themselves rather than in terms of any functions it may be assumed to fulfil for society as a whole. Ackerman sees marriage as a 'whole way of life', something that is more than sex. (Ackerman, 1966, p. 113). English and Pearson are almost overwhelmingly enthusiastic about the institution. It is a 'very valuable maturing experience', an 'opportunity for personality growth' and 'serves to meet many important emotional needs' (English and Pearson, 1947, p. 427). Pincus *et al.*, also see the opportunity for growth and self-realisation through marriage (Pincus *et al.*, 1960). In general, therefore, the assumptions reflected in a publication like *Marriage Matters* are clearly part of a much wider shared perspective on marriage.

(c) Definitions of family

The question of the definition of the family is somewhat more complex. While, as in the case of marriage, this does not appear to be an issue for many writers here, and the conventional nuclear family household is assumed to be the model, the issue is complicated by two main factors. The first is the commitment of some of the theorists and therapists to a three-generational model of family processes and structure, a concern with generational links between households as well as processes within households. Lieberman, for example, is committed to some model of transgenerational family therapy and argues for the recognition of three or four generations. His definition is one of the widest: 'those individuals bound by blood or marriage who, through their culture, make up a kinship' (Lieberman, 1979, p. 13). Therapists working within a Bowen framework also stress the importance of a multi-generational approach (Hall, 1979). The wider kinship network is recognised by several other authors, even where they do not adopt an especially three-generational approach to therapy.

The second main factor is that, while the analyst may not have a particular theoretically-based definition of the family in mind, the pragmatic question of who to include in the therapeutic intervention thrusts the issue to the foreground. Here the answers are extremely various ranging from the complete household (Bell, 1975, pp. 169–72; Haley, 1979, p. 108) through various extensions to other relations (Ackerman, 1970, p. 7; MacGregor, 1970, p. 36) to three generations (Framo, 1981) to even wider networks (Speck and Reuveni, 1970). It is rarely stated clearly whether non-related members of a household (e.g. lodgers) are to be included although one therapist notes the importance of pets (Friedman, 1970, p. 106).

Thus, the definition of the family, as revealed through professional practice rather than on the basis of a more formal theorising, reflects wider theoretical assumptions about the nature of the family. Whether the point of reference is the nuclear family-based household or the three-generational household or some other model, the central idea behind all of these is the systemic nature of family living (see Chapter 7). What is perhaps surprising is that, contrary to my expectations, the family therapists were aware of variations in the definition and understanding of the family. Haley (1979, p. 108) and Jackson (quoted by Bodin, 1981, p. 274) are clearly opposed to any stereotypical notion of the normal family, in terms of structure or functioning, while Duhl and Duhl recognise a variety of forms, 'none bad or good in itself' (1981, p. 499). Yet it must be remembered that many of the authors investigated do not provide definitions of the family or assume that the nuclear model is universal and the basic unit of society (Ackerman, 1966; Fullmer and Bernard, 1968; Satir, 1967).

(d) Sexuality

Sexuality is understood to be an essential component of marriage, at the core of what makes marriage a relationship in the strong sense of the term (Framo, 1981; Hinchcliffe *et al.*, 1978; Skynner, 1976). The strongest statement comes from Whitaker and Keith: 'Passion and sexuality are the voltage in a family system' (Whitaker and Keith, 1981, p. 192). Satir is, partially at least, an important exception in this respect (Satir, 1967). Generally, as in the frequent use of the medical sounding term, 'dysfunction', a fairly conventional model of sexuality would seem to be implied, that is of heterosexual genital contact leading to orgasm. Lack of orgasms may be seen as a sign of 'dysfunction' and, in some earlier texts, homosexuality may be seen as a sign of immaturity, 'abnormality' (Lowe, 1972) or 'fetishism' (Rayner, 1971). Generally, also, there seems to be an acceptance of conventional male/female distinctions in sexual expression.

However, there are also clear signs of a sexual 'openness' in many of the texts referred to potential marriage guidance counsellors, a striking example being Greengross's compassionate and open discussion of the sexual 'needs' of handicapped persons (Greengross, 1976). Other texts recommended by the NMGC include the well-known works of Alex Comfort and there is also reference to Singer's *Goals of Human Sexuality* (1973) which is an extended argument for sexual pluralism and a rejection of the essentialism of Freud and Masters and Johnson.

Nevertheless, whether the approach to sexuality is a conventional one or a more open one, the emphasis on sex is an important component of the medicalisation of marriage. Even where a narrowly biological approach is rejected, social and cultural factors would seem to be added to an essentially biologically based model, and emphasis is often given to the findings of sex-researchers such as Masters and Johnson. The very notion of 'sexual dysfunction' (variously understood and defined) implies the adoption of a medical model. A striking example of this medical orientation to sex may be found in Kaplan's *The New Sex Therapy* (1974) which is also on the NMGC list.

(e) The wider society

(i) Class The most striking fact is that the majority of the texts studied do not mention class – or any other form of social inequality. Most of the others have extremely brief and unsystematic references. In some cases it will be stated or assumed that class makes no difference at all. The general theme that seems to emerge from my brief survey is that while, for a variety of economic and cultural reasons, the clients tend to be middle

class in origin there is no reason in principle why the practice of therapy should not extend to other social groups. In some cases, the relationship is reversed and the therapist has been primarily, at least in some stages of his/her career, concerned with poor or deprived family systems. Minuchin spent some time working with poor and deprived families and Aponte and Van Deusen (1981) describe how structural family theory developed out of work with the poor and was extended to other family groups. There are references to the study of working class, poor or deprived families in a variety of texts. Some forms of therapy, on the other hand – such as Speck's network therapy which requires the assembly of the patient's social network in a living room – might seem to be automatically limited to the middle class. But, in general, it may be argued that patterns of social inequality are not understood to have significance in the theory and practice of family and marital therapy; the basic principles are assumed to have universal relevance even although there may be some accidental limitation to middle-class families. Where questions of class are considered it is usually in terms of economic deprivation and poverty, rather than on class as a wider system of social and cultural inequality.

(ii) Work While it may be understandable, given deep-rooted patterns of academic specialisation on both sides of the Atlantic, that marital and family therapists may not pay a great deal of attention to questions of social class, the omission of a discussion of work in many of these texts would seem to be more curious. And omissions there are: while the nature of the literature survey does not lend itself to a strict quantitative analysis, I could only find just over a dozen such references and many of these were very brief. Persons attending therapy sessions, it would seem, leave their work identities at the cloakroom. As Storr has noted recently:

> Freud affirmed that mental health depended upon the capacity to love and the capacity to work . . . the former capacity has been over-emphasised at the expense of the latter. (Storr, 1983, p. 43)

These may be some signs that Marriage Guidance may be taking this to heart, although perhaps with a middle class or professional bias (Gonin, 1984).

(f) Questions of gender

Given the fact that, in recent years, the differences in experience and understanding of family life between men and women have been recognised (Bernard, 1973; Thorne and Yalom, 1982), it would be interesting to discover the extent to which such gender differences have been incorporated into the writings of family and marital therapists. The short answer, as with the cases of class and work, would seem to be 'not much', although the subject receives a little more attention than these other two variables. The picture is, in fact, rather complex. Certainly, fairly conventional notions of gender differentiations appear, either by implication or through more direct statement. Often gender differences, presumably biologically based and relatively immutable, are simply assumed. Elsewhere, the taken-for-granted notions might be stated more openly and a more or less biological basis may be assumed or stated. Klein and Riviere, for example, write of 'the mother's loving and giving breast and the father's creative penis' (Klein and Riviere, 1962, p. 107).

In some cases it may be argued that the taken-for-granted gender assumptions that may appear in these articles and texts may possibly reflect the client's view of reality rather than the analyst's own views. In some cases, however, the picture is far from clear. Monger refers to the 'costs' of sexual emancipation (although not necessarily condemnatory) and has a slightly pejorative reference to 'militant feminists' (Monger, 1971, p. 127). He also stresses the need to accept the client's own stereotypes rather than, presumably, impose ideal versions on to the clients themselves. Lowe recognises the often stereotypical nature of gender differences (Lowe, 1972) but the complexity of the issue is neatly brought out in this quotation from Ackerman: 'Within the family, often it is unclear who is the man and who is the woman.' (Ackerman in Ackerman, 1970, p. 91.)

In many of the texts there are references to change and to the social and cultural dimensions of male and female roles. In some cases these may be simply an acknowledgment that 'times have changed', that there is increasing variety in the ways in which male/female differences are understood and the impact that these differences have upon the family. The changing role of men and women in the labour force is sometimes cited (e.g. Fullmer and Bernard, 1968). The current situation is often understood as being one of both great potentiality and great difficulty.

Other more recent writers have presented a more positive evaluation of the criticisms and contributions of the Women's Liberation Movement. Haley, for example, gives recognition to possible unjust gender hierarchies within the family (Haley, 1979, p. 102). More direct references to the WLM occur in even more recent writings. Somewhat ponderously, Gurman and Kniskern refer to the WLM as part of the 'meta-criteria for evaluating outcomes' in therapy (Gurman and Kniskern, 1981, p. 771). In other words, the Women's Movement is seen as part of the critical and ideological environment in which family and marital therapy is practised. Similar recognition is provided by Carter and McGoldrick (1980). There has also been the development of a feminist family therapy (Hare-Mustin, 1978).

Thus, while many of the texts studied did not seem to regard gender differentiation as worth mentioning or appeared to assume a conventional division of roles and labour, there is perhaps some increasing recognition of the changing position of women in society and of possible tensions and contradictions that this brings about within the family. But, generally speaking, whether welcomed or unwelcomed, these changes are seen as presenting difficulties or complexities for the practices of marital and family therapy (ones which can presumably be overcome within the existing clinical paradigms) rather than presenting a more fundamental challenge to these institutions themselves.

This survey of the literature, although incomplete, does provide support for the idea of the medicalisation of marriage and the family (see also Pearson, 1974; Reiger, 1981). In the first place, it would seem to be clear that the general assumption is that there does exist a class of human problems which can be defined as 'family' or 'marital'. These problems exist as an important subset of a wider class of problems defined as 'relational'. Such problems can be isolated, defined and treated, with little reference to other areas of human or social activity, most notably the sphere of work and employment. In the second place, orientated to these relationship problems, there has developed a cumulative body of literature, based upon case work, although referring to wider theoretical issues, deriving from Freud and communication theory, etc. Whatever variations there may be between therapies there seems to be little dissent from the model of a cumulative growth of practice and theory with, at its heart, the case work interview.

It is important not to overstate the case. At one extreme Andolfi (1979) is prepared to admit that the choice of the family as a point of entry is to some extent arbitrary; the general interest is in 'ecosystems' and the family is probably more accessible than some other areas of social life but not necessarily to be accorded any lasting privileged status. More cautiously, Skynner claims that he is opposed to the traditional medical model but also castigates the 'unscientific and unhelpful' attitudes of sociologists (Skynner, 1976, p. 165). Nevertheless, it is difficult to see how Skynner's own approach departs from a medical model, except in a very narrow sense of the term.

Several of the writers already cited do include some reference to the wider social and cultural setting. Thus, while Ackerman (1966) includes few, if any, references to social class or work he does recognise that therapy is based upon certain value judgements and that family processes do exist in a wider social context. The same is true of Satir and, to an even greater extent, Minuchin. What is important, however, is that these wider social and cultural influences are rarely theorised to any elaborate extent, neither are they significantly incorporated, it would seem, into therapeutic practice. Where the wider society does become a little more concrete is in those writings that deal with wider networks of kin and neighbourhood: Bell (1970), Sussman (1970) and Speck and Reuveni (1970) for examples. But even here the approach is still one which might be described as familo-centric.

Further, some writers do seem to recognise the political dimension of therapy. Haley (1979), for example, recognises that the therapeutic encounter is a situation of social control and feels that a frank recognition of the fact is better than attempting to maintain the myth of non-directed therapy. Walrond-Skinner and Kingston see problems of power, manipulation and reification as developing with the theory and practice of therapy (Walrond-Skinner, 1976, p. 149; Kingston, 1982). These recognitions are still fairly sparse and the central sociopolitical problem relating to the gender power relationship is still rarely a matter of attention outside writers explicitly committed to a feminist perspective.

CONCLUSION

> The fact that family therapy has evolved in the third quarter
> of this century is unlikely to be accidental and unrelated to
> the nature and state of the mid-twentieth century industrial
> society. (C. Dare, Editorial to first issue of *Journal of Family
> Therapy*, Feb. 1979)

> Sexuality, the couple, pedagogy, and social adoption are
> brought together in a single mold by the recent appearance
> of the constellation of counsellors and technicians of human
> relations. (Donzelot, 1980, p. 171)

Donzelot's *Policing of Families* represents a recent, but by no
means the only, critical account of the processes whereby
marriage and the family have become the subject of state and
professional intervention. While he does not deal specifically
with marital and family therapy, it is certain that such practitioners would be included under the general rubric of the
useful phrase the 'technicians of human relations' and that his
more general account of the growth of social work and the
gradual permeation of Freudianism would be readily applied to
this more specific area of analysis. His account, for example, of
the categories used and developed by social workers in relation
to the families which come within their orbit (*ibid.*, p. 152) could
easily be adapted to the interventions, whether voluntary or
otherwise, of family therapists. Donzelot is, in fact, dealing with
the elaboration and growth of the category of the 'social' as it is
used to qualify such words as 'work' and 'services' and the way in
which this is strongly linked to certain notions of the family.

It is important to stress that Donzelot is not simply talking of
the interventions of external agencies in some essential
institution such as the family or marriage but also, and simultaneously, the way in which these interventions construct the
entities that they are supposed to treat. Thus family therapy not
only treats families; it also, and at the same time, constructs
families and family problems. It is important to emphasise this,
since some more conservative treatments of the same processes
almost seem to suggest that the 'true' family exists prior to or
outside the interventions of state and professionals, that these
interventions represent an 'invasion' into a private and privileged area of life (Lasch, 1977; Mount, 1982).

Donzelot may be linked to Foucault, whose recent work on the history of sexuality is of particular reference. Foucault constantly stresses the dialectical nature of the processes he is analysing and seeks, largely successfully, to avoid any biological or psychological essentialism in his analyses. In his *History of Sexuality* (1979), Foucault is setting himself against a fairly traditional liberal story, namely the story of the gradual liberation of sexuality from the Church and from the constraints of a medieval society. The simple-minded account of the growth of sexual freedom is replaced by an account which seeks to demonstrate that one set of controls has been replaced by another, even though this latter set may present itself in the guise of liberation. This shift is from a complex system of power based upon ideas of sovereignty to a system based upon ideas of discipline. That this discipline seems to reside in the individual is largely illusory; 'thou shalts' may be as limiting as 'thou shalt nots'. While Foucault's analysis is directed specifically to the question of sexuality (about which more later) it clearly applies to our discussion of marital and family therapy:

> But medicine made a forceful entry into the pleasures of the couple: it created an entire organic, functional, or mental pathology arising out of 'incomplete' sexual practices; it carefully classified all forms of related pleasures; it incorporated them into notions of 'development' and institutional 'disturbances'; and it undertook to manage them. (Foucault, 1979, p. 41)

Outside the often complex theorising of Foucault and Donzelot, a more popular interpretation of the broader counselling movement is that of a substitute for religion in an otherwise secularising society. The titles of two books – *The Secular Priests* (North, 1972) and *The Faith of the Counsellors* (Halmos, 2nd edn, 1978) – bear witness to this approach, the latter indeed appearing on the NMGC list. Both North and Halmos refer to the language and assumptions of the counsellors and argue that they often seem to signify statements of faith rather than a more obviously 'scientific' orientation. Halmos is the more thoroughgoing in his analysis of the counselling movement in religious terms, looking at the use of metaphysical or theological imagery, the processes by which the decline of religious practice was to some extent replaced by the growth of medical or para-medical personnel and exploring the tension between the emphasis on the 'therapeutic gift of love' and the 'harder', more orthodox Freudian tradition (*ibid.*, p. 52). Halmos's own position is one of critical approval arguing that counselling has introduced a humanising influence into medicine.

The use of the 'surrogate religion' model is not without its theoretical difficulties. It assumes the overall correctness of the 'secularisation thesis', a thesis which has not gone unchallenged in the sociology of religion if only for the somewhat limited, official Church version of religion that is usually taken as a yardstick. Moreover, it does seem to posit some kind of inherent religious need such that a decline in one form of religious practice and worship must, eventually, be replaced by some other form, or something which should be regarded as a functional alternative. Clearly, the picture is more complex than this, and this complexity is recognised by both North and Halmos. The growing prestige of science and scientific rhetoric, the alienating effect of mass society, the growth of bureaucracy and the downgrading of politics are all cited as well as the more familiar candidates of industrialisation and urbanisation. All these factors interact with one another and with the processes of secularisation to provide the general historical and cultural background against which the rise of counselling can be understood. While these analyses sometimes seem to be getting closer to the matter than the more removed accounts of Foucault and Donzelot (where it is very difficult to find any clear statement of historical causality), it must be admitted that what we have at the moment is some broad sense of an affinity between counselling and social context rather than a carefully articulated theory or historical analysis. At the very least, there is enough in these accounts to emphasise the therapist's own accounts of their own development in terms of conceptual breakthrough, and paradigm shift must be treated with some caution.

One aspect of the debate which requires a little further attention is that of sexuality, the central concern of Foucault's book. Drawing together a number of diverse, and not necessarily theoretically coherent writings, we may make the following points:

1 In place of 'outdated' Victorian or Puritan taboos, sex is seen as coming out into the open. However, this is a superficial

liberation. While the controls have become more diffused and apparently non-repressive, there has been the establishment of a sexual yardstick against which to measure one's own performance, and an obligation to work at and enjoy sex (Lewis and Boissett, 1967–8; North, 1972, p. 225).

2 If couples become obliged to learn sexual techniques, the other side of the coin is that there are teachers there to instruct them. This is undoubtedly the case as the continual stream of books, encyclopedias, articles and videos bear witness, together with the growth of sex therapists and clinics. Most of these conform very closely to the medical model, either directly in that the 'teacher' or 'therapist' operates within a medical establishment or with a medical title, or indirectly in that the stance is that of helper and couple in need of help. Here, as in the case of marriage and the family, the professional intervention not only responds to a 'condition', it also serves to construct that condition at the same time.

3 A theme closer to the writings of Foucault is the overlapping interest in sex, truth and confession. The disclosure in the consulting room – about premature ejaculation or lack of orgasms or whatever – has close affinities with the older religious idea of confession, and both are linked to notions of ways of reaching the truth. To 'tell the truth' about another person – say in the form of a biography or a set of exposure articles – is to inform the reader about the subject's sex life. Not to do so in the required detail is to lack candour, to be untruthful (Hepworth and Turner, 1982).

4 Foucault writes of the 'artificial unity' of 'sex' (1979, p. 154). This is a very useful idea, pointing to the way in which a diversity of concerns, practices and themes are linked together under the rubric of sex. The emotional, the biological, the interpersonal and the moral are linked together and naturalised through their subsumption under the one term, 'sex', which becomes a taken-for-granted 'fact of life'. This idea of providing for the unity of a process or institution as part of its social construction is a valuable one, and clearly has relevance when we come to talk of marriage and marital, family and familial.

This emphasis and construction of sexuality is an important aspect of the medicalisation of marriage for while few writers would nowadays argue that legitimate sex is simply confined to the institution of marriage, sex is still seen as an important component of relationships of which marriage is still viewed as a paradigmatic form. (Even quite explicit sex manuals may still refer to the partners as husband and wife.) Sex, while it is not equated with marriage, is seen as an integral part of that relationship, and it is that part which is most amenable to medicalisation since it appears to be closest to the natural, the biological.

The consequences (and part cause) of this medicalisation of marriage and the family are an individualisation and a depoliticisation. The shift is away from seeking political change or communal action towards inner change, towards 'working' at one's marriage or relationship (Halmos, *op. cit.*, pp. 7–8; North, *op cit.*, p. 87). A further and related consequence is a new twist in the construction of 'women's place'. While not all of the therapists and counsellors accept conventional notions of the sexual division of labour, it is more than likely that without change in many other spheres the burden of making a relationship work, of coping in more sensitive ways with the intra-familial dynamics will fall upon the woman.

The one remaining question is whether this broad process of the 'medicalisation of marriage', this construction of marriage, family and sexuality is *ever* avoidable. The romantic conservatives such as Lasch and Mount and presumably North seem to be hankering after a society – or looking forward to such a society – where the family and marriage can stand alone, solid and impregnable defences against the ravages of mass society and the invasions of state and professional alike. Foucault, on the other hand, would seem to be arguing, more realistically, that the family, marriage and sexuality are always being constructed by forces outside themselves; that they cannot exist outside and apart from these forces however they might change. In one century it may be the Church, in another the medical profession.

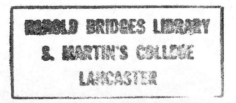

3 Politics, family, state

Neighbours had gossiped about the scandal for years, but had done nothing not wanting to interfere in a family matter. (*Guardian*, 12/6/80, on case of Portuguese girl brought up in a chicken coop)

The family is becoming increasingly subjected to control and supervision by numerous agencies of the state, all or most of which are wholly or partly under the influence of those whose faith is that of the counsellors; all that is now possible is the realisation of self within the limits imposed by these external pressures and controls. (North, 1972, pp. 251–2)

INTRODUCTION

The previous chapter examined one aspect of the wider context in which *Marriage Matters* and the current concern about divorce rates might be situated: that of the rise of the counselling function and the medicalisation of marriage. This chapter will examine the other aspect: the introduction of a specifically party political orientation into the debate. *Marriage Matters* was produced jointly by the Home Office and the DHSS and the family became an important part of the platform of the then Prime Minister, James Callaghan, as well as of the Conservative administration that followed him. Although treated in separate chapters, the two issues are linked as the quotation from North at the beginning of this chapter indicates. Many of the counsellors and therapists involved in the medicalisation of marriage are employed by state institutions or give advice to members of these institutions; the state supports the educational institutions in which the theories that underlie the work of the counsellors are elaborated and taught, and persons influenced by the theory and practice of therapy or its wider context will enter Parliament and the Civil Service. While it would be wrong to see these professionals – or any professionals – as simply being an arm of the state, nevertheless, the links between the two are too close to be ignored.

One point should be made clear at the outset. Although, for a variety of political and economic reasons, the word 'family' is more likely to receive prominent status in party manifestos in the 1980s than in other decades since the Second World War, it should not be imagined that the family has recently become politicised. There are very few aspects of state legislation that do not have direct or indirect impact upon the family (consider a more or less random list such as taxation, conscription, regulating obscene materials, education) and very few practices of state officials that do not, again directly or indirectly, have some kind of family dimension. At a more theoretical level, political philosophies have constantly been informed by, and make reference to, current understandings of the family and family relations, from Tudor theories of patriarchalism (Schochet, 1975) to the *Communist Manifesto*. To speak of the politicisation of the family is therefore, to this extent, misleading; it only has meaning with reference to a possibly greater degree of openness and explicitness about such matters than has been customarily or recently expected.

THE FAMILY AND POLITICS

A close examination of the current political debate both in Britain and the United States highlights certain complexities such that the opposition tends not to be simply a matter of left and right or socialist and conservative but a variety of cross-cutting currents. Nor is it simply a matter of pro- and anti-family. A simple starting point might be made by cross-cutting a distinction between those who give the family a more or less positive evaluation and those who do not, with a distinction between those who positively evaluate state intervention as against those who do not. This gives rise to the familiar four-fold classification shown in Table 3.1.

Table 3.1 Orientation to family and state

		STATE	
		+	−
FAMILY	+	1	2
	−	3	4

It will become clear that any Socialist/Conservative distinction does not map unambiguously into this classification.

1 The situation where a more or less positive evaluation of the family is combined with support for or a recognition of the necessity for state intervention might be seen as more or less orthodox Labour party policies. Thus, James Callaghan was reported as saying in 1978:

> 'The overriding social concern is to preserve and enhance the influence of the family. An influence which is beneficial in every way.'

> 'I do not believe that Government has done enough to consider the impact of its policies on the family when we take decisions.' (*Telegraph*, 15/5/78)

> 'The family is the place where we care for each other, where we practise consideration for one another. Caring families are the basis of a society that cares.' (*Guardian*, 23/5/78)

The second quotation identifies a fairly central theme in British socialist thinking on the family, namely the family as providing a model, in micro, of the ideal socialist society. The family is seen as a centre of caring and altruism and egalitarianism; there is no contradiction, therefore, between supporting the family and supporting wider social intervention on the part of the state. Linked to this is the notion, only just below the surface, of the working-class family where these values are most likely to be manifested but which has, so often, been tragically distorted by the ravages of an impersonal and competitive capitalism. These considerations are probably linked to more pragmatic concerns (the family is there so we should seek to enrol it as a partner), to popularist appeals (the family is popular) which slide into straightforward opportunism. Also implied in the first quotation is the idea of the 'family impact statement', an issue which will be given more extended treatment later.

One feature of the 'family impact statement' is that as a proposal it finds its supporters among the Conservative Party as well as among the Labour Party. The Conservative Party, traditionally, has seen the family as a key institution alongside the nation, the monarchy and the Church. It is more than likely that the 'family' that appears in Conservative philosophy is very different from the institution that may be cited in speeches from the Labour Party. In Conservatism it is more likely to be linked to a traditional sexual morality, opposition to easier divorce, abortion or readily available contraception. It is also more likely to mean, by 'family', a more obviously patriarchal division of labour within the household. Nevertheless, such a traditional adherence to the institution of the family may sometimes come into conflict with features of the newer Conservatism which are based upon monetarist principles and which stress the need to reduce public expenditure. It is doubtful whether this tension within Conservatism has been fully resolved in either this country or in the United States where the traditional values of the born-again Christians might contradict some of the key values of the New Right's economic policies.

2 Here a negative evaluation of the role of the state coupled with positive support for the family rests more easily with contemporary Conservative philosophy. It is this orientation that Ronald Butt (a leading Conservative columnist) has in mind when he argued, against Callaghan, that the idea of the family 'springs more readily and easily from Tory ideals and convictions' (*Times*, 1/6/78). He goes on to argue that: 'to the Tory mind, the family is the natural antidote to the undesirable power of the state.' (*ibid.*) This is a view that has more recently been argued at much greater length by another Conservative spokesperson, Ferdinand Mount (Mount, 1982). The family is seen both as a more desirable substitute for the state in all matters of care (for the aged, the sick and for children) and as a private haven, a bulwark against the encroachment of a potentially totalitarian state. As a general orientation to the family, this view has implications beyond the contemporary British Conservative Party, particularly in the debate over the writings of Lasch (Lasch, 1977; Zaretsky in Thorne and Yalom, 1982; Barrett and McIntosh, 1982). As with other orientations to the family, this approach has its built-in contradictions and dilemmas. Empirically, the notion of the state invading the family is not quite as simple as it might seem. There is the assumption of some golden age of the family and it seems likely, as Zaretsky suggests, that the impact of the state on the family has been uneven. In some cases, among the poorer sections of

society, the family may well have had its 'autonomy' challenged; middle-class families, on the other hand, may well have had their autonomy strengthened by the growth of the state since they are the groups that tend to use, rather than allow themselves to be used by, the agencies of the state. In Thorne and Yalom, 1982, p. 190, Zaretsky concludes:

> Far from the state 'invading' or 'replacing' the family, a certain kind of alienated public life and a certain kind of alienated private life have expanded together. (*ibid.*, p. 218)

More specifically, and nearer home, it is doubtful whether Mount's romantic familism – which includes support for divorce, opposition to the Church and Mrs Whitehouse as well as opposition to Marxism and state intervention – would find much support among his own party, at least in its undiluted form.

3 A positive evaluation of the role of the state combined with a negative assessment of the role of the family would seem to accord most closely to certain versions of a Marxist and/or feminist approach to the family. Certainly, the criticisms of the family are well known; it is a central institution for the suppression of women and the maintenance of gender inequality; it is 'anti-social', encouraging a narrow focus on a small set of interpersonal relationships at the expense of wider commitments to citizenship or to the public sphere; it is a major institution in the reproduction of class inequalities (Barrett and McIntosh, 1982).

Contrary to some popular stereotypes, it is doubtful whether this perspective has ever been more than a marginal one in British society and that therefore it would be misleading to regard it as having become marginalised. Certainly, it is not a view that would find much public support from contemporary politicians, whatever their private feelings and experiences might be. In the first place, the ideology of family and familism is too deeply imbedded in contemporary British culture. For a very complex set of historical reasons the opposition between family/natural/moral and anti-family/unnatural/immoral can be sustained almost without effort. In the second place, if terms such as 'family' and 'marriage' continue to have very strong positive resonances, the term 'state' has widespread negative connotations. Probably the central dilemma facing the contemporary socialist movement is that, while it can continue to make searching criticisms of capitalist society, the exemplars of 'actually existing' socialism are almost wholly, at least apparently, negative. Moreover, the largely negative connotations that surround the word 'state' are enhanced by the positive evaluations of the word 'family'. If the family stands for all that is authentic, warm and personal, the state seems to stand for all that is abstractly bureaucratic, cold and impersonal. Weber's iron cage of increasing rationalisation seems a more persuasive vision than the Marxist one of revolution leading to the classless society.

4 These kinds of dilemmas have led to the growth of our fourth category where both the state and the family receive negative evaluation although almost certainly to varying degrees. In one sense this is perhaps not new; the commune movement in many of its forms has always manifested a suspicion of the conventional nuclear family model combined with an almost equal suspicion of conventional politics and the state. The emphasis is upon constructing 'alternative realities', on exploring quite different forms of relationships and bonding. This kind of vision has been around for a very long time but has possibly received reinforcement from at least two further sources. Firstly, the criticism of various forms of social work intervention which argue – roughly following the arguments of Donzelot and Lasch – that these interventions often lean strongly in the direction of social control rather than in the direction of welfare. (Both aspects are involved in all spheres of the welfare state and social services, as many practitioners are often willing to recognise; the question is one of emphasis.) Thus, theoreticians and practitioners in the social services sometimes come to manifest a suspicion of the social control aspects of their work or subject while also maintaining a degree of scepticism about the effectiveness of traditional family-based households (Jordan in Rapoport *et al.*, 1982). Secondly, the contemporary feminist movement includes a radical critique of male-dominated conventional politics as much as it includes a critique of the conventional nuclear family. Politics are male-dominated not simply in numerical terms but also in that the standards for evaluating political practice are almost invariably male. The denigration of the women protesting against cruise nuclear missiles at Greenham Common is similar to the marginalisation of women's political

behaviour in many academic studies. It is likely that this fourth orientation will continue to grow in strength and significance in the next few years.

All typologies and taxonomies have their limitations, particularly in that they nearly always tend to present a relatively static picture of reality. Nevertheless, it is likely that this rudimentary classification has highlighted some of the difficulties that stand in the way of a more simplistic left/right or socialist/conservative distinction. Suspicion about the state is to be found over a wide spectrum of political views, and positive endorsements of the institution of the family are not confined to orthodox members of the Conservative Party. Within each broad categorisation of political views there are dilemmas and contradictions; conservatives may sense a tension between a positive support for the family and a critique of all the welfare functions of the state while socialists may experience similar contradictions between a formal commitment to sex equality and more familistically-orientated statements.

Two further points need to be made with regard to this classification. In the first place, I have used the terms 'state' and 'family' without quotation marks or qualification, as taken-for-granted generally understood terms. But such terms cannot be taken for granted and their use and meaning are an integral part of the political debate. In the case of the 'state' the term has very different meanings for the conservative and for the socialist. When the conservative uses the word state she/he has in mind a bureaucrat or tax inspector; when a socialist uses the same word she/he has a policeman in mind. The socialist will qualify the term state with the word 'capitalist', perhaps leaving open the question of the nature of the state in a socialist society. The conservative will see the state as an already existing instance of socialism which should, where possible be removed.

Similarly, the 'family' conjures up quite different images. The conservative image of the family will most likely be patriarchal, with clear lines of authority and a straightforward division of labour between the sexes. Where someone on the left presents a positive evaluation of the family, it is more likely to be one where the themes of egalitarianism and sharing are dominant. It may not be too fanciful to suggest that the family still provides images of 'the good society' and that the image of the one can still serve to reinforce the understanding and evaluation of the other, just as the family entered political rhetoric in pre-capitalist times (Schochet, 1975; Elshtain (ed.), 1982).

In the second place, it is important to note the role of institutions outside the categories of 'state' and 'family' and the role that these play in different political philosophies. In practice, this means various constructions of the terms 'the community' and 'voluntary agencies'. The use of the term 'community' in sociology has been extremely various and widely contested, and the use of the term in political rhetoric is also extremely baffling. In many cases, its use seems to be akin to some form of ritual incantation which will mend social hurts and heal cultural divisions; how else can we account for the repeated use of the word in the context of Northern Ireland or riot-torn parts of inner cities? In terms of the family/state debate, the uses are equally complex and vague. The way in which the use of the term 'community' in the context of a discussion of 'community care', to mean female members of nuclear families, has been widely noted, commented upon and analysed (Craven, Rimmer and Wicks, 1982, p. 15; Dalley, 1983; Finch, 1984; Lewis in Lewis (ed.), 1983). In these contexts, the community is viewed as a natural partner, together with the family, in welfare programmes or, in more radical versions, the family-community is seen as largely taking over or back many of the welfare functions from the state. In the socialist perspective, on the other hand, the community is seen as something which indicates relationships between different families rather than relationships which remain largely within families. Notions of 'community' or 'grass-roots' politics (which are found in liberal models as well) contain something of this idea. The difference between conservative and socialist conceptions of community may be signified simply in terms of a public/private distinction. Socialists place the community firmly in the public sphere and seek to draw individual family members into it; conservatives place the community in the private sphere and seek to draw family members back into it.

A similar distinction may be made in relation to voluntary associations and agencies. A recent controversy surrounding the role and practice of the Citizens Advice Bureaux (CAB) illustrates the dilemma almost perfectly. Some conservatives would wish to see the voluntary CAB as an adjunct to a familistic-based policy of care and welfare, as a substitute for state support and intervention, while others would wish the CAB to be essentially concerned with ensuring that the state lives up to its obligations in relation to individuals (rather than family members) and emphasises the 'rights' of citizens, and ways of encouraging citizens to realise these 'rights'. Thus, in the cases of the words 'community' and 'voluntary sector', just as in the cases of the words 'family' and 'state', there are radically different understandings and interpretations reflecting deep political and philosophical divisions.

FAMILY AND STATE: A TENTATIVE MODEL

As a tentative model I consider a set of interchanges between state, class, family and gender as shown in Figure 3.1. This provides four elements and six sets of exchanges to consider.

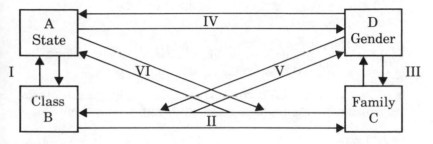

Figure 3.1

Elements

A State Without going into the complexities of the theoretical debate, I am here concerned with all those institutions, categories of persons and individuals who are involved in the framing and administration of legislation. Thus, I am concerned with governments and ministers, with the Civil Service, the judiciary, the police, with professionals working in the public sector, and so on. I am concerned with the national and the local state.

B Class More exactly, I am concerned here with the class/status system. Again, attempting to short circuit a great deal of sociological debate, I aim to indicate a system of dynamic relationships between different groupings, groups and categories of persons with different structural positions and different sets of interests, perceived or actual. I shall include class as generally understood in a Marxist perspective as one potentiality, together with classes and status groups as deriving from a Weberian model. I shall include age categories and ethnic groups; gender, on the other hand, seems to deserve a separate category.

C Family This is a deceptively simple term. The consideration of the definition of family and family members as a social process will be deferred until Part II. Here I am concerned with any one of the following:

(a) the actual distribution of the population in terms of households, that is units of residence where the members, as in most official definitions, share at least one meal;

(b) relationships between persons which are understood by these persons to be in terms of blood or marriage or which are understood to have an equivalent status as these relationships;

(c) ideals, images, understandings and evaluations of such terms as 'family', 'marriage', 'parenthood', etc.

A more complex model would show that these separate items are constantly inter-relating and influencing each other.

D Gender This is another deceptively simple term. Quite simply, I am concerned here with the understandings and evaluations around the terms, male/female, man/woman, feminine/masculine and the way in which categorisations on the basis of these distinctions form a system characterised by equality and inequality, opposition and cooperation.

Thus, although I have drawn up a set of boxes labelled 'State', 'Class', 'Family', and 'Gender' an opening of any of these boxes will reveal a complex set of processes. These 'internal' processes are both shaped by, and have an effect upon, the 'external' processes and interchanges between the elements.

Processes

1 State/class This is not the place to consider the complexities of the theoretical debate surrounding this relationship. Here it is enough to note that the set of interchanges between the state and the class/status system have to be considered in order to discuss the relationship of the other two elements with the state. In short, it is not a question of the family and the state, but the family and the state in relation to the class/status system. In considering these interchanges, I am concerned with the way in which the state attempts to regulate, police and control class conflict (and status group struggle) on the one hand, and the processes whereby class struggle and political pressure by status and interest groups affects and shapes state legislation and its administration. I am concerned, therefore, with the interconnections between the policing, in the most general sense of that term, and the welfare functions of the state. One important status group, or set of status groups, to be considered are those officials and professionals who are directly employed by the state and who are directly involved in the administration of state policies. Such groups are not to be seen simply as 'agents' of the state but as relatively autonomous status groups in their own right.

2 *Class/family* Consideration of this set of interchanges will be deferred until the next chapter. In essence, I am concerned with:

(a) the ways in which the family reproduces the class/status system; more especially the ways in which the family reproduces systems of patterned inequality;
(b) the ways in which systems of class and status inequality place limits upon or provide opportunities for various modes of family living. Thus, if we talk about 'the working-class family' or 'the middle-class family' we are talking, in a highly compressed way, about the processes by which these families reproduce the class categories and relationships so described and, simultaneously, the way in which these class categories provide some kind of loose parameters for the elaboration of certain patterns of family life.

3 *Gender/family* This too will be deferred until the next chapter. Two aspects of the interchange between these two elements are important:

(a) the ways in which the family reproduces gender differences;

67

(b) the way in which gender differences constitute a major axis
     upon which family life is organised.

4 State/gender Here I am obviously concerned, firstly, with the
way in which the state reproduces gender differences. It would
be difficult, if not impossible, to find a piece of legislation that
did not have gender implications, that did not either direct itself
explicitly to gender differences or where gender differences
were implied or unexamined and where the legislation or its
enactment did not have some consequences for the positions of
men and women in society. Even law which might claim to be
'gender-blind' might, in a society structured around gender
inequality, have reinforcing effects. Criminal law, at least in its
routine enactment, may be an example of this kind; gender
assumptions may lie at the back of the framing of this kind of
legislation (emphasis on protecting property, definitions of rape
and sexual offences, etc.) and will certainly influence sentencing
policy (Edwards, 1981; 1984).

As examples of the way in which the legal process may
reinforce gender differences we may turn to the often quoted
Lord Denning:

> 'Some features of family life are elemental in our society.
> One is that it is the husband's duty to provide his wife with a
> roof over her head; and the children too. So long as the wife
> behaves herself, she is entitled to remain in the matrimonial
> home.' (Lord Denning, 1970, quoted by Hayes, 1978, pp. 4–7)

> 'When a marriage breaks up, there will thenceforward be
> two households instead of one. The husband will have to go
> out to work all day and must get some woman to look after
> the house – either a wife, if he remarries or a housekeeper, if
> he does not. He will also have to provide maintenance for the
> children. The wife will not usually have so much expense.
> She may go out to work herself, she will not usually employ a
> housekeeper. She will do most of the housework herself,
> perhaps with some help. Or she may remarry, in which case
> her new husband will provide for her.' (Denning, quoted by
> Harris, 1977, pp. 5–10)

While not all statements from politicians or legislators are as
straightforward as this, there would still appear to be broad

assumptions that inform the framing and enactment of legislation. Lewis has listed these as follows:

(i) The assumption of the family wage; that the man's wage is designed to support both that man and his wife and family.
(ii) The separation of spheres between the public and the private, mapping on to the difference between women and men, home and work.
(iii) The sexual division of labour within the home and at work and within the labour market (Lewis, 1983, pp. 32–3).

Even where it is the case that legislators claim to be treating social reality as it is, i.e. where they address themselves to notions of what is generally accepted or desired or taken for granted, they may thereby sustain these notions by cutting off a critical examination of possible alternatives (Lewis, *ibid.*, p. 19).

The notion of the state reproducing gender inequalities is probably much too simple, for it suggests a straightforward continuity from generation to generation. We do not, however, live in a static society and the relationships between the sexes are constantly changing and being redefined. There has been legislation in favour of greater equality between men and women (equal suffrage, equal pay, etc.). However, it can be argued that whatever number of steps may have been taken in a forward direction they have been countered by an almost equal number of steps taken in the reverse direction. In some cases, a detailed consideration of legislation shows the limits of that legislation in bringing about any significant shift of power within a patriarchal society. Thus, full adult suffrage has not brought about anything approaching equal representation in the Houses of Parliament, even over fifty years after the completion of the struggle for the vote. In other cases legislation, through the narrowness of its focus, may have limited effects. The Equal Pay Act could do little about the wider distribution of men and women in the labour market, especially the concentration of women in low-paid or part-time employment (Breugel in Lewis (ed.), 1983; Walby, 1983). In some cases, there may be a shift in emphasis rather than a shift in terms of wider assumptions about men and women. Land, for example, argues that in the areas of income maintenance, taxation and family law there have been reforms but that they have been limited in their effects. The emphasis, she argues, is now on the role of women as 'carers' rather than, as may have been the case in the past, on their position as a married woman. This shift from status to role may not have had any significant effect upon the overall position of women in society (Land, 1983, pp. 64–85).

While most versions of the relationship between gender and state would either indicate some kind of improvement in the position of women as a result of the intervention of the latter, or would argue that the state more or less maintains the traditional status quo, others might argue that in some cases the position of women has actually worsened. This may be seen in terms of the erosion of traditionally-based rights as a result of state interventions. For example, Oakley and others have argued that in the area of medical practice women lost control in areas such as midwifery and obstetrics to the state and the emerging medical profession (Oakley, 1976). In more recent years, with 'women's revamped responsibilities as guardians of the nation's health' (Oakley, 1983, p. 125), the burden of much routine health care has been placed back on to women's shoulders while the concentration of medical power remains firmly with men. Gittins traces a similar, if more recent, development in respect of the area of child care and education. The development of a movement dedicated to infant and child welfare between the wars eroded the traditional power base of the working-class woman's social networks, making her more dependent upon the immediate nuclear family, the professions and the state, a process reinforced by suburbanisation and the resulting isolation (Gittins, 1982, p. 51). In both arguments, we see a loss of traditional power and support combining with new and more complex domestic responsibilities.

In this simplified model, I have attempted to suggest that there are interchanges between all of the four elements. Thus gender interest groups or movements mobilised on implicit or explicit gender lines may themselves be seen as influencing state policy. In the case of interventions on the part of men this is rarely at an explicit level; the dominating never have to justify their dominance but simply to assume it. Thus, it might be argued that some of the legislation associated with sexual liberation in the 1960s might, in retrospect, be seen more in terms of the interests of men than of women (Segal in Segal (ed.), 1983). This is even clearer in the case of masculine pressure, through the trades union movement, to resist women's employment and to maintain the idea of the family wage. Similarly, recent pressure groups on behalf of divorced fathers may be seen either as attempts on the part of fathers to claim some caring role or as an attempt to organise against women. In the case of women, the pressure is necessarily more explicit, more obvious and hence more open to criticism and adverse comment. Nevertheless, it is likely that state policy has been influenced by such organised pressure, although often in complex and ambiguous ways.

We are, therefore, dealing with a situation of considerable fluidity. Many of the articles in the journal *Family Law*, for example, show an appreciable degree of understanding of the feminist arguments, at some distance from the magisterial statements of Lord Denning recorded earlier. Freeman, for example, is in no doubt as to the nature of domestic violence:

> Violence against women is better seen as a necessary concomitant of women's generally oppressed position in the social structure. The purpose of male violence is to control women. (Freeman, 1979, p. 111)

King questions the notion of 'maternal love' and accuses judges of: 'using metaphysical notions to reinforce the role which our society imposes upon the mother of young children.' (King, 1974, p. 64.) These examples could be multiplied although many counter-instances could also be provided. It is possible that the area of family law is of relatively low prestige in the legal profession and hence attracts those with more critical attitudes towards state and society. Nevertheless, these examples remind us that the state does not present a unified face on these or other matters and that divisions and contradictions within it are as important as the conflicts between the state and various groups within society.

The reference to the pronouncements of judges and legal experts should underline the fact that in dealing with interactions between state and gender we are not simply speaking of legislation but also of many different kinds of officials and professionals who are employed by the state (or who require some kind of licence from the state to practice) and who should be considered if we are to depart from a somewhat monolithic and reified conception of 'The State'. The gender/state relationship, therefore, is much more than a question of the framing and influencing of legislation: it is also relationships between teachers and pupils in classrooms, between doctors and patients in consulting rooms, between social workers and clients in home or office and between the police and the public in the street. It is particularly in the fields of health and education that these encounters are likely to be most crucial for it is there that women, particularly as wives and mothers, are likely to come up against the state.

5 State/family Many of the issues arising out of the interrelation between the state and the family cannot be clearly distinguished from the concerns of the previous section. The family is, among other things, about gender relations, about what is taken to be the normal, natural or desirable relationship between men and women within the household, and how this relates to distinctions between home and work, the public and the private and the division of labour within the household. Since the state routinely addresses itself to questions of the nature of family living it must also be concerning itself with questions of gender.

A brief glance at the journal *Family Law* will indicate the range of issues that now concern the state in relation to the family: battered children and women, 'sham marriages', incest, custody, the sterilisation of minors, the value of a wife and so on. Take any one of these issues and explore the debates and ramifications surrounding it and you will eventually discover, and perhaps after not too long a search, the deployment of understandings about correct family relationships, about marriage and about parenthood. As in the case of gender, persons involved in the framing and enacting of legislation both draw upon conventionally held notions of familial relationships (or more complicatedly, upon notions of what these conventional notions are – the 'man on the Clapham omnibus' syndrome) and, in so doing, reinforce these notions through their public pronouncement or through their deployment in law and judgement.

At the most fundamental level, the state is involved in the definition of what constitutes a family, marriage and parenthood. What counts as a genuine and legal marriage, the claims of 'natural' as against step-parents, definitions of dependants, family and household are all called upon the framing of legislation or the enactment of judgements to do with inheritance, custody, taxation or eligibility for state benefits and the collection of official statistics. Judgements concerning the right or otherwise of members of immigrant families to stay in this country, whether their marriages are 'genuine' and so on, draw upon conventional models drawn from the ideal-typical Christian family. The growth of census taking and official statistics entailed the growing crystallisation of such notions as 'head of household', 'housewife' and 'dependant'.

One central aspect of this involvement of the state in the family is the assertion of the natural. This is well illustrated in an article by Alec Samuels on the Children's Act of 1975 (1976, pp. 5–8). Samuels notes that the Act gives new legal rights to the Minister, the local authorities, the foster parents and the adopters. He deplores the loss of rights for the natural parents, 'especially the mother'. He argues that the family is being devalued by the Act and that the vital 'love tie' that every child requires is most likely to be provided by the natural mother, 'the bond of nature'. This he feels is true even if the mother is unmarried or unsupported. Samuels is drawing upon his understanding of people like Bowlby as well as more traditional religious or moral notions. The 'natural' is therefore simultaneously being called upon and reinforced. Samuels is here arguing *against* the state and its interventions in his defence of the 'natural', much in the same tones as Mount argues against state interventions into the family (Mount, 1982). The paradox is that even where the family is the site of contested versions of the family and of the proper role of the state in relation to it, it continues to be socially and ideologically constructed even by those who wish to retain or reassert its purity.

Thus, the basic coinage of family relationships, the understanding of the central terms of marriage, family and parenthood are built into the relationships between the state and the family. In an important sense, the state is a key agency in telling or reminding us what the family 'is'. Legislators, interpreters and practitioners of the law are constantly addressing themselves to notions of normal or good family practice. For example, Poulter considers developments in the question of child custody (Poulter, 1982, pp. 5–12). A list of loose guidelines are provided, based upon recent legal practice. Thus it will be assessed which parent or set of parents will be best able to meet the child's physical and psychological needs. The author notes that in the majority of cases, young children under ten will normally go to the mother. Here the judges seem to be influenced by 'views expressed by leading child psychologists in the 1950s' (*ibid.*, p. 5). Among this list of guidelines are considerations relating to the behaviour and character of the adult parties and the likelihood of a parent being denied custody if he or she 'participates in social practices which do not conform with majority values' (*ibid.*, p. 8). Examples here are membership of minority religious sects such as the Exclusive Brethren or the Jehovahs Witnesses, and homosexuality.

Thus there are all sorts of ways in which the family is constructed anew by the variety of state interventions in which it is involved, directly or indirectly. But here too I am talking of an interchange between the two elements. In Marxist analysis it has been argued that the family reproduces the class relationships upon which the state depends and which constitute the state and, further, functions as an ideological state apparatus (Althusser, 1971; Morgan, 1979). The family, together with the educational system, may be understood as an essential ideological adjunct to the state. Even conservative thinkers will argue in a variety of ways that the stability of the state depends upon the stability of the family. It is possible to sketch out, in a very provisional way, some of the family 'inputs' into the maintenance of the state:

(i) The so-called socialisation function of the family, particularly the way in which the family serves as an agency for promulgating the nature of obedience, conformity and discipline. In the simple patriarchal model, the family stands for the wider society, and obedience to rulers is learnt through obedience to parents, especially the father. In a more complex model, what is being taught is not obedience to any one person or thing, but a general understanding of the nature and importance of obedience itself.

(ii) The notion of responsibility, the idea that parents accept responsibility for the behaviour of their children. Parents, within the family, are seen as an important agency of social control.

(iii) The creation of 'subjects' in the dual meaning of the word: as subjects in a system of hierarchical authority and as persons with identities as individuals. The family, as we have seen elsewhere, is understood as a major site of authenticity and individuality, notions which simultaneously devalue the public sphere, especially for women, and which strengthen the family as the natural focus of our attentions.

In these, and in a variety of other ways, therefore, the family is not simply constructed by and at the receiving end of state interventions and definitions but also contributes, directly and indirectly, to the maintenance of that state.

The use of the troublesome word 'ideology' at this point opens up further complex theoretical issues. What is important now is to highlight the complexity of the relationship of the multiplicity of strands that link state and family. Something of this complexity is indicated by Voysey:

> Official agencies both construct and maintain an absolute public morality. Individuals may believe that there is an absolute morality governing their lives and act in accordance with it, even if privately they do not agree with its rules. . . . Whether or not he agrees with the official morality is irrelevant since it is to this that he is held accountable for those of his actions that are public or 'private' but held to have consequences for the public realm. (Voysey, 1975, p. 42)

We are dealing here with a circular, or if preferred, dialectical relationship. Parents have certain notions as to what constitutes good parenting. The state draws upon such notions, and their elaboration in scientific theories, in its legislation and daily practices. In so doing it reinforces these notions. Since these notions are around themes of responsibility, obligation and authority, parents will draw upon these ideas when something 'goes wrong', thereby again reinforcing these ideas and the agencies which support and promulgate them The location of these notions in the sphere of the natural effectively removes them from the more temporal or ephemeral vicissitudes of political practice.

Here too, as in the case of gender, it should not be supposed that we are dealing with a solid, monolithic state with extensive and effective control in all areas of life. We are dealing with areas of contest, of change of opposition and struggle. Thus, within the area of family law we can find considerable debate over the meanings and uses of some of the key terms and it is possible, as already indicated, to find recognition given to ideas arising out of the Women's Movement as well as to ideas deriving from psychologists such as Bowlby. Bradney, in an article in *Family Law* (Bradney, 1980, pp. 244–8) considers some of the definitions of marriage and the family and recognises the contested nature of these definitions, citing myself, Aubert, Laing, Cooper and Kropotkin as well as the more familiar list of cases. Polak writes:

> The popular meaning of family was not fixed for all time; it was not restricted to blood relationships and those created by a marriage ceremony; it included *de facto* as well as *de jure* relationships. (Polak, 1975, p. 207)

The debate over the definition of marriage in recent years is instructive for while, on the one hand, we may have the recognition of various forms of cohabitation not blessed by clergy or state, we also have the tendency of judges to use the old fashioned word 'mistress' in this connection.

6 Class/gender The final relationship in this model does not properly belong in this discussion although it is clearly of relevance. The inter-relationships between class and gender have, indeed, been the subject of considerable debate and discussion (see Gamarnikow *et al.*, 1983a) although it seems clear that class and gender both reinforce and cut across each other. These issues become relevant later.

My model, let it be stressed, is simply an attempt to isolate some of the important elements in the family/state relationship and to examine their interconnections. But it must also be remembered that we are dealing with processes which may often be obscured by the presentation of a static diagram and secondly, that the relationships that we may be concerned with often involve three or more elements. In order to take the argument a little further let us consider some more concrete examples.

1 THE FAMILY WAGE

Virginia Woolf, in *Three Guineas*, expressed the idea of the family wage thus:

> Ah, you will interpose, here is another misunderstanding. Husband and wife are not only one flesh; they are also one purse. The wife's salary is half the husband's income. The man is paid more than the woman for that very reason – because he has a wife to support. The bachelor then is paid at the same rate as the unmarried woman? It appears not. . . . (Woolf, 1943, p. 64)

Traditional economic theory, Marxist as well as classical, has enshrined the idea that the wage of the man should be enough to support not only himself but his wife and children as well. The notion of the 'family wage' incorporates in stark form the conventional model of the patriarchal nuclear family. As Land has argued (Land, 1980) the debate over the family wage highlighted some of the tensions between class and gender in relation to the state for, partly opposed to the idea of the family wage was that of 'family allowances' which would be paid directly to the mother. Trade union and labour movement pressure for the 'family wage' underlined conventional conservative models of the patriarchal family. The workers pay packet should be large enough to provide a reasonable standard of living for the man and his family. This should be a basis for any wage claims and industrial action, and underlying that was the very powerful idea of the man as 'the provider', as someone who took on the responsibility of caring, economically, for others. To be unable to provide for one's family was, in some sense, to be less than a man. The claim for the 'family wage' also reinforced, therefore, certain notions of masculinity. The movement for 'family allowances' on the other hand was seen in some quarters as undermining this traditional authority of the working-class father and weakening and dividing the struggle of the labour movement in its attempt to secure a decent standard of living for all working people.

Thus the struggle around 'the family wage' involves a three-cornered tug between class, gender and the state insofar as the last may be either an employer or in some way involved in the economy. The state is also involved in other ways. The construction of the man as the supporter, as deriving status and identity from having people who depend upon his labour and earnings, accords well with the general ethic of capitalism. It provides a motive for work; it gives a sense of responsibility directed towards the family rather than towards the class or the wider polity; it underlines the rhetoric that can be mounted against the scrounger, the person dependent upon social security (Golding and Middleton, 1982).

That the idea of the family wage works at an ideological level is evidenced by the fact that it never accorded with experience. From the earliest days of industrial capitalism, working-class households relied upon a variety of earning strategies including, most crucially, the wife's employment outside the home (Rushton, 1979). The notion of the breadwinner has never matched actual experience even where it still retains its rhetorical power. It may be noted, however, that the power of this rhetoric is seen up to the present day where even in two earning households, the earnings of the wife may be treated as marginal or extras (Hunt, 1980; Cunnison, 1983).

The idea of the family wage also introduced another familiar figure in political rhetoric, that of the housewife in her guise as consumer: on the one hand, the man seeking to enlarge his earning power either through individual efforts or collective struggle; on the other hand, the woman, anxiously scanning the shelves of the supermarket, planning and budgeting for the week to come. The idea of the one reinforces the other.

2 THE FAMILY IMPACT STATEMENT

The 'family wage' debate showed, among other things, paradoxical alliances at the level of gender ideology between some working-class leaders and some conservative and business leaders. The idea of the 'family impact statement' has something of the same flavour, being suggested by representatives from both Conservative (Bottomley) and Labour (Field) Parties. The essence of the family impact statement may be expressed in this quotation from Patrick Jenkin, a Conservative spokesperson and minister:

'Ministers would . . . be asked to accompany any new proposals with an assessment of their impact on the family. . . . In this way Parliament, Cabinet and the people

can be vigilant to safeguard and enhance the quality of
family life.' (1977, quoted in Craven, Rimmer and Wicks,
1982, p. 35)

In other statements – 'our tax system must be more family
orientated' (quoted in Study Commission on the Family, 1983,
p. 31), Jenkin seems to refer less to the 'quality of family life'
than to the needs of the children, and this latter emphasis is
more obviously the concern of Labour supporters of the idea of
the family impact statement (Field, 1980). When the term
'family poverty' is used, the emphasis again is usually focused
on the needs of children.

The idea of the 'family impact statement' (which in fact
derived from the United States) is one which shows links
between state, class, gender and family. The gender issue tends
to be muted here but, insofar as the idea of the family impact
statement has also built into it conventional notions of household structure, gender is at least implicated. It is necessary to
ask, however, what work the word 'family' does in this context.
It is perhaps best seen as a linking concept, a role which the
family is often called upon to assume in political debate.
Fogarty calls family policy (a stronger version of the family
impact statement in most accounts) the 'cement' blending
different policies together (quoted in Rapoport *et al.*, 1982,
p. 497). Wicks traces interesting similarities between the
family policy movement and the consumer movement (In *ibid.*,
pp. 469–70). The political construction of 'the consumer' (or 'the
rate payer') is based upon some notion of common interests at a
very general level which override other differences in terms of
level of income or consumption, occupation, gender or class.
It presupposes linkages to be made between daily purchases of
food from the supermarket and occasional purchases of cars,
videos and continental holidays. The 'family impact statement'
or 'family policy' presupposes linkages not merely between
individuals or separate households but between different
issues, represented by different government departments. It is a
recognition that all policies have an impact on 'the family' and
that this impact could and should be calculated in advance.

Different political and social orientations have different
understandings of the term 'family' here. In the more conservative model, the family is seen as a central value, a structure

79

that should be preserved and supported. This unit is, it would appear, a fairly standard and traditional model. In more liberal perspectives – such as in most of the statements of the Study Commission on the Family for example – the 'family' here is simply a recognition that most people live in households which they would describe as families, and that these units – nexuses of interdependence – should be considered when looking at any proposed legislation. No one form of family is being privileged, it is argued. Nevertheless, the use of the term 'family' (rather than household or referring directly to needs of children, the elderly, etc.) does appear to make use of an ideologically charged word and to privilege certain patterns of living against others. 'Family' does – even in the more extended versions – privilege households centred around a heterosexual couple and their biological or adopted children. It says little about the needs of single people or the possibility of other kinds of domestic arrangements (Coussins and Coote, 1981).

3 THE ALLOCATION OF BLAME

'We have the highest ever rates for divorce, truancy, violence, vandalism in schools, drug abuse, alcoholism and terrorism.' (J. Anderton, quoted in *Manchester Evening News*, 3/3/78)

'Women's Lib. blamed for Violence' (*Times* headline, 14/6/78)

During the riots and civil disturbances which took place during the Summer of 1981, several leading figures showed an inclination to point the blame at the family. There was, it was argued, a lack of discipline in the home; children were inadequately supervised and this led to their going out on to the streets and getting 'into trouble'. Links were often made to the rising participation of mothers in the labour force and hence 'to women's lib' (also blamed for divorce rates and wife battering) and it was occasionally argued that parents should pay for the cost of their children's escapades.

The family and particular family members have been blamed for all kinds of things in the past and the recent past including schizophrenia (particularly the schizophrenogenic mother) and all kinds of delinquency (Spiegel, 1982). In the United States there was the popular idea of the pathology of the black family, a variation on the culture of poverty theme (Rapp, 1982). Social science may apparently support many of these arguments.

If the idea of the family impact statement sees the family as a kind of junction for the meeting point of many different concerns, the family as a source of blame tends even more to remove the family from its surrounding context. A variety of ideological themes and issues find their point of intersection in the allocation of blame on to the family.

(a) The notion of parental responsibility. It is assumed that parents choose to have children and can therefore be reasonably expected to assume responsibility for their actions. The idea of parenthood is a natural given; it is so basic and widespread that ignorance cannot be taken as an excuse (Voysey, 1975, p. 50).

(b) The notion of the sexual division of labour. The father is seen as breadwinner and source of authority (perhaps in a more egalitarian form) and the wife as having prime responsibility at home for the care of her children. Employment outside the home on the part of the mother carries with it the connotation of irresponsibility unless very clear steps are taken to show otherwise.

(c) A variety of psychological notions which see childhood disturbances or anti-social behaviour primarily in terms of problems 'at home'. (Notions of 'the broken home', 'maternal deprivation' etc.)

(d) The idea of the family unit and the way in which family members in their dealings with the outside world may be said to reflect upon that family, rather like rowdy football supporters are said to 'let down' the good name of their country. The behaviour of one family member may reflect upon the behaviour and attitudes of others (Voysey, 1975, p. 132).

These themes once again show the complex linkages within my model. These notions are clearly widely held (although like most notions not consistently) and hence it cannot be said that politicians and social scientists are simply 'indoctrinating' the public when they call upon these themes in the analysis of social issues. They clearly have important consequences for the ways in which gender roles are understood in our society and present one of the most serious challenges to the full equality of the sexes. They also have class and sometimes ethnic connotations, as the reference to the pathology of the black family and associated notions of cycles of deprivation indicate. It is the rioting of children in inner cities that gives rise to notions of inadequate family structures and poor family practices; we do not call upon the same frame of reference when an adult is charged with embezzlement, fraud or dangerous driving.

One further point might be noted and that is the reverse process of the allocation of praise. Voysey, for example, shows this process at work in the case of families of handicapped children. Parents of such children, she argues, present a test of the legitimating power of familistic ideology (*ibid.*, p. 219). They are informed by everyday notions of normal parenting and may become exemplary models – 'coping wonderfully', etc. – which thereby sustains the force of ideology. The allocation of praise, like blame, has a single point of reference: the ideological construction of the normal family, of good family practice.

4 Unspoken themes: inequality and conflict

INTRODUCTION

It is a commonplace of political or social debate to say that such a text – a speech, a manifesto, a report – is more significant in what it excludes than in what it includes. This is not simply a question of a failure to 'cover the field' as if the text were expected to reproduce in miniature the whole area to which it purports to be addressing itself. What we have in mind here is a stronger sense of exclusion, a sense in which the omissions may be said to 'speak volumes', in the double sense that these omissions tell us something about the authors of the text and also that these omissions have the effect of underlying the overt written or spoken message of the text. That which is excluded, by virtue of the fact of its exclusion and the claims to authority on the part of the text, is deemed to be unimportant, irrelevant, extreme or the view of a small minority.

Marriage Matters is no exception in this respect and this chapter will deal with two such omissions, that of inequality (class and gender) and of conflict and contradiction. Before proceeding to these substantive issues, I shall raise some further questions about *how* these exclusions and omissions are achieved. It is assumed, then, that the omissions and exclusions of a text are not the result of personal ignorance, bias or malice on the part of the authors, that they are not the result of any particular conspiracy of which the authors form a part and, finally, that they are not the outcome of a simple process which sees the text as the end product of some abstracted interplay between state and ideology.

Consider, for example, the following passage:

> Our evidence, and the experiences of our members, confirm
> that the Report was accurate in saying that 'all strata of
> society are involved', that 'physical violence is not necessarily
> any less tolerable than verbal or emotional assault' and that
> – particularly in the wider sense – men are 'battered' by
> women as well as vice versa. Violence in marriage is indeed
> 'a wide and difficult subject' with a 'complex origin'.
> (Working Party on Marriage Guidance, 1979, para. 7.48.
> The quotations come from the House of Commons Select
> Committee on *Violence in Marriage*, 1975)

Here, the Report deals with one particular aspect of domestic
conflict, that of violence in marriage. The passage achieves
several things. It states the authority of those presenting the
Report: 'our evidence and the experience of our members'. It
again seeks to convey a sense of judicious balance, making
claims for legitimacy and competence in dealing with a 'wide
and difficult subject'. The sense of balance is achieved by a set of
oppositions: on the one hand 'physical violence', on the other
'verbal or emotional assault'; on the one hand 'women are
battered' and the other 'men can be battered too'. It is clear that
this paragraph (and other paragraphs dealing with this issue in
the Report) has the effect of neutralising the original moral and
political critique, of edging out the feminist perspective which,
had it been considered in more detail, might have provoked a
much wider critique of the model of marriage being endorsed in
this particular Report. One thing that the 'balance' presented in
this paragraph achieves is the parallel sense of marriage as a
symmetrical relationship, whereas, of course, the feminist
critique has been directed at all aspects of this assumed
symmetry. This striving for balance and representativeness
sometimes gives the Report a kind of vagueness which
approaches obscurity:

> Another paradox is observable in that, while living
> standards and the quality of life have risen and inequalities
> in this regard have shown some reduction, the differences
> between the 'haves' and 'havenots' are made much more of,
> and are still as controversial. (Working Party, *ibid.*,
> para. 2.24)

This quotation is a whole paragraph and one of the few which treats questions of inequality. It may be possible to make something of this paragraph taking it in context, but the abiding impression is one of obscurity. It may be noted that some of the more obscure passages of this kind occur when the Report attempts to deal with socio-historical factors as compared with the relatively more concrete style adopted when dealing with matters of marital counselling and its organisation.

It may be said, therefore, that the text uses a variety of devices to present its case and, at the same time, to make claims for its own authenticity and legitimacy. These are:

1 *Normalisation*. Throughout the text there is a constant strain towards a consensus. The 'we', signifying collective authorship, comes to stand for a wider body of expert and experienced opinion.
2 *Exclusion, evasion and omission*. The examples cited illustrate these devices whereby wider controversial issues are displaced. It is to be stressed that there is nothing sinister or conspiratorial about this. Such processes are doubtless features of all texts, including the present one. It may be noted in passing that where some exclusions are mentioned this is presented as a technical problem, one of lack of time or resources, etc. Thus, the Report acknowledges that it was not able to get the views of laypersons, potentially or actually at the receiving end of marital counselling.
3 *Objectification*. This is found throughout the text in the adoption of the medical model and the emphasis on administrative or technical solutions to the problems. The emphasis is on better training, better coordination and better (i.e. more scientific) research.

It must be recognised that almost any official document, produced by a committee or a working party is under a particular set of constraints to present its findings as objective and as a fair representation of the evidence rather than the personal views of a set of individuals. Where a report does not conduct research itself, the tendency is to rely upon a body of 'informed opinion', the opinion of experts and practitioners in the field. This is doubtless particularly the case where the object of the report is seen as being particularly contentious. When confronted with views ranging from the Catholic Church and other religious groups stressing the sanctity of marriage to contemporary feminist critiques of the very same institution, the temptation must be to strive for some sense of the middle ground, excluding the extremes or incorporating them where possible.

But to point to the difficulties facing a committee entrusted with the production of an 'official' report is not to tell the whole story. In Chapter 1, I outlined some of the features of the Report in terms of the membership of the Working Party, the range of persons and institutions consulted for evidence and the range of published sources used and cited. It was suggested that this range of sources might be expected to produce something approaching a medical model of marriage, and this is not necessarily surprising given the particular terms of reference of the Working Party. What we have here is a very complex inter-relationship between the terms of reference of the Report (and the factors shaping these); the routine understandings of the workings of an official committee and the desire to produce a balanced, objective report, these understandings themselves shaped by wider societal expectations; the similarity of approach in many of the sources consulted, particularly in terms of a professional, medical model of marriage; and the way in which all these factors interplay to squeeze out discrepant views. These discrepant views are to do with gender and class inequalities and with conflict and contradictions within the institution of marriage.

INEQUALITIES: GENDER

It is possible to find some references to feminist perspectives in the Report. The National Women's Aid Federation presumably was consulted on the sections dealing with violence in marriage and the advice columnist, Anna Raeburn, might be claimed as someone close to a feminist perspective. However, it cannot be said that the theme of gender inequality appears much to the fore in the Report. In most cases, the male pronoun is used throughout the text to refer to persons who might, in theory, be of either gender. The sense of a feminist critique of the institution of marriage might be subsumed under more general references to 'radical changes in the relation between men and women' (para. 2.21) but might also be said to be generally excluded by reference to the 'fact' that only 3 per cent of Britain's sixteen-year-olds state that they do not wish to marry (para. 2.22).

This is not to criticise the Report for excluding a full-scale feminist critique of the institution of marriage, although a recognition of some of the literature coming out of, or influenced by, this movement might have caused the authors to hesitate before putting in passages about the growth of 'symmetrical' or 'companionate' marriages. The omissions are not so much in terms of a set of feminist texts, but rather in terms of a wider set of women's experiences, *differential* experiences of marriage and the family. Against the view, presented in the Report, that marriage has become an interpersonal relationship with the emphasis on personal growth and development, it should be possible to present the argument that marriage is still, to a large extent, an unequal relationship between men and women. This inequality is still significant enough to question the very use of the term 'marriage' insofar as the use of this term masks important differences between the spouses in terms of experiences and understandings.

The version of marriage presented in the Report closely resembles, at some points, the version presented by the widely reprinted paper by Berger and Kellner (1964). While this paper is not actually cited in the Report it is likely that, given its wide circulation in a variety of places, it formed part of the background understandings of at least some members of the Working Party. I have discussed Berger and Kellner's paper in more detail elsewhere (Morgan, 1982) but a summary of the main points may not be out of place.

The article is an extension of Berger's central concern with the sociology of knowledge and his understanding of the world as socially constructed which, as mediated to and actualised by the individual, is in constant need of validation. Both societies and individuals require some constant process where the precarious reality of the social world is reaffirmed as being incontestably real. Such validation is chiefly 'sustained through conversation with significant others' (Berger and Kellner in Anderson (ed.), 1980, p. 305). In contemporary society, marriage can be seen as a key institution in this collaborative process of reality construction and reaffirmation.

Issues

There are certain features of marriage in contemporary society that underscore its crucial role in this validation process. Marriage is supported by a massive and pervasive ideology defining the centrality of the nuclear family, the nature of romantic love and the importance of personal and sexual fulfilment in the context of a stable, heterosexual relationship. These ideological prescriptions are reinforced in an urban, industrial society which, for a variety of historical reasons, defines marriage and the family as central concerns, gives special priority to the private sphere in the face of a relatively impersonal occupational and political world and which defines the marital relationship as a major arena within which to exercise individual choice and autonomy. Berger and Kellner's account is very much in line with Parson's functional account of marriage and the family (Morgan, 1975, Ch. 1) and with *Marriage Matters'* account of the shift from institution to relationship. One consequence of Berger and Kellner's approach to marriage (and here they miss the insights of their chief mentor in this project, Durkheim) is that the relationship is treated as an undifferentiated unity. Differences between women and men within the relationship are obliterated. However, at about the same time that Berger and Kellner's paper first came out, Betty Friedan had already published her *Family Mystique* with its sensitive charting of 'the problem that has no name' and its indictment of much contemporary social science in its treatment of marriage and the family (Friedan, 1963). Some ten years later, Bernard's *The Future of Marriage* spelt out in considerable detail the differences in perceptions and experience of marriage between men and women implied in Friedan's earlier book (Bernard, 1973). While there is clearly much room for argument over her statistics and interpretations, the general premise on which Bernard's work was based can scarcely be disputed: 'Anyone . . . discussing the future of marriage has to specify whose marriage he is talking about: the husband's or the wife's. (*ibid.*, p. 4.)

This is not simply a matter of an argument being disproved by subsequent research or of a position coming under attack from the feminist movement that developed in the late 1960s after the publication of Berger and Kellner's paper. It is rather that the authors, in seeking to highlight, ideal-typically, some of the taken-for-granted features of contemporary marriage, fail to present one of the most taken-for-granted features of all, namely the inequality between men and women.

FAMILY AND GENDER

In terms of the 'model' outlined in the previous chapter, I am concerned here with a set of interchanges between gender and the family. The central strands in much of the current debate about marriage and the family tend to marginalise or minimise questions of gender. In contrast, this section will attempt to show not only that gender is a major axis of differentiation that we need to take into account if we are to understand these institutions but that, further, these institutions are central to understanding the processes of the reproduction of gender inequalities. Central but not causal in any simple linear sense, gender inequalities exist and are sustained and reproduced in 'the wider society' and these wider understandings feed back into and influence relationships within marriage and the family. The wider theoretical issues will be deferred until Chapter 9; here I shall deal with more empirical and political issues.

In legal terms, inequalities are still often written into the marital relationship, defining the status of the wife as that of a dependant. It is also likely that, even where there have been some formal changes in the direction of equality, official attitudes may still reflect more traditional values. The status of a dependant, enshrined in legal and fiscal terms is also reflected in the economic dimensions of the marital relationship. It is difficult to find any reference to economics in *Marriage Matters*, reflecting the belief in a transition from institution to inter-personal relationship and the professional involvement of the practitioners in the psychological aspects of the relationship. While research should have destroyed, once and for all, the 'myth of the male breadwinner' (Land, 1975), it is clear that the myth still has considerable sway at all levels of society and is reflected in actual practice. Thus, while most women will expect to undertake paid employment for a large part of their lives, some women indeed will earn sums equal to or greater than those of their husbands, and while many women will be sole breadwinners, the expectations remain that the male job is primary. In times of high unemployment these expectations are reflected in calls for a return to a more traditional model of marital living and that wives should 'make way' for the men in the market-place.

The long debate within Marxism and feminism over the theoretical status of housework did at least underline one vital point, namely that home and work are not separate spheres, economically, but formed part of the same system, although often articulated in very complex ways. Housework is an economic activity. It contributes to the maintenance and reproduction of the economic system, it is very clearly understood to be work by those who undertake it and its value can, under certain conditions and at certain points of family crisis, be calculated. Moreover, it is an economic activity which remains the responsibility of women, even where these women may also be undertaking full-time paid employment. While there are many modifications to, and in some cases departures from, the ideal typical model of male-breadwinner/female housewife it is still the case that the household still manifests strong tendencies in this direction, and that these tendencies are reflected in legal judgements, official pronouncements and commonsense understandings.

These legal and economic differences are further reflected in another dimension of marriage, that of power and decision making. Earlier studies of the effect of the wife's employment on decision making in the home suggesting a move to a more egalitarian domestic political system have been found defective because of the failure to differentiate decisions in terms of importance and because of the limited notion of power that was being used. This notion seemed more concerned with overt negotiation than covert vetoes, ignored questions of the wider power to define the rules and expectations within which the bargaining should take place and failed to consider the more subtle features of the 'deferential dialectic' (Gillespie, 1971; Bell and Newby, 1976). The rediscovery of domestic violence must be fed into the analysis, not simply in terms of actual violence, but also in terms of the threat of or potential for violence.

I have, for the purposes of the argument, isolated the legal/fiscal, the economic and the interpersonal. In practice, of course, these all inter-relate and reinforce each other. This is most dramatically illustrated on such occasions as wife battering, where the man's greater capacity for violence is demonstrated and where the wife's dependence is, or was until fairly recently, demonstrated in her inability to escape, physically, and often psychologically, from a dangerous and intolerable situation. But even outside the more dramatic or public demonstrations of marital power, inequality and dependence, actual marriages would seem to be at some variance from the model proposed theoretically by Berger and Kellner and practically by *Marriage Matters.*

The case of middle-class or professional marriages provides an instructive case study. Young and Willmott argued that the middle classes would stand, at the head of a marching column, as some kind of exemplars of symmetrical marriage (Young and Willmott, 1973 (Penguin, 1975)). This argument, together with the belief that affluence is positively associated with egalitarianism plus a dash of class stereotyping, might lead one to suppose that middle and professional classes would manifest some kind of model of marriage close to that of Berger and Kellner. However, a variety of studies, including the Pahls' studies of managers and their wives (Pahl and Pahl, 1971), Young and Willmott's own chapter on managing directors (*op. cit.*, Ch. 9), Edgell on middle-class couples (Edgell, 1980) and Taylorson on women academics (Taylorson, 1980), all point in the opposite direction. We may instance the following contributing factors: the dominance of the husband's career, particularly at the early stages of the family life cycle where the wife is left to care for small children while the husband is advancing; the expectation, at higher levels, for domestic entertaining; the greater earning power of the husband in many cases; the prestige of not working and of participating in voluntary activity, again at the higher levels; and the almost universal tendency to define the husband's participation in the running of the house and childcare as 'helping'. In many middle-class or professional households, the wife retains the major responsibility for the domestic economy, even where the husband may assume some responsibility for some portion of the domestic system.

There may be two possible objections to this account of gender inequality in marriage. The first would be to argue that the discussion has confused differences with inequalities. Berger and Kellner's account of marriage would not necessarily preclude a recognition of differences; this is also possibly the case with *Marriage Matters*. The differences are summed up in the term 'sexual division of labour'. I have not, in fact, begun to map the complexities of this sexual division of labour and the multitude of patterns possible around the oppositions of home and work, male and female, public and private and so on. To do so, I should have to make some fairly rigorous distinctions between differences, asymmetries and inequalities; I should need to ask whether these differences were structured or individual; and I should have to ask whether these differences were reflected in the subjective evaluations of the partners concerned. From what has been said so far it should be clear that at least some of the differences within the marital relationship are also asymmetries and inequalities; that these asymmetries and inequalities are structured in that they are not the simple product of individual choice on the part of the partners; and that some of these asymmetries and inequalities are felt and perceived as such, at least by the women. The studies of housework alone should provide the evidence (Oakley, 1974).

Another kind of objection to my discussion so far may be stated in socio-historical terms. Thus, it could be argued that while there are still some differences, asymmetries and inequalities within marriage, these differences are less frequent now than in former times. This is implied in Berger and Kellner's brief attempt to locate contemporary Western marriage, in *Marriage Matters'* discussion of the shift from institution to relationship, and Young and Willmott's account of the stages from pre-industrial Britain to the present time. The history of this period can be seen, adopting a classical liberal model of progress, as a steady removal of the inequalities facing women within marriage. Landmarks would include the Married Women's Property Act, the various Divorce Acts, the acquisition of the right to vote, the expansion in employment opportunities and equal opportunities legislation. Some of these changes were more to do with the public arena but all of them had some impact on marriage itself. Thus, it might be argued, while there may still exist some inequalities within marriage, these are less numerous and less onerous than in former times. Where such inequalities persist, they may be seen as anomalies awaiting early rectification or, more conservatively, evidence that legislation 'cannot change human nature', that many couples actually prefer a more or less traditional arrangement.

There is little doubt that this kind of view is fairly widespread, one which notes the considerable progress over the past century or so, acknowledges existing inequalities and anomalies and expects that more or less steady improvement to continue. It would be foolish, moreover, to brand these accounts as simply examples of bourgeois or patriarchal ideology. It is also important to realise that many of these developments were the result of collective action on the part of women themselves and not simply concessions made by a patriarchal establishment. That there remains a lot of work to be done does not obliterate the fact of achievements already accomplished.

There are a couple of questions that need to be asked, however, of the liberal progressive model of the expansion of women's rights in marriage. The first is to do with the question of feelings, experiences and expectations. We can, with some difficulty and considerable inexactitude, begin to map out patterns of feelings and expectations among groups of people in contemporary society. The difficulties are, however, considerably multiplied when we attempt to map the feelings and expectations of former generations (see Chapter 7). Thus, while we can record, after some diligent research, the sexual division of labour in former times, it is much more difficult, perhaps impossible, to trace the structures of meanings and feelings that accompanied these more formal differences. In short, we do not know the extent to which these differences were understood by the women as inequalities; evidence from the more literate or articulate strata of society is always suspect to some extent. There is the danger of projecting current feelings and experiences on to patterns of living of earlier generations.

The consideration of the possibility of there being differing expectations in relation to marriage at different points of time also suggests the well-known theory of the dislocation of expectations and actuality. Stated in its baldest terms such a theory would consist of the following elements:

1 An initial state where there is a more or less stable match between expectations and reality. The normal assumption is that expectations are low or moderate although, theoretically, high expectations could be matched by actuality. Such departures from this match as exist will be interpreted in terms of individual failure, rather than in structural terms.

2 A period of social change where expectations are raised. The processes whereby these changes come about are very complex; certainly they are not simply generated out of the air. We may note, for example, the presence of actual institutional change in certain sectors of society which may lead, through education, the media, political action and so on, to these sections of society being presented as exemplars or models of what is possible and desirable.

3 The perception of the gap between these rising expectations and actuality for large sections of society.

4 Diffuse unhappiness and discontent giving rise to more organised, coherent patterns of protest acting back upon and possibly changing the institutions that are found wanting.

The application of this model to marriage should be clear and, indeed, variations of this account have been applied to the growth of feminism in the post-war years. Mitchell, for example, lays particular emphasis on the expansion of higher education in the early 1960s, although placing this within a wider discussion of the contradictions of capitalism (Mitchell, 1971, pp. 28–39). Education, particularly higher and further education, is *formally* based upon universalistic, egalitarian premises, premises which come into conflict with actual experiences of marriage. We may also note the possible effect of sociology here; the egalitarian family model in its many variations disseminated through countless undergraduate courses, extra-mural classes, television and radio discussions and articles in popular journals and newspapers must have made some kind of impact and have caused some women to pause and examine, quizzically, their own marriages or relationships. Even where the impact of these contradictions was not direct, it was perhaps mediated more sharply by women's groups and individual feminists. In place of the liberal evolutionary model, therefore, we can substitute a more dynamic, dialectical model, one that stresses the contradictions and strains between expectations and reality such that even where, as is undoubtedly the case, there have been changes within these institutions of marriage, the rising expectations have risen faster than these actual changes.

In the second place, and related to this discussion of the relationship between actuality and experience, we must

94

consider the possibility that in some respects things may have worsened within the marital relationship. Two such aspects may be given brief consideration:

1 *The deskilling of housework.* Here we may note the following inter-related features: the loss of personal prestige within the wider family or neighbourhood based upon the possession of certain particular household skills; the removal of certain skills and knowledge to others such as doctors, health visitors and cookery experts; the growth of mass-produced products and appliances; and the increasing isolation and fragmentation of the actual practice of housework.

2 *The burdens of working wives.* Innumerable studies on either side of the Iron Curtain have shown that the entry of women into the labour market or into full-time paid occupations outside the home has not led to a *concomitant* increase in the husband's participation in the home. It would be a fine and complex task to attempt to enumerate the actual changes in the total number of hours worked (at home and in paid employment) by women. Such a calculation would have to take into account changes in hours of paid employment, the possible (and not necessarily straightforward) impact of labour saving devices in the home, the increased ability to purchase the labour of others for some domestic tasks, distances between home, work, schools and shops and the possibilities of speedy travel between these points. There are enough questions here to challenge the simple liberal evolutionary model of the move towards egalitarianism in the home; certainly we would expect, in the light of these potential calculations, to find considerable variations in terms of class and, equally certainly, we would expect to find evidence of only minimal real change for some sections of society.

It has been argued, therefore, that the egalitarian model of marriage can be called into question, both in actual terms and in terms of the expectations surrounding it. Such qualifications have a variety of consequences. In the first place, they point to a need to undermine and question the reificatory character of the term 'marriage' and the desirability of distinguishing between the experiences of husbands and wives. In the second place, such differences in experience and perception may be a valuable clue to the 'problems of marriage' themselves. The fact that the majority of petitions for divorce are initiated by women, a fact made little (if anything) of in *Marriage Matters*, should itself point to this discrepancy. Finally, insofar as the differences are ignored or muted in favour of a stress on the 'relationship', the Report provides ideological support for a particular model of marriage and for a particular version of the world by editing out, as it were, the perspectives of feminists and the experiences of women, not all of whom would describe themselves thus.

While this section has concentrated on the ways in which marriage in particular, even those marriages which might be supposed to be more egalitarian, reproduces gender inequalities, there is also a reverse process. Whatever their origin, gender inequalities exist and persist in labour markets, in public representations, in legal and political processes and in education. The statement 'a woman's place is in the home' is both a public statement, used to legitimise inequalities in employment for example, and a private resource to be deployed within the micro-politics of the home. In most cases, here as elsewhere in social life, we are dealing with circular, inter-dependent and dialectical relationships. Traditional models of domesticity are used to legitimise and maintain a labour market structured around gender inequality. As a consequence we find women concentrated in relatively lowly paid, routine and sometimes unpleasant working conditions (Gamarnikow *et al.*, 1983b). Moreover, within the home, their earnings are marginalised or treated as extras. Consequently, in terms of some simple cost-benefit analysis, home may be preferred to work, hence reinforcing the traditional structure of beliefs.

Moreover, we are not dealing with a static situation. While the gender-family link may appear to be one of the strongest and most durable links within the model (and it is certainly ideo-logically constructed that way) it is subject to change. Changes in the roles and statuses of women in education and work can be seen as having some kind of cumulative effect on relationships within the family, although these processes are not always as straightforward as some of the sociological analyses of the effects of work on domestic power relationships would seem to suggest. Increasing participation in the labour force, implying a wider range of experiences outside the home and (in some cases) an independent income, together with the impact, direct and more indirectly diffused, of the WLM can be seen as having some kind of effect on relationships between husband and wife. To this extent, and with all the necessary qualifications, the feminist movement can be apportioned some of the 'blame' for rising divorce rates. Similarly, the development of alternative models of the marital or family relationships or even of 'non-family' households and their dissemination through the media has some kind of effect on wider understandings of gender relationships. There is perhaps a danger in playing down these relatively unexplored areas of change and their multiple reverberations in favour of a relatively static model of unchanging inequality. That this particular link, gender-family, is a central link cannot be denied and this is nowhere more manifest than in the fact that most of the change and adjustment seems to be focused upon the women rather than the men. Nevertheless, it is important to monitor and analyse these processes of change and their effects throughout the system.

FAMILY AND CLASS

The other form of inequality with which I am concerned here is class inequality, using the term as a loose form of shorthand for a whole set of inequalities, chiefly, although not wholly, focused upon the economic sphere. Class, and the wider question of the reproduction of economic inequalities is very much an 'unspoken theme' in *Marriage Matters*. There are some brief references to poverty, 'family poverty', in the final publication of the Study Commission on the Family, *Families in the Future* (1983), but no serious treatment of inequality or class. Class and inequality feature a little more in the Rapoport *et al.* volume *Families in Britain* (1982), but again it cannot be understood to be a central concern.

It is also the case that where some issues of stratification might be raised (questions of poverty, unemployment, ethnicity, etc.) these are understood to be sources of variation on what is otherwise a central family theme. This is particularly true in the case of ethnicity where different family forms are recognised while the wider structures of racialism and discrimination are ignored. In this chapter I shall be concerned with emphasising a stronger point. Not only are family/household structures *different* according to a variety of indicators of social stratification but there is a strong connection between the household/family forms and the continuation of these inequalities. In short, the family may be seen as an important institution in the reproduction of class differences, just as it may be seen as an important agency in the reproduction of gender differences. A more complex model would look at the interplay between gender, class and family.

Without going into complex theoretical debates, I see social class as involving differences in terms of income and wealth, differences that have a considerable effect on the life chances of the individuals involved. This is not, of course, the whole story but it is an important part, especially when considering the influence of the family. Looking first at the influence on the family of poverty we may distinguish two levels of analysis. In the first place it is possible to list a variety of 'family' conditions – single parent, large number of children, old age, etc. – which, other things being equal, give rise to a condition of poverty. In these cases it is the ratio of persons labelled as 'dependants' in relation to the household as a whole which seems to be the crucial factor. The word 'family' is often used in such a context (see previous chapter) but this is a convenient reflection of ideological centrality plus common practice rather than a strictly logical use since 'dependency' need not necessarily be defined in familistic terms.

In a stronger sense we may see the variety of family and household situations that are conducive to poverty at some stage as being situated in a wider class structure. This is partly a reflection of the obvious point that the conditions listed above (such as single parenthood) do not necessarily give rise to poverty in the households concerned; it is the combination of class and domestic factors that is important. In this sense we may see class as being reproduced through the patterns of dependence associated with the family. Certain tendencies within working-class families – earlier marriage, large families, etc. – will combine with other economic features such as lower job security, poor housing and educational disadvantages to produce a mutually reinforcing system of disadvantage and poverty. The family cannot be said to 'cause' the condition of poverty but it is a major institution in its reproduction. We need to distinguish this argument from other popular ones about 'the culture' of poverty and biologistic notions of transmitted deprivation.

The central weakness of many discussions of poverty is their tendency to be isolated from an analysis of wider patterns of class inequality. Writers, such as Field and Townsend, have reminded us that it is important to consider the wealthy or the relatively well-off at the same time as conducting any kind of survey of the poor. The variety of mechanisms through which wealth, and all the advantages and privileges that accompany it, is inherited have been recorded in a variety of places and are well known (Field, 1980; Townsend, 1979; Scott, 1982). The surprising thing is that these economic dimensions of family living are so often ignored in discussions of the family; similarly, if less frequently, the family dimension of stratification is not always given the emphasis that it might. If, in the case of the poor, we see a variety of more or less family based strategies being adopted in order to minimise the effect of poverty, in the case of the more wealthy we find a set of family strategies being adopted in order to maintain wealth. The resilience of the patterns of wealth inequality is well known and it is clear that family-based strategies are central to the understanding of the processes by which the top 5 per cent may be said to own over half the nation's wealth while the bottom 5 per cent own little or nothing (Townsend, 1979, p. 343). We need to look at patterns and methods of inheritance and gift-receiving and of differential patterns of house purchase and ownership. Domestic property may be seen as a crucial linking variable; on the one hand being a major resource or limitation for individual households and, at the same time, a public resource with a market value (Fletcher, 1976). We need to note that not only do the wealthy deploy a variety of family strategies which enable them to maintain and reproduce their wealth but that they are also more likely to create the standards and rules by which such familistic standards continue to be possible. At an ideological level, they are able to define standards of and explanations for poverty and inequality (Townsend, 1979, p. 367). All this forms part of what Townsend calls the 'cumulative command over resources' (*ibid.*, pp. 389–90; Scott, 1982, p. 119).

Thus, at all levels of society, marriage has an economic dimension and economic consequences and the family and family-based strategies are central to understanding both the lives of the poor and the privileges of the wealthy. They are also important in understanding households in the middle levels of society in, for example, the patterns of owner-occupation and inheritance of domestic property (Townsend, *ibid.*, pp. 524–5). In short, we may see the family and marriage as crucial in the reproduction of class-based inequalities. In all cases, the very language used – such as 'cumulative command over resources' – indicates that we are dealing with an interactive process. The family not only reproduces inequalities, these inequalities form the parameters defining what resources are available to families to reproduce themselves within the life span of a household and over generations.

Classes are not static and social mobility is an important feature of industrial society. Certainly, if we take absolute rates of social mobility, then, as Goldthorpe and his colleagues have noted, there has been considerable upward social mobility in England and Wales since the beginning of this century and not all of this is to be accounted for by relatively short moves (Goldthorpe *et al.*, 1980). The 'service class' of professionals and managers has increasingly been recruited from diverse social origins. Similarly, in educational terms, Halsey and his colleagues call into question the notion of a cultural capital which is passed on by middle-class parents to their sons (women were excluded from the analysis). At all the selective schools, fee-paying and grammar, we find the dominance of first-generation pupils (Halsey, *et al.*, 1980, p. 88). In class, occupational and educational terms, therefore, we find a considerable amount of social mobility. Insofar as the family plays a part in this, it would seem to be a combination of material and cultural circumstances that is important, although the surveys do not really tell us a great deal about the circumstances that are favourable to mobility.

However, that is not the whole story. In a perfectly stable class society, upward social mobility could only be achieved through the replacement of persons in the higher classes, i.e. it would need to be matched by downward mobility. With an expansion of positions in the service class, however, it is possible to achieve the pattern which we actually find, that is an asymmetrical pattern of social mobility. In income terms, *men* from lower levels are more likely to rise than men from upper levels to fall (Brown and Madge, 1982, p. 64). Although the service class is increasingly recruited from all levels of society, at the same time it is able to transmit its advantages to its young. The service class tends both to 'solidify' – to begin to constitute a genuine social grouping – while also expanding, thus providing opportunities for outsiders (Goldthorpe *et al.*, *op. cit.*, p. 256). In the ways that Townsend and others have described, this new service class is well able to preserve and maintain its advantages, not simply cultural capital, but material and cultural capital in combination. This is certainly the case if we consider access to private schooling, especially private primary schooling (Halsey *et al.*, *op. cit.*, p. 103). Similarly, looking down the scale, the present-day working class is 'overwhelmingly at least second-generation blue-collar in its composition' (Goldthorpe *et al.*, *op. cit.*, p. 259). In sum it would seem that people at the upper levels (even more so if we consider particular elites in society) are well able to pass on their advantages through school and family while at the same time opening their expanding ranks to men from lower strata while the manual working class shrinks, drawing the largest proportion of its members from its own families, perhaps over three or more generations. Classes may be seen as having both a stable core – of varying size – and a mobile periphery; hence the social structure is characterised by both mobility and stability (*ibid.*, p. 12, p. 147).

The family is, therefore, a crucial source of social stability in our society, using the term in its least controversial sense as an opposite of social mobility. It may also be central in understanding social mobility but that will require some further investigation. It is necessary at this point to refer to one body of literature and debate which might be felt to have some bearing on the topic: the theory of transmitted deprivation. The term itself lacks precision as it could range from the narrowly biological and genetic to the more social. In general, however, the idea is the simple one that social disadvantages are transmitted from generation to generation through the medium of the family. The simple version was developed by social theorists influenced by the Eugenic movement of the late nineteenth century. In its more extreme version it was argued that the state could not afford to leave the family to its own devices as the poor, already numerous, would continue to breed at a faster rate than the

101

diminishing better classes who were more likely to practice some form of family limitation. Middle-class women going out to work would exacerbate this tendency (see Lofthouse, 1912, for an example of this argument, p. 200, p. 210). While these more extreme eugenic-type theories may not be so much in evidence, the notion that a whole range of deprivations may be the responsibility of the family is still very much with us and may be seen as a version of the 'allocation of blame' processes noted in the previous chapter.

Detailed research shows that the 'transmitted deprivation' argument is much too simple. For one thing the term 'cycles of disadvantage' is preferred with the emphasis on the plural rather than the singular (Brown and Madge, 1982, p. 2). It is true that particularly unfavourable crises in one generation may be associated with problems in the next; this may be true in the case of domestic violence, for example. Multiple problems in one generation may, similarly, increase the likelihood of difficulties in the next. But such continuities are not inevitable; there is 'no general sense in which "like begets like"' (*ibid.*, p. 143). Moving away from these particular issues it can be seen that large and single parent families are important but not necessarily in any simple causal sense. Such households may be the site of a whole 'constellation of deprivations' and for understanding of this we need to look beyond the immediate domestic environment (*ibid.*, p. 211). Such an approach would lead us back to issues considered elsewhere in this section, the processes by which the social structure as a whole reproduces itself over generations, not just the poor or the socially deprived.

CONCLUSION

This chapter has looked at certain issues that have been marginalised in many of the current discussions of marriage and the family; issues of inequality in terms of gender and class. We could, of course, consider other forms of inequality such as ethnic group inequality, bringing in aspects of racialism into the model. One line of investigation here would be, for example, the way in which a certain ideal typification of white, middle-class family life is taken as the norm against which to judge, and find wanting, the family life of other ethnic groups. Or, as in the case of immigration laws, a certain middle-class model of marriage and the family may serve as a legitimation for certain legislation against ethnic groups. It would also, in a more extended treatment, need to consider questions of age and ageing and their relationship to class and gender inequalities (Phillipson, 1983).

A great deal of work needs to be done in this area and in other areas linking the family and patterns of inequality. Nevertheless, so much is clear: the family continues to be a major agency for the reproduction of class and gender inequalities. Class, family and gender are, as we have seen in the previous chapter, already related in a variety of complex ways to the state. One further relationship may be the ideological one, the process whereby the link between family, marriage and inequality is obscured or ignored in favour of a model of marriage which emphasises the interpersonal and the relational as against the economic.

5 The construction of a public issue

Social problems do not emerge of their own volition, thrusting themselves to our attention by virtue of some inherent and overriding quality of urgency; at the same time it is in the nature of the social construction of such problems that they should appear such, their apparent naturalness and obviousness both drawing attention to the issue at hand and diverting attention away from other potential issues. Such is the case with divorce and behind it the concern with a wider threat to the institution of the family and to a society which is held to be based on familistic values. That divorce is on the increase and that it brings in its wake a variety of emotional, medical and economic problems is not denied; that these problems are inherently more disturbing than those sets of problems which might be attributed to the institution of marriage itself is, however, a point of contention. Thus, it is not simply the scale of the problem, measured in terms of the divorce rate or in terms of the economic cost that accompanies it, which gives divorce its social problematic nature, it is also a set of wider social concerns and pressures which serve to focus attention on divorce as opposed to some other possible set of problems.

To talk of the social construction of a problem or public issue is to run the risk of propagating some version of conspiracy theory or some relatively simplistic functional theory. Thus the problem may be framed in such a way as to suggest that members of various elites – moral entrepreneurs – have both the ability for, through their greater access to media of persuasion, and the interest in the construction of a particular public issue. These elites may be seen as a loosely linked set of interested parties: clergy with moral and religious interests; members of the legal profession with occupational and pecuniary interests; politicians with personal or party political interests and so on. Alternatively, and more subtly, it may be argued that the framing of a particular public issue serves to, has the function of, perpetuating a particular social system, a system which, among other things provides greater rewards to these moral entrepreneurs.

The discussion of hegemony should alert us to some of the difficulties and complexities of this kind of analysis. An account purely in terms of alleged functionality or interests, while it may have some persuasive arguments in its favour, does not account for why the presentation of one particular public issue should take root more readily than another. The attention on divorce and the crisis of the family may well serve to perpetuate patriarchy or capitalism and may well be in the interest of a variety of political, religious and professional parties but the relative ease with which such an issue takes root is something that must be explained in a wider cultural context. And that kind of explanation, while eschewing any references to human nature or the human condition, will probably take us beyond the confines of a particular political regime or social system and deeper than an account of the persuasive powers of the mass media.

Such questions clearly take us well beyond the particular issue of the differing interpretations of the causes and consequences of the rising divorce rate and it is one of the purposes of this book to take this public issue as a case study of these wider problems of interpretation and sociological analysis. In this particular chapter I shall attempt to draw together some of the issues raised in the previous few chapters and point towards a wider analysis.

The beginnings of a framework for the understanding of the social construction of divorce as a problem has been provided by Brannen and Collard (1982, pp. 222–43). In a postscript to a study of the processes by which individuals come to define themselves as having a marital problem and to seek help for that defined problem, Brannen and Collard attempt to situate their empirical analysis in a wider context. They outline three sites where the discussion of marriage and marital problems has taken place, considering all three as important in the construction of divorce as a problem. The first site is roughly the area covered in my second chapter, the area constituted by inter-linked circles of politics, law and the Church. Here we would consider a variety of statements, publications and programmes from leaders in these three areas and would focus in particular on the way in which family and marriage matters entered overt political debate from the late 1970s to the present day. Liberals, as well as conservatives, will be found taking part in the debate within this first site. The second site that Brannen and Collard discuss is something outside this broad orthodox convergence (if not exactly consensus), that consisting of more radical critics of marriage and the family in contemporary society. Central among these is the Women's Movement which, while it contains a variety of differing orientations (radical feminist, Marxist feminist and so on) focuses much of its attention on oppressive and exploitative relationships within marriage and the family. The final site is the area covered by my third chapter, the growing number of professionals and semi-professionals generally indicated by the label the 'human sciences' industry (a somewhat similar analysis, although differently evaluated, appears in Berger and Berger, 1983).

In practice, it is not always easy to distinguish between these three sites, particularly the first and the third. *Marriage Matters*, for example, could be seen as falling into either camp although the emphasis (as Brannen and Collard indicate) falls very much within the third area. The publications of the Study Commission on the Family tend to the first site although have some elements of the third and so on. The second site, that occupied by the feminist movement, is clearly not quite of the same order since its 'interest' in divorce and marriage is radically opposed (for the most part) to the interests of the other two groups. Nevertheless, the approach of Brannen and Collard provides a useful point of departure.

1 POLITICS, CHURCH, LAW

It is not necessary to provide further illustrations of the converging concerns about marriage and divorce on the part of those who might be characterised following Becker, as 'moral entrepreneurs'. It *is* necessary to indicate why these concerns have been articulated at this particular time. This will necessarily be speculative and incomplete.

(a) The simple explanation might be the actual rise in divorce rates, giving rise to a public concern. As I indicated at the beginning of the chapter, this is too simple. For one thing, as Brannen and Collard indicate, the relationship between divorce statistics and marital problems leading to marital breakdown is not an obvious one. The sheer fact of collecting statistics and making these statistics more available, together with the fact that statistics have become a 'natural' part of official discourse, suggests that what is important is the visibility of the problem rather than any objective social or personal conditions (Brannen and Collard, 1982, p. 224). Moreover, there is no natural or inevitable link between the publication of sets of statistics and the growth of official or public concern. For one thing, the causal connection may quite easily be seen as working in the opposite direction, the 'concern' giving rise to the production of the statistics. Nevertheless, the production of divorce statistics is an important part of the account and one which links, perhaps, to members of the third state, members of professional or semi-professional bodies.

(b) The members of this first site may be seen as members of more traditional elites in our society, although the occupants of these positions may not necessarily themselves come from traditional backgrounds. Members of these elites, have traditionally seen themselves as guardians of public morality, as having a natural right and duty to speak on matters of morals. This is particularly true in the case of members of the churches and the legal profession, and is particularly true in the case of family matters since members of all three groups have seen crucial links between the family, morality, social order and personal and social well-being. (The particular 'mixes' of these elements may, as I demonstrated in Chapter 3, vary between different political persuasions.) In recent years, particularly since the Second World War, the apparently 'natural' right of these elites to speak on matters of morality appears to have come under challenge. The growth of a 'youth culture' and some of its more publicised manifestations such as 'hippies', 'student activists' and 'football hooligans'; the growth of 'sexual permissiveness' symbolised by the publicity given to 'swinging

107

London', the pill and Lady Chatterley; the growth and influence of the media, particularly television; the growth of areas of concentration of Commonwealth immigrants, seemingly challenging the concept of a British nation: all these and several other factors may have been defined as challenges to traditional right and authority, presenting a diffuse, spectral legitimation crisis. Groups, such as the Centre for Contemporary Cultural Studies have demonstrated in some detail how all these issues have themselves been socially constructed: but this does not detract from their power or the cumulative way in which these trends may be perceived as threats to 'traditional values'. Even the growth of sociology itself has been seen as part of this threat: 'Instead of "Ask the Archbishop" it is now "Ask the Professors of Sociology"' (Latey, 1970, p. 168). Jordan suggests that outside, but possibly related to the concern of the more traditional elites, is a specific set of concerns among the middle classes. The middle classes have (largely influenced by groups of people in the third area with whom they have many elective affinities) developed a variety of expectations about marriage and, more generally, about relationships, in the strong sense outlined in Chapter 2. They therefore develop considerable anxiety about divorce and perceived divorce rates and project this anxiety on to the working class as a kind of scapegoat. The anxieties of sections of the middle class are therefore linked, psychologically, to the processes of the allocation of blame (in Rapoport *et al.*, 1982, *op. cit.*, p. 458). This is an interesting suggestion and could, if true, add to the character of the concern shown by members of the more traditional elites about the apparent erosion of their moral privileges. Analytically we may see this as part of a wider debate seeking links between middle classes and traditional status concerns (Gusfield, 1963; King and Nugent, 1979; Tracey and Morrison, 1979).

(c) One or two more specific factors may be mentioned. In the first place there has been the rising rates of unemployment, coupled with the fear or realisation that these rates are not easily reversible by traditional policies of economy management. The relevant effects of this are manifold, but the following may be indicated:

  (i) The reassertion of the belief that a woman's role in the labour market is a secondary one, that her proper place is back in the home. Hence, the reassertion of a more traditional domestic model.

(ii) Youth unemployment, a particular focus of concern, has an effect since young people who might otherwise have left home may find themselves as semi-dependants remaining within the traditional nuclear family of origin.

(iii) Unemployment is seen as influencing a variety of other social problems, such as delinquency and vandalism. Blame, however, is allocated to the family, and to its apparent breakdown.

(d) The next set of more or less specific factors, is the 'concern' over and desire to reduce 'public expenditure'. This is often accompanied by pleas for more community and voluntary care (especially for the young, the sick and the aged) which in practice means the woman located within the traditional family structure.

(e) The 'moral panic' over educational standards may lead to a downgrading of the educational role of the school in favour of the family, especially in matters of morality and discipline.

(f) Finally, and related to the next section, are the challenges, real and apparent, that have been levelled at patriarchal power. The growth of the Women's Movement, the passing of legislation dealing with equal pay and equal opportunities, the introduction of words like 'sexism', 'sexual harassment' and 'male chauvinism' into the language may all in various ways be seen as a set of challenges undermining male patriarchal power. Rising divorce rates and the 'crisis of the family' may be seen as both the consequence of these challenges and as an opportunity for mounting a counterattack.

2 THE WOMEN'S MOVEMENT

Brannen and Collard see this as the most important element in the development of critical or radical perspectives on the family. Clearly, people within the movement are not concerned with the 'problems' of divorce or marital breakdown *per se*. However, a major stream within the movement has been the critique of the institutions of marriage and the family and of the role of these institutions in the reproduction of gender inequality and oppression. Whether this movement has contributed to the rise in divorce is difficult to assess, although it has certainly been blamed for it. Feminism, it is argued, has encouraged women to seek identities outside the traditional family-based roles. Opportunities to develop other interests and to meet other people plus the chances of an independent income have led women to become more willing to sever relationships with men and families. It is certain that this line of argument is too simple. For one thing, as has already been shown, women's earnings are not always treated as separate earnings and, for another, many women seem to leave one heterosexual relationship for another (as, of course, do men), rather than depart from the institutions of marriage or coupledom as such. What is important, however, is that the Women's Movement is perceived as a threat to traditional notions of marriage and the family (in Mount's, *The Subversive Family*, 1982, for example) and as such is correctly located as an important oppositional element in the debate about divorce.

3 PROFESSIONALS

This issue has been dealt with at some length in Chapter 2 and need only be mentioned briefly at this point. We are dealing with:

(a) The long-term rise of professions and professionalism, associated with, among other things, the growth and prestige of science and scientific models.

(b) In particular, the growth of the 'human services' industry, consisting of professionals and semi-professionals. Within this we may emphasise the growth of an overall medical discourse or orientation, one that is brought to bear on a whole range of human and relational problems.

(c) More specifically again, the growth within this movement of marital and family therapy with a particular emphasis on (i) sexuality (underlining the elaboration of a medical model) and (ii) the marriage or family as relationships in themselves that cannot be reduced to the sum of their parts.

The growth of these sets of specialists both reflects the anxieties and concerns of members of the first category (and often overlaps in terms of life styles and social networks) and develops special interests of their own which feed into the more general concern.

Thus, these various elements feed on each other in the construction of divorce as a social problem, aided by the presentation and dramatisation of these issues in the mass media. These concerns and debates take on a wider resonance, and individuals in marriages or families will have a new set of terms, rhetorics and legitimations to describe and understand their conditions. Thus, the terms of the debate become publically available and deployed and the use of these terms – 'marital problems', 'relationship problems', 'sexual problems' and so on – in turn confirms the guardians and the professionals in the rightness of their initial diagnosis.

Two features of this problem construction should be emphasised. The first is the role of marital problems as a linking concept. In other words, marital breakdown is seen and defined as a problem which links a whole set of other concerns, moral, economic, interpersonal and so on. Thus, the often cited statements about the costs of divorce 'to the nation' include not simply the narrow legal costs but estimates in terms of medical and psychiatric aid, and loss in terms of production. Secondly, is the use of marital problems as an explanation for wider problems and issues: hooliganism and breakdown of authority, for example. In both these we may be witnessing the elaboration of a refinement of methodological individualism: methodological familism. Conservative and liberal thought, while rejecting the holistic orientations which they see as characteristic of socialism, must also feel uncomfortable with a purely individualist orientation. 'Methodological familism' does allow for one particular collectivity which may be seen as a fundamental building block of society. Any threat to or weakening of this institution may be seen, therefore, as a threat to the wider social fabric. In more traditional conservative thought there are easy routes from family to nation but 'methodological familism' may be seen as tempering the somewhat starker individualism of some strands of contemporary conservative thought.

The consequence of this, as noted in the previous chapter, is the exclusion, minimisation or obscuring of other concerns. An orientation which provides an explanatory link between various areas of life also, simultaneously, cuts out other issues, particularly issues of division and opposition. The definition of the problem and the proposed solutions to it both have the effect of minimising other areas of potential concern.

In the course of this brief discussion of the construction of a particular public issue I have had occasion to refer to a variety of theoretical orientations, schools, movements, and paradigms. These may be seen as relevant to various points of the argument. In the next section I shall take up some of these more general theoretical issues directly.

Part II
THEMES

In this second part I shall deal more explicitly with issues of theory. Yet, throughout this book, and most explicitly in the conclusion, I hope to argue for the intimate interconnection between theory and theoretical concerns and issues of public policy and practical application. This is most obvious in Chapters 6 and 7; the work of the Rapoports has been highly influential in much of the policy-orientated research in contemporary Britain, and versions of systems theorising have underlined much of the practice of marital and family therapy. History, the subject of Chapter 8, may seem more remote, although I hope to show that historical assumptions and understandings lie behind many of the current interpretations of the contemporary debates around marriage and the family. Phenomenological approaches, paradoxically, seem most removed from issues of public policy although they claim to be dealing with the most everyday and immediate issues of family living. Rendering the everyday unfamiliar and strange may always be seen as a somewhat threatening activity and this sense of challenge and opposition is, of course, reflected more directly in the approaches I group together rather loosely under the label of 'critical'.

6 The Rapoports

INTRODUCTION

The Rapoports, Rhona and Robert, are certainly ubiquitous figures in the study of the family and have been so for some years although it is difficult to assess their influence. Indeed, in the second edition of their study of dual-career families they comment upon the absence of reviews of the first edition (1976, p. 7). Yet, on the same page, they also claim with some justice that the term 'dual-career family' has 'now passed into general usage'. They were members of the Study Commission on the Family which produced a series of working papers in the early 1980s, some of which attracted press comment and discussion and, with Fogarty, were editors of *Families in Britain* (1982). They gave evidence to the Working Party on Marriage Guidance which produced *Marriage Matters* and they are also quoted in the same report. They have written or have been associated with a wide range of publications on family matters over several years.

Whatever the actual influence of the Rapoports, they can certainly be seen as representative of a central strand in family research and theorising. It is a strand which is empirically-based, unconcerned with abstract theorising and policy-orientated. The tone is generally liberal, rational and optimistic. It is aware of feminism and other sources of criticism of the family just as it has become aware, in more recent years, of the greater articulation of more conservative approaches. There is something of the cautious 'on the one hand, on the other' especially in their contribution to *Families in Britain* but that never fully masks a basic humanistic commitment.

Themes

One apparently obvious feature of their work, and one which might militate against their wider assessment in academic journals, is that of apparent eclecticism. This eclecticism may, indeed, reflect their different intellectual backgrounds. Rhona's background is more in psychiatry, Robert's in social anthropology with both having developed an interest in sociology over many years. There would seem to be little point in attempting to disentangle the separate contributions of each. Certainly, the topics they have covered have been various enough; while they are undoubtedly best known for their work on 'dual-career families', they have also written on the honeymoon, on the community as patient, on the interrelationships between home, work and leisure and on parenting. Their list of sources is also impressively wide and various; almost any of their works will contain references to psychoanalytical literature, to social anthropology, to policy-orientated documents, to all kinds of sociology, to writings of feminists and critics of marriage and the family. In some cases this eclecticism may seem to be at the expense of any critical discrimination. It is rare to find any critical assessment of the sources which are used or cited; the fact that something is written, or at least published, would seem to be sufficient. This may lead to some unlikely linkings; Young and Willmott's *The Symmetrical Family* is frequently referred to as is the work of Ann Oakley on housework without any apparent recognition of the possible contradictions here. Yet, clearly, this eclecticism is part of their overall optimism, a belief that social scientific enquiry is cumulative and more or less progressive. Almost anything may contribute to this goal:

> From the more circumscribed views of early Marxists, early Freudians and early cultural relativists we can now put together derivative views which seek to use what seems valid in each of them while avoiding their rigidities.
> (1976, p. 361)

Yet it would be wrong to overstate this eclecticism or simply to describe their work in these terms without probing a little deeper. What may appear to be an almost promiscuous use of different disciplines may in fact reflect a commitment to a project that, as I shall attempt to argue later in this section, lies at the heart of the study of the family.

116

In *Dual-Career Families Re-examined* (the source of the last quotation) the authors talk about the processes of social change, arguing for a need for change at each of four levels: the societal, the institutional, the interpersonal and the personal (*ibid.*, pp. 361–2). This reflects a desire, expressed in various parts of their work, to relate the macro and the micro in the study of the family. In some of their work, their early study on 'community as patient', for example, the psychological or psychoanalytic interest and influence becomes obvious. Later, in a discussion of the problems of interviewing, they talk of issues of 'transference' and 'counter-transference' (*ibid.*, p. 33) and such references are not uncommon. But generally, they would describe their work variously as 'holistic' (*ibid.*, p. 27), 'a more open systems approach' (Rapoport, Rapoport and Strelitz, 1977) or 'anthropological' (Rapoport and Rapoport, 1976, p. 27). In their study of leisure they argue for the importance of relating the macro and micro levels (1975, pp. 18–19) and seek to elaborate the idea of 'resourcefulness' as linking the organisational level with processes of human development (*ibid.*, p. 26). Thus the concern is not simply with assembling information about the family from whatever source but rather, and more importantly, to examine the links between these different sources, to explore the processes that link different levels of analysis. Their work remains sensitive to both individual expressions, statements and feelings (witness the long case studies that make up the large part of *Dual-Career Families* and the interviews in the leisure study) while seeking also to understand these statements in terms of the wider social structure. While such an aim may seem obvious, even trite, it is not insignificant, particularly in the study of the family.

CENTRAL THEMES

Within this central project, and reflecting it, some major themes can be seen to emerge from the work of the Rapoports. These are themes which are sometimes the subject of a single book or paper but are also likely to appear more or less regularly across the different specific subjects of their investigations.

Themes

(i) Home and work

The importance of the first theme in the sociology of the family would seem to be so obvious as to be hardly worth noting were it not for the fact that it is so often overlooked in, for example, the literature on family therapy and in *Marriage Matters*. Yet, the mainstreams of family theorising – functionalist, Marxist, feminist – have always recognised, in different ways, the relatedness of the two spheres and this too is a distinctive feature of the Rapoports' studies. Traditional models of the family saw the link between the two spheres as being through the male breadwinner, and this allowed for the elaboration of relatively simple models in terms of sets of interchanges between the family and the occupational sphere along the lines of the adult male. The Rapoports have been consistent in their recognition that this traditional model does not hold, and argue that working couples (and not simply dual-career families) have at least two sets of links to the world of work, links which, in their turn, make for more complex patterns of interaction within the family (1978, p. 13). The separation between home and work never proceeded to its logical conclusion and has, in our own times, been modified further by increasing patterns of female paid employment and the growth of more egalitarian marriage (in Ackerman (ed.), 1970).

Adopting a framework based upon the assumption that both partners in a marriage will want or need to spend at least some time in paid employment, the Rapoports often see the sphere of work as presenting a set of constraints on family-based projects. In an article on the relationships between home and work (in Moss and Fonda, 1980, p. 160), they make a distinction between structural and event impacts. The first is more long term and often presents itself as a set of historically-based constraints: the way in which work is organised in terms of time and space, the sets of expectations structuring the labour market and so on. The latter, event impacts, refers to more specific short-term events that have an impact upon the family and its members; a cited example is that of unemployment although that, increasingly, takes on a more structural dimension. Nevertheless, in both cases we see the worlds of work and employment as having an impact upon, as presenting a set of constraints upon, and sometimes opportunities for, members of

118

the family. Similarly, the business of 'parenting' exists in a context of constraints partly provided by the occupational sphere (Rapoport, Rapoport and Strelitz, 1977, pp. 245–60). The demands and expectations of work often limit the opportunities for parenting on the part of the father, often to the extreme of creating a 'one-parent family' situation, even where there is, formally, a family with two parents. Work, and associated institutions such as nurseries, also provides limits for mothers and their opportunities to find work outside the home. The Rapoports reject the idea that the impact of work on the home is simply a question of 'the problem' of working mothers and seek to encourage a more wide-ranging discussion.

Moreover, the relationship between the two spheres is not seen as one-way. In their study of dual-career families they see family structure as a 'crucial determinant' of the careers of the partners concerned (1976, p. 11). Family is important in the lives of these couples in two ways: in terms of the structure and influence of the individual's own families of origin and the availability of appropriate role models and, secondly, in terms of their current domestic situation and the way in which their lives at home are organised. 'Behind every worker outside the home', they argue, 'there is a domestic back-up' (*ibid.*, p. 301). Reciprocally, changes in the way in which work is organised will provide the opportunities for the future growth of dual-career families as a chosen option for couples.

(ii) Processes

Central to almost all of the Rapoports' work is the understanding of the family in processual terms. Again, while this is scarcely a novel idea – the Rapoports acknowledge a variety of sources for their thinking on this point – it is one which often tends to elude thinking on the family which often leans towards a more static analysis. From Alice Rossi, for example, they borrow the concept of 'role cycles' in the analysis of some of the problems faced by dual-career families. Family roles may be analysed in terms of specific role cycles which can be seen as going through distinct phases, those of anticipation, establishment and plateau (1976, p. 317). Analysis of families in terms of processual or cyclical elements also implies that, from time to time, there are crucial turning points or points of status transition and these too are treated in their work (e.g. Rapoport, Rapoport and Strelitz, 1977, p. 161). Thus, family life consists not so much as a set of relatively static roles but rather a set of intermeshing careers or cycles, with crucial turning points that involve both the careers of individual family members taken separately, but also seen as having impacts upon the careers of other family members. Parenthood is an obvious example, involving the two parents (in different ways and to different degrees) other children, kin and so on. The decision of a married woman to return to work is another such turning point, of central concern to the Rapoports, having reverberations throughout the family unit.

This last example reminds us that the Rapoports are never simply concerned with *family* processes in some narrow sense. In their work on leisure, for example, they outline their life-cycle framework which they see as having three lines: work, family and leisure. Each can be seen as following an individual and separate trajectory but also simultaneously involving the others. These three lines may be likened to coloured threads of different thicknesses which are woven together by individuals, couples and families in order to construct a 'life career' (1975, pp. 19–20). That this processual approach, the interweaving of a variety of career strands, has a strong future orientation is underlined when, in the same work, they talk of 'satisfying life investments' (*ibid.*, p. 186). Again, parenthood may serve as an illustration of this and also of the ways in which the three lines of work, leisure and family are mutually affected and affecting. The effects on family careers or role cycles have already been noted; parenthood will also have an effect upon work for one or both of the partners and upon leisure activities, perhaps meaning a shrinking or a growing segregation of these activities. There are strong affinities here with the 'life course' approach adopted by some recent social historians and sociologists (see Chapter 8).

(iii) Variety and diversity

From Roberts' earliest work on 'community as doctor' the Rapoports have recognised the variety of models for family role performance (1980, p. 231) and this sense of diversity has been a constant theme running through their work. This is both an empirical observation and a value premise. Empirically, they have frequently drawn the attention of readers to the diversity of household forms in a contemporary society. The Rapoports were probably not the first and are certainly not the only investigators to make this observation; nevertheless, it is a fundamental premise underlying their work. At all points in their separate studies they are keen to underline this theme of diversity and variety. Thus, there are a variety of parental situations (Rapoport, Rapoport and Strelitz, 1977, Ch. 3), of leisure needs (1975, p. 337) and of possible futures for working couples (1978, p. 183). Whatever the subject under discussion the reader is bound to be warned at one time that there is 'no single pattern' applicable to that subject.

This theme of empirical diversity was very much the concern of the edited collection, *Families in Britain* (1982). Not only do the separate articles themselves reflect variety (one-parent families, families of different ethnic groups, step-parents, etc.) but each subheading seems (one presumes under their editorial guidance) to give rise to more diversity. Thus there are a variety of pathways to becoming a step-parent, a variety of situations subsumed until the title 'single-parent family' and a variety of meanings attached to the term 'dual-worker family'. In their concluding essay to this collection, the Rapoports usefully outline some of the sources or types of diversity. These may be listed as: organisational (i.e. types of household structure); cultural (ethnic or religious differences, for example); class differences; life-course or stage in career or family-life cycle and cohort (*ibid.*, pp. 479–83). It will be noted that this analysis of diversity does link to their other concerns of adopting a processual approach.

But it is clear also that this is not simply a set of empirical observations but a reflection of a fundamental ethical and political orientation. It is, after all, a matter of choice and judgement as to whether one sees variety and diversity or whether, more narrowly, one simply sees slight variations on a fundamental family theme. The pluralism is not simply some-thing which is discovered by the Rapoports; it is also positively welcomed and endorsed. They welcome dual-career families as modes of domestic operation which extend the range of choice open to individuals while not claiming that this should be a model for all families. Their values are unequivocably pluralist, welcoming all except 'Mafia' type families or the mutually destructive systems analysed by Laing and his associates (1976, p. 359; Rapoport, Fogarty and Rapoport, 1982, p. 470). One of their ideals is that of the 'protean family', which is not simply a passive 'chameleon' type of family, simply responding to external change, but rather a purposive, 'enabling' structure adapting in a rational and coherent fashion that does not do violence to the needs and wishes of the individuals within it (1978, pp. 184–5). The values, then, are those of choice, freedom, maturity and growth.

(iv) Gender

It might seem that the Rapoports are simply presenting a some-what more sophisticated version of the 'family as a success story' theme (Morgan, 1975). There is something to be said for this assessment although it is not the case that they entirely mistake their values for the reality they seek to examine. They are aware of conflicts and tensions within family relationships. In their analysis of dual-career families, for example, they are certainly aware of the tensions, difficulties and conflicts within this particular family form. They consider a whole range of dilemmas that such couples face, the question of 'overload' being a prominent instance. Within this account there is an interesting discussion of what they call the 'identity tension line'. These are the limits, the boundaries that partners individually draw for themselves, beyond which they are, for the moment, unprepared to go in the direction of further change or modification. These boundaries, these *de facto* statements of 'so far and no further', are not in fact fixed for all time but are subject to change. While the Rapoports see these 'identity tension lines' in the context of their discussion of dual-career families, where indeed they have a particular salience, they are not confined to such couples. The concept, therefore, points to a source of tension which can almost be said to be built into a marital relationship, especially one that is subject to processes of change and experimentation (1976, p. 312).

One aspect of 'identity tension lines' which is given emphasis in their account is that of the difference between husbands and wives. Husbands have different 'striking points' about how much they should be involved in the home and how much occupational achievement on the part of their wives they should tolerate in relation to their own occupational involvements. Wives' tension lines, on the other hand, relate to 'their self-conceptions as good wives and mothers', partly in the eyes of others (*ibid.*). Thus there is, here, some notion of gender conflict within marriage, of gender as a major axis around which domestic life is organised. Whether this amounts to a full recognition of gender inequality within marriage is more open to question.

Throughout their work, the Rapoports make a kind of comparison between the 'traditional family' and the family of today, especially the family that has developed in Britain since the Second World War. As we have seen in Part I this understanding of what has happened to the family is quite widespread and it is a matter for some discussion as to how far the Rapoports have themselves contributed to this general understanding. In essence, the argument is not dissimilar to that presented by Young and Willmott in their *Symmetrical Family*, although without the historical elaboration. The main lines of change are in terms of choice and variation as analysed in the previous section, and particularly in terms of greater equality between the spouses. They outline some of the main influences on these changes, giving particular emphasis, as one might imagine, to the greater involvement of married women in the labour market. If the family is not necessarily 'symmetrical', there is a suggestion of growing opportunities for women and a decline of the traditional patriarchal model. Dual-career families may be very much a minority option, a small subset of a much wider category of dual-worker families; nevertheless, they maintain that these families are of much wider interest than their apparent rarity suggests. They are important as indicators of deeper changes in the relations between men and women inside and outside the family and as models, exemplars of change to come (1976, p. 15).

Again, it is difficult to disentangle the Rapoports' empirical mapping of processes of family change from their overall values about the desirability of such change. They provide criticisms of the child-rearing theories of Bowlby and Winnicott and the ways in which these theories have been used to justify traditional or conservative models of family living (in *Fathers, Mothers and Others*, 1977). Of particular concern here is the way in which these analysts played down the role of the 'father' in child-rearing and this is a central concern in their study of parenting. They believe strongly that both men and women should be able to undertake parenting tasks traditionally allocated to women and that this shared parenting will be of benefit to the individuals themselves, the children and presumably to society as a whole (Rapoport, Rapoport and Strelitz, 1977, p. 23). Again, the Rapoports were not the first to call for a more positive re-evaluation of fatherhood, but their book almost undoubtedly contributed to this debate.

However, despite references to Oakley and Bernard, there is relatively little to suggest that gender inequality may still be a major factor of family living in contemporary society even, one might say especially, in the middle-class families that form the core of their analysis. In their discussion of leisure, for example, there is some recognition that leisure activities might differ between men and women, but little discussion of the more fundamental issues that might be at stake here, that the very conceptions and understandings of leisure might differ between the two genders (Deem, 1982).

(v) Policy

The work of the Rapoports is firmly linked to questions of policy. This is not simply something which is found in the concluding section of *Families in Britain*, but is something that runs throughout their work; policy suggestions or implications occur in the concluding sections of all their major texts. In *Families in Britain* they distinguish between three aspects or levels of family and social policy:

(a) *Research*. Here they would presumably include their own work which is both original (dual-career families) and a synthesis of other studies (parenting). The commitment is simply to the rational provision of information and conceptual understanding in order to guide policy makers and to correct prevailing myths or misunderstandings. They write of a 'massive socio-cultural lag' (Rapoport, Fogarty and Rapoport, 1982, p. 490) between what has actually happened to the family, especially since the Second World War and the assumptions built into many areas of social policy (see Chapter 3).

(b) *Dissemination*. Much of the work of the Rapoports could
also be included under this heading, although the
examples they cite are the series of publications of The Study
Commission on the Family. This is a necessary extension
of the first strand, research, and points to a commitment to
creating an informed public opinion on family matters.
(c) *Advocacy*. Again, the Rapoports could also be listed under
this heading, given their undoubted belief in the values of
pluralism and choice. The example they use is a body called
Family Forum, a body pressing for a greater, more overt
family dimension to social policy. The Rapoports argue for
the 'fruitful interplay' between research, dissemination
and advocacy (*ibid.*, pp. 498–9).

(vi) Optimism

Running through all the themes mentioned up to now, constituting a qualitative link between all of them is an undeniable
and, it might also be said, an unfashionable optimism. One more
theoretical influence on this optimism is possibly in the work of
Emery and Trist who suggest a variety of shifts in cultural
values in the transition to a post-industrial society. These
include shifts from achievement to self-actualisation, from self-
control to self-expression, from independence to interdependence
and from endurance of distress to capacity for joy (Emery and
Trist, 1972, p. 154). Like the Rapoports, Emery and Trist see the
value of pluralism developing in the transition to a post-
industrial society (*ibid.*, p. 188). While this aspect of their work
has probably been obvious in what has been said up to this point
it may be worth emphasising some of the inter-related themes
in this optimism. The first strand is the strong sense of a turning
point in the history of Britain and probably other industrial
nations as well. 'We are,' they state, 'at what seems to us to be a
pivotal point in history. . . .' (Rapoport, Rapoport and Strelitz,
1977, p. 349). The contrast is between the convention bound
model of the past (and not very distant past) and the openness of
the future. The subtitle of *Fathers, Mothers and Others* is
'towards new alliances'. Wherever Young and Willmott's
Symmetrical Family (1975) is mentioned it is with seeming
approval.

These shifts towards more open family living based upon greater freedom of choice are found in several areas of life. Thus, they trace the shifts in parenting from a society where parenting was idealised to one where there is a more balanced appreciation of the joys and sorrows of being a parent; from a society where parents were supposed to adopt an attitude of total sacrifice to a more balanced sense of sacrifice; and from unitary parenting, i.e. mothering, to shared parenting (Rapoport, Rapoport and Strelitz, 1977, p. 58). While they take note of and recognise the work of critics of the family – Laing and Cooper, Bernard, Oakley, etc. – their general belief is that the family, in its newer more protean form, is here to stay and that it does not necessarily have the deleterious effects sometimes claimed for it. Thus, in the work on leisure, they argue that leisure that tends towards home-centredness does not necessarily stifle creativity and social participation (1975, p. 269).

Another aspect of this optimism is the notion that we can learn from the examples of couples and families that may, in some ways, be seen as being in the vanguard. Research, dissemination and advocacy meet, for example, in the collection on *Working Couples* where they argue in favour of such a book, demonstrating the difficulties and opportunities faced by such couples in order that others may learn from them (1978, p. 17). This argument is even more strongly marked in their work on dual-career families. A minority, yes, they argue but also an impressive portent of future possibilities. Thus, they argue that the mothers in dual-career families in particular may be as radical a challenge to conventional sex-roles as more dramatic communal experiments (1976, pp. 22–3). Given the tendency for communes often to develop fairly conventional sex-role patterns, they may well have a point here (Abrams and McCulloch, 1976).

The movement, then, is towards diversity, a process of questioning and searching for new models. Changes in the family and marriage reflect wider societal changes towards the direction of increasing the 'possibility of making our own futures' (1978, p. 184). This makes for healthier, more creative individuals:

Our emphasis on rationality, communication and planning ahead may reflect middle-class values, but we believe that they are also means for attaining healthy and enjoyable lives. (Rapoport, Rapoport and Strelitz, 1977, p. vii)

In their recent article in *Families in Britain* there is some recognition of a conservative backlash (a shift back, in marriage guidance, from counselling to more directive interventions, for example) but generally the overall sense of optimism remains undiminished.

DISCUSSION

The optimism manifested throughout the works of the Rapoports does not exactly identify them with those who see the family as one of the success stories of the twentieth century. For one thing, they are much more sensitive to the variations in patterns of family and domestic living than say Fletcher, McGregor or, more theoretically, Parsons. For another, and this is a difference in emphasis, they are more interested in individuals and individual growth and development than in the functions that a family may be said to perform for society. This is manifested in their orientation to divorce. While the more traditionally orientated will point to the maintenance of high rates of marriage and re-marriage in spite of higher rates of divorce as a cause of optimism, the Rapoports would be prepared to acknowledge the positive side of the rise in divorce rates themselves.

I would not wish to condemn such optimism, still less the values that underlie it. In an area where, as we have seen, traditional, more conservative values and models are receiving new emphasis and publicity, it is good to have such unequivocal advocacy of humanistic and rationalistic values. However, there is some cause to question the kind of optimism being advocated here. Consider, for example, the frequent use by the Rapoports of the term 'doomwatcher' to describe the kind of pessimism that they are opposed to. In my earlier book I suggested that we could see two strands of pessimism in relation to the contemporary family (Morgan, 1975, pp. 204–5). The first strand, from the left, saw the family as both strong and destructive to individuals; the second strand, from the right more often, saw the family as weak or in decline to the detriment of the social fabric as a whole. Doomwatchers would presumably be found in either camp although it would appear that it is the first grouping that the Rapoports have in mind for the most part when they use the term. These would include people like Laing and Cooper and more recent feminist critiques of the family. It is not clear whether Oakley's work on housework (and indeed her whole body of work) or Bernard's work on marriage would come under the label of 'doomwatcher', although clearly at least some of the conclusions and arguments of these two authors (not to mention many others) would run counter to the general orientations of the Rapoports' work. They are cited but never engaged. Important differences seem to be smoothed over here, perhaps in the name of some idea of a unified and progressive social science. The use of the rather imprecise and pejorative label 'doomwatcher' seems to be a way of avoiding controversy, of smoothing over real divisions and contradictions.

We have seen that the grounds for the optimism, apart from the more general adherence to humanistic, rational values, would seem to be in the diversity of individual practices, the presence of a growing variety of role models to serve as exemplars for the future. The future seems to lie, therefore, in terms of individual solutions and options, of people taking advantage of the increasing opportunity for growth and experimentation open to them. Social change, they seem to argue – or rather desirable, purposive social change – is a product of this growing variety of individual practices together with the increasing rational use and dissemination of social science findings. There seems to be little recognition of the role of more collective forms of action as a basis for social change. The Women's Movement is accorded considerable importance, but largely in terms of influential individuals it would seem. There seems to be little place for collective political action, feminist, working-class, socialist or whatever, in their benevolent model of social change for the future. Such individually based optimism does become more unreal in a context where the very liberal humanistic values which the Rapoports advocate are being challenged and eroded.

All this, and the general tenor of the Rapoports' work, could be summed up in terms of a middle-class bias. At various points of their work – in dual-career families and in the quotation on p. 126 for examples – they appear to acknowledge as much although would claim that this is not a limitation. While they do not seem to accept the simple 'moving-column' idea of Young and Willmott, whereby the middle-class families of today set the standard of family life for the working class of tomorrow, there does seem to be a suggestion that the middle classes are more likely to provide a wider range of exemplars for future patterns of family living than any other sections of society. The accusation of a middle-class bias, therefore, is one that the Rapoports would not necessarily seek to deny.

If the notion of 'middle-class bias' is to have any use beyond that of a pejorative label (rather like the Rapoports' own use of the term 'doomwatcher') it must be broken down a little more. In the first place, while the Rapoports recognise class as one basis for variation in family patterns, their own examples tend to come from the middle class. This is, of course, very much more pronounced in their work on dual-career families but the other books also show a bias towards middle-class illustrative material. While some illustrations may come from the lives of manual workers and their families, the majority of the cases, whether we are talking about their studies of parenting, of leisure or of working couples, do come from the middle and professional classes.

In the second place, again as they acknowledge, their values are largely those of the middle class. They are not necessarily to be condemned because of that; nevertheless, they provide a potent source of bias. Acknowledging the methodological and conceptual difficulties in assigning a set of values to a given social class or strata, it can be seen that the Rapoports' emphasise choice as against constraint, individualism as against collectivism, rationality as against traditionalism and freedom as against equality or fraternity. Generally, such values can be identified with the middle class. Certainly, they come easier to those sections of society that have more leisure, higher incomes and better chances for interesting and stable employment than is usually found among the manual working class. Divorce may, for example, provide opportunities for growth and personal development at all levels of society, but the opportunities are perhaps more likely to be realised where the material conditions for this realisation are more favourable.

Finally, there is a more general bias against the consideration of class as a possibly central intervening variable in their analysis. The emphasis is, for example, upon *work* and the family, rather than work, employment and occupations as key elements in the class and status structure of society as a whole and the family as an important institution in their social reproduction (see Chapter 4). A somewhat similar point may be made about gender, although here the picture is more ambiguous. Certainly, the Rapoports are aware of differences between men and women in the home and in the labour market and, in a somewhat diffuse way, of the critiques levelled against contemporary marriage and the family by feminists. But, while there is this clear recognition, together with due acknowledgment for the contribution of some individual feminist writers, there seems to be a reluctance to see gender as a major axis for the analysis of family relationships or, even more so, to see family and marriage as institutions central to the reproduction of gender differences. Thus, there is the tendency to talk of differences rather than inequalities, and inequalities rather than oppression or exploitation. There is the tendency to suggest that patterns of gender inequality belong to a more traditional patriarchal past which, while it is still with us, is a survival from some earlier times and is 'on the way out'. The persisting patterns of gender inequality within middle-class marriage which have been documented by Edgell, the Pahls and Backett among others, are not really given searching attention. There is a sense in which feminism is held at arm's length by the Rapoports; its presence is acknowledged and sometimes even incorporated, into their work but the full force of the feminist attack is somehow neutralised. This is not to criticise the Rapoports for not being feminists; whether or not they would accept such a label is probably not a matter of great significance. The point is that the combative, critical and oppositional nature of the feminist perspectives on marriage and the family tends to get lost in the Rapoports' optimistic syntheses.

All this is to suggest that the Rapoports ultimately present a fairly familiar liberal version of history. This is history as a relatively steady progress of reform and improvement. As history it is very much a 'before and after' affair, a contrast between the present with all its opportunities and potentialities and some relatively ill-defined traditional and patriarchal past. In fact, among the range of references deployed by the Rapoports, few seem to refer to works of historical scholarship. The nuances, the ambiguities, the contradictions of the past do not emerge and hence their opportunity to inform our present understanding is not taken up (see Chapter 8).

Another aspect of this general liberal version of progressive history is the absence of any sense of contradiction. There are conflicts, strains and tensions within individual couples and families, but these are things which can be overcome through the adoption of enlightened policies by the state and employers and through greater self-understanding on the part of the couples themselves. A sense of real, deep contradictions, between and within classes, between men and women and so on, is never really acknowledged. Perhaps, one day, the families will be in accordance with the models that the Rapoports advocate; it is perhaps not a bad vision after all, although one that is limited to a relatively small and privileged section of the globe. Yet there does seem to be a huge gulf between the families described by Townsend in his studies on poverty, or the working-class gender relationships described in a variety of recent sources (Gamarnikow *et al.*, 1983a; Hunt, 1980; Pollert, 1981; Porter, 1983; Purcell, 1982; etc.) and the relatively affluent families and liberal values so persuasively advocated by the Rapoports.

7 Systems theorising

INTRODUCTION

Some of the more confident claims for General Systems Theory and its application to the study of the family occasionally prompt the irreverent suspicion that, like prose, we have been speaking it all the time. Certainly, the actual links and proposed parallels within this orientation would suggest that systems theorising represents a shift in perspective, a striking rearrangement of existing themes and materials, rather than a major paradigm shift or Copernican revolution. Parsonian functionalism can in one sense be seen as standing at a point looking back to the classic tradition, especially Durkheim and Weber, and forward to systems theorising. From Durkheim can be derived the holistic approach, the sense of the irreducibility of social facts to their individual components and of the impossibility of understanding individual facts, processes and manifestations outside of their connection to other facts in a social context. From Weber can be derived the idea of the interacting pair, not the individual as being the basic unity of social investigation, of social action being understood in essentially relational terms, rather than in terms of individual motivations or processes. Indeed, many of the postulates of systems theories would appear to be the assumptions of any kind of genuinely social enquiry, however unfamiliar the actual working might be. And while Parsonian functionalism might wish to remain relatively silent on the point, Marxism is no stranger to the holistic approach, or indeed to many of the other themes of systems theorising.

But General Systems Theory would seem to have developed outside the mainstream of sociological theorising and sociology, on the whole, and would appear to have reciprocated by marginalising systems thinking, in name at least. This reflects the fact that a whole host of influences from outside sociology and social thought have contributed to the systems approach. Here might be noted cybernetics and, more recently, ecology, both of which contribute the sense of process and time as well as the themes of inter-relatedness, of feedback and mutual causation. Closer to the family there are the continuing attempts, especially within the United States, to rework Freud. Here, once again, the idea of connectedness is given a temporal dimension, a linking between present and past, adulthood and infancy, between generations. And from the communications approach identified with Bateson (1973), the familiar notion of 'the double-bind' stands more generally for processes of paradoxical communication, for meta-rules, rules about rules, within the family and elsewhere.

This last reference reminds us of the central, most important aspect of systems theorising in relation to the family; its connection with the theory and practice of family therapy, as discussed in Chapter 2. This is not to say that all family therapy is based upon systems thinking – far from it. But family systems theory is closely identified with the essentially practical aims of family therapy. Indeed the very name, *'family* therapy', with the sense of a distinction from individual therapy, suggests some of the major concerns of systems theory; the sense of the family as a whole, the sense of processes and so on. In this country, the work of the Rapoports shows direct and indirect influences from systems theorising, especially in their emphasis on processes and on the connectedness between the family and other institutions in society. A likely influence, in the case of the Rapoports, is the Tavistock Institute, especially the work of Emery and Trist (Emery and Trist, 1972). Indeed, *Towards a Social Ecology*, is referred to, albeit very briefly, in *Marriage Matters*. Outside the work of the Rapoports, the influence of systems theorising on sociological writing about the family remains minimal.

Perhaps the most pervasive image of systems theory is the diagram, with its boxes, its arrows and feedback loops. Like most more or less coherent bodies of theorising it is easier to point at than to describe. Indeed, and again in common with other ways of indicating bodies of theory (e.g. structuralism, Marxism, feminism, etc.), closer examination sometimes reveals considerable differences in emphasis, marginal over-laps between texts and authors as well as slight and possibly revealing linguistic differences. For example, Epstein and Bishop outline the following 'crucial assumptions' of systems theory:

1 the parts of the family are inter-related;
2 one part of the family cannot be understood in isolation from the rest of the system;
3 family functioning cannot be fully understood by simply understanding each of the parts;
4 a family's structure and organisation are important factors determining the behaviour of family members;
5 transactional patterns of the family system shape the behaviour of family members (Epstein and Bishop, 1981, p. 447).

Cromwell and Olson, on the other hand, outline the following key features of systems theory, although here this is more related to their desire to understand power in families rather than the more practical applications of family therapy. Here, they list:

1 the concept of circular causality;
2 the concept of family rules, which includes the concept of meta-rules, rules about the application of rules;
3 the idea that the family can either be operating to maintain the status quo or can be responsive to change. This is the closed/open distinction, and brings in the use of feedback loops;
4 the importance of moving beyond the individual, to dyads and triads within the family and beyond that to wider kin and societal networks (Cromwell and Olson, 1975, pp. 34–6).

The difference between these two characterisations of systems theory, as applied to the family, represents two different sets of theoretical and practical interests, two different sets of languages, the latter being more strictly social and sociological than the former. Other examples could be provided but this should, for the present, be enough to remind us that here, as elsewhere, apparent similarities and identities begin to disappear the moment we begin to move in close.

As the name of Parsons has already been mentioned at several points, it might be helpful to examine some of the similarities and differences between his version of functionalism and systems theory, in both cases with particular reference to the family. It might appear that the two are similar if not identical. However, Parsons' name seems to appear infrequently in many of the writings under the 'systems' label and while this may reflect the relative insulation of disciplinary or theoretical traditions it may also indicate real differences in emphasis. The following would appear to be some of the main points of similarity:

1 The isomorphism of systems. All systems have underlying similarities and can be analysed in similar terms. Whatever important differences there might be, a personality system, a family system and a social system (and also an economic system, cultural system, etc.) can be analysed in similar parallel ways.
2 The idea of levels. These systems can be arranged in some kind of hierarchy (although stressing interdependence rather than domination and subordination), the relationships between the levels being characterised in terms of sets of mutual interchanges.
3 The idea of the whole, irreducible to its individual constituents.

In terms of the differences, the following would seem to be of importance:

1 While Parsons writes of boundary maintenance, this is given considerably greater emphasis in the systems analysis. Further, systems may be differentiated in terms of their boundaries, i.e. whether they are relatively open or relatively closed.
2 The much greater emphasis on precessual elements within systems theory. While, as I have suggested, the dominant image in systems theory is the arrow suggesting movement, interchanges within and between systems, the dominant image in Parsons' work is that of the box, divided into four, or as Craib suggests, the filing cabinet (Craib, 1984).

3 In systems theory we find greater emphasis on dysfunctional systems, i.e. those systems that fail to adapt to changing environmental conditions or whose adaptations are to the detriment of the subsystem itself or its constituent parts. Parsonian theory, on the other hand, is more functional in emphasis (see Morgan, 1975).

While these may be seen as differences in emphasis in that it cannot be maintained that these points are entirely absent in Parsonian theorising, the cumulative effect of these and other differences is to produce more substantial differences in tone, style and application. Systems theory, perhaps because of its interdisciplinary origins, is clearly being taken more seriously in practical terms than Parsonian functionalism ever was. Whether these differences add up to a Copernican revolution is, however, more dubious.

THEMES IN SYSTEMS THEORISING

(a) Parts and wholes

Epstein and Bishop's list of features of systems theorising clearly gives great emphasis to the link between parts and wholes. This orientation (which is scarcely peculiar to systems theorising despite some of the claims which are made for it) is conventionally summed up in the phrase, 'the whole is greater than the sum of the parts'. Angyal, who likens the paradigmatic shift from relational thinking to systems thinking to a shift from three-dimensional to four-dimensional geometry, considers that this formulation is a little imprecise. He distinguishes between aggregations and systems: in the former, the parts are added; in the latter the parts are arranged (in Emery (ed.), 1969, p. 26). In a strict sense, therefore, the parts are not summed at all in the case of a system.

Turning to the family, the holistic emphasis is, as we have seen, the one which is underlined in all the writings on family therapy. In the controversial case of understanding schizophrenia, for example, the shift has been from a concentration on the individual patient to an examination of that patient in relation to another family member, usually a mother, and finally to seeing the patient in the context of the family system as a whole (Morgan, 1975, pp. 105–8). In short, and more generally, the shift is from treating the individual to treating the family as a whole.

Even this formulation, however, tends to blur a variety of ambiguities involved in treating the family as a whole. Before examining these, however, it is worth pointing out that it is doubtful whether anyone within sociology has ever considered the family as simply a collection or aggregation of individual units. Politically, as I have already suggested, methodological individualism would be best relabelled 'methodological familism'. The extent and way in which the family may be treated as a whole, however, does vary. At the simplest level of terminology, the individual terms 'father', 'mother', 'daughter' and 'son', etc. can be said to hang together and to derive their commonality from the shared point of reference in the family. Conversely, 'family' when defining, refers back to notions of parenthood and marriage which lead us back to these 'individual terms'. The ethnomethodological notion of 'membership categorisation devices' points in the same direction; so too does Wittgenstein's metaphor of 'family resemblances'.

But the treatment of the family in terms of part/whole relationships does not remain at the terminological level. At the next level, the argument is about the understanding of 'individual' behaviour on the part of family 'members'. Thus the anorexic daughter cannot be understood without reference to her relationships with her father, her mother and her siblings and to the relationship between these relationships and other family relationships such as those between husband and wife and between each of the parents and the other siblings. Note that there the 'parts' are not so much individual *roles* or *statuses* (father, mother, daughter, etc.) but particular *relationships* (f-m, f-d, m-d, etc.). Moreover, these relationships do not have to remain at the dyadic level; we may (as in the case of Laing's early writings on the family) be required to view the family as a set of overlapping triadic relationships (f-m-d, f-m-s, d-s-f, d-s-m, etc.). These triads may be analysed simply in terms of mini-political systems of shifting alliances and coalitions based on shifting power (Simmel, Caplow) or as Freudian psychodramas (Laing). The apparently simple discussion of the family in terms of a systematic relation of parts in a whole rapidly spirals off into increasing realms of complexity.

Themes

The 'parts' of the family may not, indeed, be anchored to named roles or relationships at all. Kanter and Lehr, for example, refer to a system of roles that does not depend upon traditional family names (see next section). Or the 'parts' may be pieces of behaviour or communication. Take the following exchange, witnessed by the author when he was an undergraduate living with a family:

> Father (reading local newspaper): 'Oh, I see Alex Thorgumbald is dead.'
> Mother: 'Who's he?'
> Father: 'Don't know. Never met him.'

This exchange, with increasing elaboration, took place around the dinner table regularly. This little exchange may be classified as a 'family joke' or (bearing in mind my presence) a 'family performance'. As an item of behaviour it could not be fully understood without reference firstly to previous occasions on which similar exchanges took place and secondly, one might assume, to the pattern of dyadic and triadic relationships within that particular domestic unit. The parts, then, may be seen as exchanges, which are not necessarily permanently anchored to particular individuals or roles.

At the highest level of complexity within the boundaries of the family system, it is not simply a question of being unable to understand one individual item without reference to its position in relation to a whole system of other such items but also a question of not being able to understand that part without reference to the family as a whole. This relates to the understanding that a family, as a system, exists in an environment, maintains a set of exchanges with that environment while also maintaining its boundaries with respect to 'the world outside'. Thus, my use of the term 'family performance' in the context of the previous illustration reminds us that families, to varying degrees, have identities, self-images, themes and mystifications and that these have to do with the presentation by the family as a whole or by individual members to the outside world, in this case a lodger. Thus the 'whole' is not simply the outcome of a set of inter-related dyadic and triadic processes nor a set of inter-related personalities or a nexus of careers but an entity in relation to the outside world.

It should be stressed that systems theories see the part/whole relationship in terms of processes rather than in terms of static roles or building blocks. This should be clear from the examples that have already been provided and certainly becomes clear in the examination of any case material from the growing literature of family therapy. This has the consequence that the whole may be seen as a particular running or ongoing outcome rather than an institution in terms of conventional sociological under-standings.[1] The 'whole' may therefore be another well-known sociological friend, 'the paradox of unintended consequences' in another guise. Various bits of behaviour may be understood in terms of their consequences for the family 'as a whole', conse-quences which may be only dimly apprehended by individual family members involved in making the decisions or in con-ducting the exchanges. These decisions and practices will be shaped by the outcome of earlier decisions and exchanges just as the outcomes of present decisions will provide the context for future bits of family behaviour.

Thus, the statement 'the whole is greater than the sum of the parts' as applied to the study of family systems (indeed as applied to the study of any systems) is fraught with complexities and ambiguities. These ambiguities arise out of the difficulties involved in the identification of the whole, the parts and the nature of the links between them.

(b) Non-linear causation

Angyal distinguishes between causal and systems thinking (in Emery (ed.), 1969, p. 29). Cromwell and Olson emphasised, as we have seen, the notion of 'circular causation'. We may add, although few systems therapists in fact do, the notion of 'dialectical thought'. It is implied in much of the previous discussion of the relationships between the parts and the whole, and again the discussion is not without its ambiguities. Nevertheless, the basic notion is straightforward enough and not at too great a distance from common sense. Sheila leaves Bruce. She says it is because of Bruce's repeated affairs with other women. Bruce says that he has affairs with other women because Sheila is frigid. Sheila argues that being a full-time housewife with little help from Bruce does not make her feel sexy, glamorous and she resents Bruce for the fact that she does not feel sexy or glamorous. Bruce says that he works hard in order to earn the money to provide the things that Sheila demands or expects. And so on. We are not dealing with Bruce's defects or Sheila's defects or with any simple cause-effect relationship, but with the relationship of marriage itself as both cause and effect. And that relationship itself can be understood in terms of relations in Bruce and Sheila's families of origin although, again, not simply in terms of cause and effect. Moreover, the apparent explanations on the part of family members in terms of 'cause and effect' – 'you made me do it' – are themselves part of this process of circular or non-linear causation. Family and marital therapists, generally speaking, would claim that what they are doing is not so much seeking out the real cause of a particular problem (a child running away from home, a wife's affairs) but rather attempting to untangle the patterns of distorted communication and dysfunctional behaviour in terms of which any individual piece of behaviour may be rendered intelligible.

Some of the elements in this notion of circular causality may be identified a little more closely:

(i) Feedback. For example, a child is hospitalised and the responses of the parents affect, feed back into, the relationships between parent(s) and child and between mother and father.

(ii) The fact that, as in the classic Weberian tradition, family members anticipate the responses of others and build these anticipations into their actions. Billy storms off angrily into the kitchen and starts the washing-up as instructed, but very noisily. Mother goes after him saying 'OK, I'll do it before you break everything'. Billy protests that Mother is not letting him do the washing-up. . . . Here too we would include the Laingian 'knots' and spirals of interpersonal relations.

(iii) The paradox of unintended consequences. Strictly this may be seen as more complex causation rather than non-causal thinking except insofar as these unintended consequences may themselves – as in the case of (i) – feed back into the continuous stream of family living.

(vi) In the case of family living, the idea of non-linear causation may reflect particularly sharply the distinction between the therapeutic analyst's perspective and the

perspective of the family members themselves. One
feature of family living – perhaps all kinds of living – is
the allocation of blame, that is, the attribution of
motivation plus causal efficacy to some family member.
'It's all your fault', 'you started it' and 'she made me do it'
are part of the regular small change of family living. The
therapeutic intervention involves, in some measure, a
recognition of the blame-allocation processes as being part
of the problem rather than constituting explanations for
behaviour.

Whether in the social sciences the notions of non-linear or
mutual causation are so novel as to constitute a revolution in
the way of thinking about the family is a moot point. While,
clearly, there is much sociological writing on the family that
does appear to adhere to fairly straightforward causal notions
(writings about predictors of marital success, for example, or
attempts to assess the effect of a wife's employment on the
domestic balance of power), it might be supposed that the
influence of Marxist, critical, phenomenological and even some
versions of functionalist thought might together have been
enough to suggest models of causality considerably more
complex than these. This emphasis is clearly a useful corrective
to some of the more simple psychologistic approaches to the
family, but the claim of novelty does not seem to accord fully
with either experience or with an examination of what has
actually been written on the family.

(c) Systems, open and closed

Discussions of systems in general always include a distinction
between open and closed systems and it is always agreed that
living systems – biological organisms, human groups and
organisations, including families – are examples of open
systems. While there are considerably complex ways of characterising these systems – Katz and Kahn list some nine common
characteristics of organisations as open systems (in Emery (ed.),
1969, pp. 92–100) – the essential points would seem to be
straightforward enough. Open systems are systems which
maintain continuous processual exchanges with their environment. In very simple terms there are inputs from the

environment, through-puts and out-puts. A family, for example, receives a variety of inputs from its environment: money and material resources, prestige or stigma, ideological messages, etc. These do not simply pass through families but are used, worked upon, shaped in terms of the families own 'internal' system. Similarly, there are outputs into the environment; work and workers, socialised human beings, political values and so on. The importance of this stress on families as open systems – which would appear to be obvious once stated – lies in its underlining of the previous point about non-linear causation and in stressing that families cannot be analysed on their own. There is a tendency in sociology to see families as either at the receiving end of social and economic processes or, alternatively, as independent sources of social behaviour and processes. Some of the simpler distinctions between 'the working-class family' and 'the middle-class family' come close to the former error while explanations of gender differentiation, for example, in terms of family socialisation tend towards the latter. In principle, at least, the open-systems approach does emphasise both inputs and outputs, seeing the family as maintaining some kind of balance or dynamic homeostasis with its environment. In the case of more psychologistic orientations to the family – as we saw in the case of family and marital therapy – there is a tendency to focus on internal processes altogether to the exclusion of wider environmental considerations.

While in the context of general systems theory all family systems might be viewed as open systems, a variety of theoretical and empirical traditions would lead to the commonplace assumption that some families are more open than others. Bernstein's distinction between 'positional families' and between 'person-orientated' families, for example, would seem to convey a distinction that in part, at least, implied an open/closed distinction (Bernstein, 1971, Vol. 1, pp. 152–3). A positional family, for example, would not simply be concerned with relatively stable, traditional and ordered patterns of authority and role differentiations but would also be concerned with fairly clear demarcations between that family and the outside world. A person-orientated family, on the other hand, would be more likely to maintain relatively loosely defined boundaries in relation to the outside world. A stress on personal characteristics, uniqueness, individuality or whatever would normally imply a tendency to downgrade familial identities and hence to imply relatively weakly defined familial boundaries. Interestingly, Bernstein instances one kind of indicator of the kind of family system under examination as the symbolic ordering of space (*ibid.*, p. 184).

Within a different tradition, that of social work practice, Jordan makes a useful distinction between families with segregated roles combined with a high involvement in community networks and families which tend to be closed, integrated and relatively homogeneous. This distinction, which clearly owes its origin in studies such as Bott's classic study of social networks and family, is a useful one and one which Jordan feels therapists should note (Jordan, 1972, p. 21). Jordan would wish to emphasise that it is not a case of one kind of family system being 'better' than another; rather therapists, social workers and others may make grave errors if they approach one kind of family system through the perspective of a different kind of family system.

The most thoroughgoing elaboration of this view is provided by Kanter and Lehr, the subject of the next section. They distinguish between closed, open and random family systems, again arguing against the evaluative ordering of these family types. While, in terms of a general systems theory perspective, all families are necessarily open systems, some families are more open than others and the degree or otherwise of openness of a family is one important, although for the present, imprecise basis for a distinction between family systems.

(d) The family and its environment

The emphasis on openness as a central characteristic of living systems inevitably, as we have seen, raises questions about the relationships between the system (the family in this case) and other systems and its environment. Three kinds of relationship may be distinguished although any one approach may have elements of each included within it:

(i) There is the 'Russian doll' model of subsystem within systems, these systems being themselves subsystems of some wider systems. This is approximated in Parsonian theorising in his distinction between the personality system, the family system and the social system (see Morgan, 1975 for further elaboration).

(ii) There is the systems-exchange kind of model, one which may also be seen as deriving from Parsonian theorising although most clearly expressed by Bell and Vogel (see Morgan, 1975, pp. 48–51). Very simply, a total system may be seen as a political system, an economic system, a family system, a community and a value system. There are regular patterns of exchange and interchange between them.

(iii) There is the 'system in its environment' model. This would seem to be the one most favoured in General Systems theories and their application to the study of the family. In short, there is little concern with the nature and character of the environment as such; it is treated as a 'given' for the purpose of analysis. The analysis of the system, then, is concerned with the analysis of two processes: the process whereby the system maintains its boundaries in relation to the outside world and the processes of input and output or exchange that take place between the system and its environment. Focus would be, then, on the various feedback loops involved in the system and its relationships with the outside world.

Emery and Trist's social ecological approach has elements which, while they tend to focus on organisations, would seem to have some applicability to the systems study of families. Their emphasis has constantly been upon the organisation as an 'open socio-technical system'. Looking at the system as a whole they suggest, in a somewhat unelaborated fashion, an 'order of social magnitude' which seems to be close to the Parsonian Russian dolls. There is the individual, the family and kinship system, the community and, finally, transnational entities (Emery and Trist, 1972, p. 128). At this fairly unelaborated level, this approach would seem to be relatively unhelpful. More interesting, however, is their recognition that the analysis of systems cannot continue to make the assumption that the environment is itself a neutral, unstructured and unspecified 'space' surrounding the system under examination. The environment itself has varying degrees of interconnectedness – 'the causal texture of the environment' – and the character of the environment itself has systemic properties and these need to be considered in the analysis of any particular system (Emery and Trist, in Emery (ed.), 1969, pp. 242–3). They suggest four ideal types of environment ranging from the placid and randomised to the turbulent (*ibid.*, pp. 256–7). This last term, although little else, was taken over in *Marriage Matters*. While the technicalities of their characterisation of different kinds of environment need not concern us here, the notion that the character of the environment has vital consequences for the analysis of any particular system under consideration is a matter of some importance. Systems and environment do not simply co-exist; they interact 'to the point of mutual-inter-penetration' (Emery and Trist, *op. cit.*, p. 43). The relevance of their approach to the study of the family can be seen in their discussion of the turbulent environment, in short our own times. One kind of response to turbulence is dissociation, a form of passive adaption to the environment. It is an individual response but one supported at the societal level. This kind of approach seeks to reduce the complexity of choice by denying the relevance of others. It may be seen as a form of privatisation (*ibid.*, p. 65). Some versions at least of the 'closed family' may be viewed in this light, as families 'against' the environment.[2]

Thus, in adopting a systems approach to the family we are implying at least the following:

(i) An orientation which considers the interdependence of parts and whole.

(ii) An orientation based upon the assumptions of non-linear causation.

(iii) An orientation which sees the family as an example of an open social system.

(iv) An orientation which examines the family in relation to its environment, which examines the interchanges that take place between the family and its environment and which may also see that environment itself as structured in crucial ways.

An illustration of how these ideas could be applied may be provided by recent accounts of studies of television and children. The traditional model was an individualistic, causal one moving from television to child. A more systemic approach would examine the role of television in terms of the complex patterns of relationships within the family as a whole with past events influencing the way in which current messages are received, current messages often being mediated through frameworks of interpretation of other children and adults and TV talk being part of the general pattern of family talk, even away from the set (Goodman, 1983). To develop these ideas further I shall examine one especially thorough treatment of the family in systemic terms: Kantor and Lehr's *Inside the Family* (1973).

KANTOR AND LEHR: *INSIDE THE FAMILY*

Kantor and Lehr's *Inside the Family* (1973) partly originates from the practice of family therapy although its main desire is to get away from the therapist's office and from families labelled as 'problems' and towards everyday family practice. Understanding of family processes should begin, they argue, with the banal, the routine, the everyday rather than the especially dramatic or extraordinary. Hence most of the illustrations, indeed most of the sources, of the systems theorising presented here come from such everyday events as weekend outings, playing games of Monopoly and making decisions about adolescents' time-keeping. These everyday observations, however, are woven into a framework of considerable complexity and elaborateness, a welter of new terms, classifications and conceptualisations. There is an obvious tension throughout the book between the vivid and affectionate portrayals of everyday family living and the somewhat cumbersome apparatus of systems theorising, although it may be fairly argued that these two elements stand in some kind of reciprocal relationship with each other, that the theorising guided the authors towards the recognition of the everyday and the everyday provided the raw material for the theorising.

Inside the Family is a complex book to summarise, but an outline of its main components may indicate something of the flavour of the work and its relationship to systems theorising in general. Briefly, the authors consider five main components in their theory of family process. In the first place there is the analysis of the family as a network of three subsystems: the family unit subsystem, the interpersonal subsystem and the personal subsystem. These can all be understood to relate to each other (at the 'interfaces') and to the outside world. These distinctions are often understood in socio-spatial terms. Thus, an outsider may gain access to a family dwelling relatively easily without becoming part of the various interpersonal sub-systems that are present within that dwelling. Within that interpersonal subsystem it is important to distinguish between those occasions when individuals are acting as part of these subsystems or in terms of their own personal subsystem.

The second and third components are what the authors call, respectively, the 'access' and 'target' dimensions. The 'access' dimensions are three in number – energy, space and time – and may be seen as the media or resources which families and family members deploy in everyday family processes. Each of these three dimensions are further broken down into headings and subheadings. These detailed refinements need not concern us but the emphasis on time and space is of considerable importance and is intimately connected with their desire to map the ordinary. Both time and space are, it is important to stress, *social* dimensions, however they may appear to take on a 'thing-like' status. Thus, when a father looks at his watch and says 'I haven't got the time right now, son' it is a statement about power, about an ordering of priorities rather than the ruthless imposition of external timetables. Space too is a social dimension, which is recognised in everyday speech in phrases such as 'space in which to breathe'. In a more complex example, designations of parts of the city as dangerous areas may be paralleled by the ranking of children's acquaintances into some kind of order of desirability. The most difficult of these three dimensions is the notion of 'energy', a concept whose elaboration probably owes much to the general background in systems theorising. It is part of what makes families the way they are or as they appear to outsiders although it does not have the same kind of observability as we find for space and time. What may be energy in one family may be a sign of the reverse in another family. Thus, just sitting quietly may be, in one context, a 'recharging of one's batteries' and a vital part of the daily flow of family living while it may simply indicate apathy or disassociation in another context. The notion of energy as an 'access dimension' is a valuable sensi-tising notion, alerting the investigator to probe beneath the surface of everyday family exchanges and processes.

'Access' to what, it may be asked? This, the authors argue can again be seen as three 'target dimensions'. These may be seen as the valued end-points or goals of families, of each of the three subsystems. These 'target dimensions' (not analysed in the same depth as the access dimensions) are 'affect', 'power' and 'meaning'. Family members, therefore, may be viewed as engaged in the business of gaining access to targets, and the three access and three target dimensions may together be seen as constituting a six-dimensional social-space grid.

The fourth dimension is a classification of family types. These ideal typical formulations are, it would appear, not simply an external classification or taxonomy of families but represent an attempt to capture the way in which families develop some kind of coherent thematic understanding of what they are about. These types, therefore, are statements about what kind of a family we are, how we present ourselves to the outside world, an overall framework of interpretation providing points of reference for the evaluation of day-to-day events and decisions. The difference between these three types may be seen in terms of certain mixes of the access dimensions of space, time and energy as shown in Table 7.1.

Table 7.1

TYPE	SPACE	TIME	ENERGY
Closed	Fixed	Regular	Steady
Open	Movable	Variable	Flexible
Random	Dispersed	Irregular	Fluctuating

As an illustration of the three types in action let us consider what happens when Jane arrives to ask if Lisa can come round to her house to see her new kittens. The response of the closed family might be to respond that Lisa may come after she has done her homework, meaning we have strict timetables in this house and it is important that they be adhered to. (Or alternatively, permission may be granted on the clear understanding that it is an exception that proves the rule.) The response of the open family might be to argue 'certainly, after all new born kittens are a valuable educational experience'. The response of the random type family might be a little more difficult to predict, depending upon the current 'state of play' within that family, its particular thematic emphasis and so on.

Two points need to be made about these family types. In the first place they are ideal typifications and few actual families will conform clearly to one or the other. The Ewings of Dallas may seek to be closed in some respects although they include some open subsystems and often end up closer to the random. Moreover, a family subsystem may be open at one stage of its life cycle and move to be more closed at another stage, with the arrival of children, for example. In the second place, the authors stress that these are not evaluations of the family. There is not one homeostatic ideal, and a random type family may be responding equally effectively to its environment as an open or closed type. Closed families may seem to be patriarchal or oppressive to some observers (Laingians for example), while random families might well raise the hackles of more traditionally orientated family therapists or case workers. But, argue the authors, each can be effective in its own way and each can spiral off into its own form of aberration.

The fifth and final component the authors examine is the psychopolitics of family life. Here the major metaphor seems to be derived from games theories, and the authors outline four parts or roles that family members play and which can be singled out in the analysis of any piece of family living. Family players may be movers, followers, opposers or bystanders. These type of players are not necessarily anchored to any formally based system of family roles. A father may be a mover in one situation but a child might easily play the same part in another context.

The fitting together of these given components is a matter of some complexity and the authors' own analysis of a microincident where a child knocks on his parents' door on a Saturday morning in terms of all of these dimensions, threatens to collapse under its own conceptual weight. Nevertheless, it is clear that the authors' sustained attempt to think about the family in systemic terms does reap dividends even if this particular whole might seem to be somewhat less than the sum of its parts.

It might be useful to conclude this section by indicating the ways in which Kantor and Lehr's approach derives from systems theorising. In the first place, they clearly state the kinship of family systems with other social systems: 'Family systems, like all social systems, are organisationally complex, open, adaptive and information-processing systems.' (*ibid.*, p. 10.) By 'organisationally complex' the authors mean that in examining the family as a system we are looking at interdependent causal relationships. Kanter and Lehr see the 'feedback loop' as the key concept to be derived from systems theories in their study of the family (*ibid.*, pp. 12–15). Moreover, they see the terms 'system' and 'process' as being virtually coterminous (*ibid.*, p. 9). Hence the subject of their analysis is not a fixed structure of family roles or positions but processes, acts, exchanges and events. These are the building blocks and not, as in the Parsonian system, a set of positions derived from some external theorising about leaders and followers, instrumentality and expressiveness.

It is striking how, in the central part of Kantor and Lehr's book (the part dealing with access and target dimensions and with the delineation of family types), the triad seems to predominate as opposed, again to Parsons, to bimodal oppositions or two by two property spaces. While it would appear that the authors run the danger of being intoxicated by threefold divisions in the way in which other authors are bogged down in dualism, the meaning of this emphasis is fairly clear. A triadic imagination, if one may coin such a phrase, would seem to be one more alert to process, to variation, to the possibilities of alliance and coalition. The overall metaphor or image of their thought does suggest a greater tolerance of complexity and flux. Dyadic thinkers tend to be found among some Marxists and structuralists and most functionalists. Triadic thought may claim the ancestry of Simmel, Sartre and Laing.

In conclusion, Kantor and Lehr are not, in the final analysis, totally wedded to the whole-hearted application of systems theorising to the study of the family, or indeed to any other social system. Wearing their liberal hearts on their sleeves, they are unhappy about the tendency to 'blame the system' (whether familial, political or economic) with the implied abdication of individual responsibility (*ibid.*, pp. 236–7). They, like most family members, seek 'space' for individual personality and responsibility and in their analysis of the everyday psychopolitics of family living they welcome the position of the bystander (who may remain such or may move into the centre of the action) as representing the unpredictable or ungovernable element in family systems processes.

CRITICAL ISSUES

The application of General Systems Theory to the study of the family raises a variety of critical issues. It is not part of the purpose of this study to consider whether these critical issues may be raised in relation to the wider body of theorising although it is likely that some of them will have this wider applicability.

(a) The general and the particular

The first issue, in fact, deals with the relationships between the general level of theorising which is seen to pertain to all open systems and the particular level of theory which is to do with the family. The whole thrust of General Systems Theory, as its name suggests, is towards making general statements which apply not only to social organisms but to single biological organisms, to ecological systems and to cybernetic systems. The family, therefore, is just one such system. Certainly, as we have seen, Kantor and Lehr strongly suggest that their theoretical insights might be relevant to a much wider range of social systems; their discussion of psychopolitics would certainly seem to have a much wider relevance while all manner of organisations might be classified according to their threefold typification of open, closed and random. Insofar as they would seem to assign any particular features to the family it would seem to be in terms of its basis in biological relationships:

> We define a family strategy as a purposive pattern of moves toward a target or goal made by two or more people who are systematically bound in a socio-biological arrangement. (*ibid.*, p. 18)

This definition of the family or family relationships is almost smuggled into the argument; it is never discussed or evaluated. Other theorists, also working in a systems and therapeutic tradition, similarly see a biological basis for family relationships (Hall, 1979).

151

Themes

The understanding of family relationships in socio-biologistic terms would certainly seem to strengthen the argument for placing the family in a wider systemic analysis, especially since much of the inspiration for systems theory came from, and probably still comes from, biology and ecology. Indeed, it is strange that it seemed to take so long for analysts to get around seriously to treating the family in a systemic form and even recent volumes on system theorising fail to contain any specific articles on, or references to, family processes. Nevertheless, the tendency to treat the family in biological terms does, of course, raise all the old problems: the problems about the distinctions between biological and social parenthood, the social construction of family membership, the differences, assumed or otherwise between family and non-family relationships. There are also the problems about the apparent differences in family, marriage and household structures between societies and over time. Kantor and Lehr's families, for example, all seem to be very much of mid-twentieth century America.

Whether or not there are real and effective differences between family relationships and other kinds of relationships is a point that we shall defer until a later chapter; it is certain, however, that people *think* that there are important differences and act upon these assumptions, within families, in relation to other families and, as we have seen, in framing public policy. The family is a central ideological construct to which people, to varying degrees and in varying ways, respond and which they use and deploy in their day-to-day understandings. And this sense of a *difference*, that family relationships are fundamentally unlike other kinds of relationships, is something which, it can be argued has historical roots which can be examined. However, to admit the social constructedness of familial relationships – even where there might be some biological material woven into the construction – is to raise a whole range of other difficult questions to do with the designation of familial boundaries.

(b) Family boundaries

Very simply, boundaries in social life may be understood in one of three ways: administrative, theoretical and expressive. Administrative boundaries are those social boundaries which

152

are established by political (in the broadest sense of the word) authorities such as tax brackets, nation states, postal districts or households as defined by the census. Theoretical boundaries are those which are established by the analyst for the purposes of theoretical investigation such as classes, organisations, social systems and reference groups. Expressive boundaries are those boundaries to which people actually make reference and which are meaningful to them in their everyday lives. Your sense of where you live, for example, differs from the postal district or the church parish just as it differs from the sociologists' ecological zone or whatever. Sociological investigation, properly conceived, should move between all three sets of boundaries. (For a further elaboration see Morgan, 1965.)

Systems theorising would seem to involve the rigorous construction of theoretical boundaries and the movement from these theoretical constructions to actual entities would seem to be a matter for further theoretical and conceptual work. 'Would *seem to be*' for, as was shown in the section on family therapy, such practitioners (often influenced by the systems approach) would seem to be relatively unconcerned with such problems. Thus, to take the example of Kantor and Lehr, the 'family' which they attempt to get inside is bounded in a variety of ways:

1 In terms of the biologically based relationships suggested in their definition. However, this does not itself deal with the question that not all ties based upon 'blood' are recognised for everyday practical purposes.

2 The household. This would seem to be the usage most in keeping with their actual illustrative material. They are dealing with a small group of people usually related or assumed to be related by marriage and blood who share a dwelling and cooking facilities. This is close to the everyday nuclear-family household, although it is never fully explicated.

3 A more phenomenologically-based unit. Kantor and Lehr's distinction between three subsystems reminds us that to gain access to a dwelling, the outer representations of a familial subsystem, is not necessarily to gain access to an interpersonal subsystem. There is, in fact, the beginnings of a relatively sensitive understanding of the differences between the ways in which the family is understood by its

153

members and presented as such to the outside world and the categories and classifications which are deployed by the analyst in order to understand these relationships.

However, the constant use of the term 'family' to describe relationships which are not always encompassed by their observations (since a family may effectively include dead or distant members) or which may include effective and meaningful relationships which are not biologically based tends to reify where it might illuminate. What is missing from this and other systemic analyses of the family is the use and availability of the labels 'family', 'marriage' and 'home' as ideological terms which are not simply imposed from above but which are deployed and evaluated by the persons so subsumed under these labels. The business of boundary maintenance, a central concern of systems theorists, is a somewhat more complicated business than the cybernetic models would suggest.

(c) *Relations to the outside*

The definition of an open system entails some recognition of the family in relation to its environment. But the nature of this environment and the natures of these relationships often remain obscure. Some of the modes of relating a family system to its environment have already been mentioned: the Russian dolls of systems including subsystems; the patterns of exchange and interchange between subsystems placed within an overarching social system or the simple use of analogy whereby a wider social or political system may be seen to function as if it were like a family system and the principles derived from the study of the latter could be used for the study and the understanding of the former. In family studies there are further links between the family and the outside world, more of a spatiotemporal nature through the examination of inter-generational connections. Nevertheless, systems theorists like family therapists seem happiest when dealing with an entity which is closest to the standard nuclear family model and the further they stray from this model the hazier the world becomes.

With the possible exception of Emery and Trist's discussion of the way in which the environment itself is structured (which while interesting, remains at too great a level of generality to be of great help in understanding the family) the environment remains a mysterious, fuzzy area in the kinds of analysis we have examined. Very simply, three kinds of connections between the family system and the outside environment might be suggested as worthy of further investigation and elaboration:

1 *Inclusion.* In Kantor and Lehr's study there are a variety of references to the environment in their discussions although these references are rarely taken up. There are white families in black neighbourhoods, black families in white neighbourhoods. There are patterns of mobility with families moving in and out. The neighbourhood itself is not an undifferentiated mass either, for there are dangerous areas and desirable areas, areas which are part of a family's 'natural' sphere of influence and areas which are strange or alien. The environment, therefore, is not simply or passively a kind of ether in which the family is enclosed and which surrounds the family. It is itself actively constructed by the family in its work, collective and individual, of making sense of the world and making sense of itself. The family deploys understandings and symbols in terms of wealth and poverty, power and helplessness, men and women and black and white in building up the environment in which it is enclosed. The family and its environment not only mutually influence each other but manually construct each other.

2 *Overlap.* Individual family members are also included in other systems. Adult members belong to work, leisure or political organisations. Children belong to schools, youth groups or informal gangs. Again, these 'outside' influences do not simply impinge upon the family but are actively processed through the family. In more mechanistic terminology, the family may be seen as an amplifier or transformer for these outside influences.

3 *Network.* A special form of overlap occurs through particular ties that individual family members may have with other individuals who are in some senses deemed to be outside that family. These differ from other relationships of overlap in that it is the singularity and particularity of the tie that is important rather than the fact of inclusion in the same extra familial organisation. Here, we are dealing with friends, workmates, kin and neighbours. Such sets often provide

audiences for the family in question and are, reciprocally, filtered through and assessed by other family members. The relationships within the network are again mutually influencing.

There are, therefore, different ways in which the family may be related to its environment. These ways of understanding the links between a family and its environment do not require us to see family members as passive recipients of outside forces just as they do not require us to understand the family as a fixed, closed or reified entity. To date, the systems approach to the family has yet to explore those more subtle variations in the way in which a family system may be related to its environment.

(d) Time, change and history

These elements relating to the temporal boundaries of the family are brought into the systemic approach to the family, in very unexplored ways. In Kantor and Lehr, for example, we have the following hints:

1 Time is a resource, one of the access dimensions which are deployed within the family. Included here is the sense of past, present or future orientation on the part of family members. Family members do have some sense of 'where they have been' and 'where they are going' and use these understandings in day-to-day family interactions. The simple adolescent cry of 'you're old fashioned, Daddy' may provide one such illustration.

2 Although, in common with other systems theorists, Kantor and Lehr see the notion of mutual causality and feedback as central to their understandings they do offer the suggestion that:

> We believe that there is a relationship, though not necessarily an immediately visible relationship, between immediate cause-effect-cause phenomena and ultimate causal phenomena. (*ibid.*, pp. xiii–xiv)

This would seem to suggest some kind of historical perspective.

3 There is the recognition, all too brief, that families are linked to other families over generations. Models of family

behaviour – open, closed or random – are carried over from one generation to the other, although not in any simple pattern of inheritance. The inter-generational theme is taken up in much more detail by Hall and, indeed, by all the systems analysts who derive more from the Freudian tradition than the information processing tradition.
4 There is also the recognition, again brief, that families themselves change over their life cycles.

While there are these recognitions of change and generational influence in family systems theory it cannot be said that they form a major focus of attention. And where this is brought in, as in the analysis of family life cycle processes, it cannot be said that the wider context of historical change receives much systematic or detailed attention.

VALUES

In conclusion it may be argued that the very emphasis of systems theorising, at least as it is applied to the study of the family, is in the direction of developing models of universal applicability, of developing a unified model of scientific enquiry and a neutral, scientific language for the study of family behaviour. But is this language so neutral? Consider some of the terms that Kantor and Lehr deploy under the general heading of the Access Dimension of Space:

Bounding: Mapping, Routing, Screening, Patrolling.
Linking: Bridging, Buffering, Blocking out, Channelling,
            Referencing.
Centering: Locating, Gathering, Designing, Arranging,
            Spreading.

To work through these terms, and in particular through the instances of these terms, is to realise their reference to a particular kind of family at a particular point of American history. It is a family centrally concerned with space, with distance, with privacy and invasion. It is a family often located within a neighbourhood that is perceived as threatening; terms such as 'patrolling' have a slightly sinister, even military ring to them. The family as a fortress conforms closely to Lasch's *Haven in a Heartless World* (1977). Whatever this family is, it is not a

157

universally valid entity, but one very peculiar to its own time and space. The search for apparently scientific language, the attempt to link to universal scientific generalisations has the effect of smoothing over the historical particularity of the institution under examination.

Another effect is to obscure other ways of examining the family, especially, although not exclusively, in terms of gender differentiation. Whether gender is or is not a major theoretical category, must be left to a later chapter. In Kantor and Lehr, however, we have husbands and wives, mothers and fathers, sons and daughters and brothers and sisters, but never men and women. Here, as elsewhere, gender and other inequalities – perhaps the basis for major contradictions within or between families – are obscured or blurred over in favour of the elaboration of a neutral, scientific and universal model of family processes. Kantor and Lehr's investigation inside the family, probably one of the most thorough and searching systems approach that we have to date, remains tantalisingly open to wider, more critical issues while remaining firmly within a kind of scientific paradigm that seeks to expunge such issues.

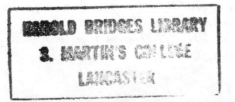

8 Family history

How then can a historian conscious of the political conflicts of his own time fail to be interested in the 'private life' of our forefathers?
J-L. Flandrin (1979)

INTRODUCTION

In the *Subversive Family*, Ferdinand Mount (1982) took sociologists and others to court for their alleged misuse of historical evidence in conducting what was essentially a political debate. A widespread agreement among academics, Mount maintains, is that the present family 'as we know it' is possibly unique and certainly of fairly recent origin. Categories which are popularly regarded as fixed and unchanging – love, childhood, parenthood and the nuclear family – are held to be 'socially constructed', the product of particular sets of historical experiences. An influential version of this kind of thinking was Philip Ariès' *Centuries of Childhood* (1972). Mount calls Ariès, Shorter, Stone and others into question, criticising their evidence and arguing instead for a relatively unchanging nuclear family (and relatively unchanging sentiments accompanying it) which has through the ages served as an effective opposition to totalitarian thinkers of all kinds.

Historical work enters into Mount's argument in a variety of ways, therefore. In the first place, the writers of recent large-scale histories of the Western family – Ariès, Stone and Shorter in particular – are held to have drawn unwarranted conclusions on the basis of slender evidence. In general, and here, Mount would doubtless be supported by some other social historians and scientists – the evidence is drawn from sources which are questionable (reports of priests or doctors) or unrepresentative (data drawn from the elites or the literate sections of the population). Folk sayings about the relative worth of cattle as

159

opposed to a wife cannot be taken as direct evidence of an absence of loving marital sentiments any more, presumably, then it would be possible to derive the same conclusions straightforwardly from jokes about 'the wife' made by music-hall comedians.

But Mount is not, of course, engaged in a scholarly debate about the use and misuse of historical data. He is more concerned with, as he sees it, the misuse of historical writings for ideological purposes, that is for the purposes of undermining the family and for the advocacy of collectivist social systems. Sociologists and others who believe these versions of history do so because they want to believe them, because such beliefs are consistent with their overall collectivist, anti-family orientations. Here Mount is more concerned with questions of values and the ways in which these shape scholarly enquiry. Presumably it would be possible for, say, Shorter's account of the rise of the Western family to be correct without necessarily implying an anti-familial stance. Indeed, such evidence might well be used to support the equally popular view (not seriously recognised by Mount) that the family has adapted well to changing conditions, the views of British optimists such as Fletcher and McGregor as well as of functionalists such as Parsons.

Nevertheless, it would seem that here too Mount has a useful point, one about the way in which 'fiindings' become established as such. In how many student essays do we now read that: 'Ariès showed that in the past children were treated as miniature adults' or that 'love developed with the growth of capitalism'. As in the game of Chinese whispers, complicated arguments become blurred certainties. That this is a process which takes place with most social science 'findings' should not deter us from suggesting that it is time to look again at some of the arguments about the history of the Western family.

Finally, and somewhat contrary to his other arguments, Mount seeks to use a 'proper' historical account to provide a basis for his assertion of a relatively unchanging nuclear family form, one that is constantly in opposition to Church and state and all forms of collectivism. Here he calls upon the work of Laslett as well as adding some literary sources of his own. The use of literary sources may be criticised on the same grounds as the use of similar source material by historians of different persuasions: that they are unrepresentative, that they refer to the lives of a literate elite and so on. In the case of the work of Peter Laslett and the Cambridge demographers it can be claimed that there too an orthodoxy has been created; the orthodoxy of the unchanging household composition, at least from 1600 to the present day. Mount seems to be happy to accept this orthodoxy while ignoring, for example, the fact that Laslett is dealing with households rather than families.

Mount's debate with the historians certainly reminds us of one thing: the extraordinary explosion of historical work on the family. Anderson has noted the rapid growth of family history as a subdiscipline and the bewildering variety of projects that are subsumed under that label. The point of this chapter is not to attempt to summarise or make sense of this growing mass of material but rather to assess the kinds of contributions that such material can make to sociological understandings of the family. That sociologists have always used versions of history is probably indisputable. The classic tradition gave rise to an understanding, rarely subjected to detailed examination, of a 'before' and an 'after', the turning point usually being identified as the Industrial Revolution. Before the Industrial Revolution there were traditional families, peasant families, extended families; after, there were modern families, urban-industrial families, nuclear families. The effect of the growth of historical studies of the family was both to call into question these simple before/after models (Laslett) and yet also to provide more detailed and sophisticated arguments for the peculiarity of the modern family form (Shorter). Historical writings, therefore, have often influenced the work of sociologists whose interests are primarily not historical. The purpose of this chapter is to examine some of these influences and uses rather than the work of the historians themselves. As Mount has reminded us, these influences and uses do have wider political and ideological reverberations.

VARIETIES OF FAMILY HISTORY

In examining the varieties of forms of family history I can do no more, initially at least, than summarise the main points in Anderson's brief but admirable guide. The reader should refer to this and the useful bibliography for more detailed discussion and references (Anderson, 1980). Anderson outlines four main schools of family history:

1 *Psychohistory.* Anderson dismisses this severely in a couple of sentences; a representative work of this school would be DeMause's *History of Childhood* (DeMause, 1976). Poster makes an interesting but brief attempt to merge historical with psychoanalytical insights in his *Critical Theory and the Family* (Poster, 1978).

2 *The Demographic Approach.* This is the approach identified with Laslett and the Cambridge Demographic school. Its characteristics are the detailed collection of statistics from sources such as parish records and the increasingly sophisticated use of computers in the analysis of detailed numerical data. Such data now relate to a wide range of European countries. The data relate to the main concerns of demographers: rates of birth, death and marriage, of illegitimacy and household composition. The chief finding – or the one which has been given the greatest publicity – has been to do with household composition:

> Laslett demonstrated that the mean household size in England (including servants) has remained more or less constant at about 4.75 from the sixteenth century right through the industrialisation period until the end of the nineteenth century when a steady decline set in to a figure of about 3 in contemporary censuses. (Anderson, 1980, p. 23)

Contrary to earlier theorists (notably Le-Play) the pre-industrial household was no more likely to include more than two generations than is the present day household.[1] As data began to accumulate from different parts of Europe, Laslett concluded that 'a nuclear familial form may have been one of the enduring and fundamental characteristics of the Western family system. . . .' (1980, p. 25).

It is hardly surprising that such material has been the basis of continuing and lively scholarly debate and criticism. Questions have been raised about the reliability of some of the sources (it is always necessary to consider the purposes behind any collection of statistical information and the understandings and coding procedures adopted by the keepers of such records) and about the extent to which the mean figures produced for marriage rates or household composition might not obscure some interesting variations. But perhaps the most fascinating set of questions, sociologically speaking, deals with the question of meaning. Put at its simplest we might have two households, one in the seventeenth century and one at the beginning of the nineteenth century. They may contain an identical number of persons, equivalent in terms of generation, age and gender. But the actual meaning of living in a particular household to the members of that household may differ radically in each case. Sociologically the two households may not, in any sensible way, be the same even where they are demographically very similar. As Flandrin notes, such studies are 'merely . . . a snapshot of the occupants of accommodation in a given locality at a given moment' (Flandrin, 1979, p. 3). One important question is the place of these intra-household relationships in the context of wider sets of relationships, with kin, neighbours, friends or with other households. To quote Flandrin again, parish census material cannot give us the structure of relationships between 'dominant large households and dependent small ones' (*ibid.*, p. 65). Another set of questions would deal with the structure and balance of obligations between household members, another set with the allocation and deployment of resources within the household and so on. Certainly many of the issues which might be of interest to feminist historians are not treated in the demographic approach (Jordanova, 1981, p. 46).

3 It is these questions of meaning that form the province of Anderson's third category, the 'Sentiments' approach. The work of these historians has probably had the wider popular appeal and is particularly associated with the names of Ariès, Stone and Shorter. The basic concern of these historians, Anderson argues, is the emergence of 'modern' social relationships in and around the family (1980, p. 39). The focus of these studies differs in each case. Stone is concerned with Britain from the period 1500–1800 and his source material is largely from accounts of upper-class and aristocratic family life (Stone, 1977). Ariès's somewhat mistitled book deals largely with French material (again with a largely upper-class emphasis) over a slightly longer, if more indefinite, period (Ariès, 1972). Shorter's is the most comprehensive in scope, seeking to deal with the whole of Europe (although with an emphasis on Western Europe with some glances at the United States) and making courageous and

often ingenious attempts to capture everyday family life and its changes. What each of these writers shares is a concern to delineate the processes of change which lead to the growing separateness and distinctiveness of the conjugal-based family. In many respects they can be seen as working within the classic sociological tradition, tracing the growth of the concept of romantic love, the development of motherhood as a full-time and largely separate status, the increasing focus on the marital couple as the main axis of family life, the increasing distinctiveness of the category of childhood and the growth of the family-based household as the locus of private, personal relationships, relationships which became increasingly prized and valued. They differ from the earlier and simpler 'before and after' models of sociologists in a variety of ways. Stone, obviously, completes his story before the full emergence of an industrial society although the implication is that 'modern' family relationships were installed before the onset of industrialisation. Ariès remains very much within a tradition of thought established by Durkheim, among others, and can be seen as a pioneer in the use of sources rarely tapped by previous analysts of the family. Shorter writes with the knowledge of Laslett's argument, one which he acknowledges and to some extent praises. He differs from Laslett in that he would claim to be filling in some of the emotional content necessarily left out from demographic analysis and in arguing for different family patterns developing in different parts of Europe.

It is important to stress that the writers loosely described as belonging to the 'Sentiments' school are not arguing for a shift from an extended family system to a nuclear family system. They are, instead, arguing for an overall shift in emphasis in patterns of control and in the relationships within the family and between the family and the wider society. In the first place they are arguing for a shift in emphasis from issues of descent and lineage to a stress on marriage and conjugality, from vertical relationships to horizontal relationships. In the second place they are arguing for shifts in terminology and meaning, particularly in the emergence of the modern meanings attached to the word 'family', one which is based on relationships of marriage and parenthood and which is seen as largely equivalent to the household in terms of composition. Finally, they are arguing for a weakening of community controls over domestic relationships and the consequent greater distinction between the public and the private: 'Perhaps most important of all, however, is the stress laid on the embedded position of the individual and household in the wider community. . . .' (Anderson, 1980, p. 42.) The dramatic symbol of these community controls was the charivari, the 'rough music' provided by the villages to exercise control over the sexuality and reputation of local inhabitants, especially womenfolk.

When Mount criticises sociologists and historians it is clearly these historians that he has in mind and he uses Laslett as a stick with which to beat them. But Mount is not alone and the whole 'school' has been subjected to some severe criticism largely in terms of their practice of generalising on the basis of slender or unrepresentative evidence. Evidence, varying considerably in quality and scope, is brought together from different countries (especially in the case of Shorter) and different historical periods. Both Ariès and Stone tend to generalise on the basis of evidence from the upper classes. Theoretically, the studies have been criticised for their failure to make any clear analysis of the processes of causality at work. There is considerable discussion and description of the processes of domestic change that are supposed to have taken place but relatively little as to how these changes came about, little about the relationship between familial change and other patterns of social and economic change.

Before leaving the 'Sentiments' school it might be worth mentioning a group of writers who might in some way be loosely identified with this school, namely those influenced by Foucault, especially in this case Donzelot. While not strictly historians (indeed Foucault defies easy categorisation) they do share some of the same concerns as these historians, namely an attempt to trace major shifts in the structure of societal sentiments. The concern here is the use of historical material to ask questions about the wider structure of power, control and knowledge. The approach may be roughly stated as a movement to and fro between the particular and the general, the outlining of a particular piece of behaviour (the punishment of a criminal or the treatment of orphans) and moving out into the wider society to ask: 'what kind of society is it where such practices would be regarded as normal?' While clearly this is a different enterprise and involves a different kind of treatment of evidence it does

165

point to one kind of use that might be made of historical material.

4 The final category, outlined by Anderson, is what he calls the 'Household Economics' approach. Anderson's own work on Lancashire families could be cited as an example of this 'school' of orientation, one which is much closer to traditional sociological and social anthropological investigation. This emphasis is largely upon the case study, of part of a region, a small town or a village, and the typical product is perhaps more often the paper in a learned journal rather than the full-scale or popular book. The central concern is very much with placing the household in its wider environment and, especially, with identifying the structural constraints that confront households in particular regions or localities at particular points of time. The key notions are the resources that are available to households and individual household members, the strategies that household members individually, or in collaboration, adopt to deal with economic issues using these resources and the power relationships that arise out of and shape these strategies and use of resources (Anderson, *op. cit.*, pp. 65–6). Key issues are patterns of inheritance, marriage strategies, the various sources of monetary and other kinds of income, the patterns of social support and social control within and between households. For working-class families, for example, the issues might be the problems of dealing with the cycles of poverty outlined by Booth and Rowntree, the use of kin in enabling mothers to seek paid employment outside the home, the use of minors as sources of income or the taking in of lodgers. It can be seen that many concerns traditionally associated with social anthropology have been taken over in this approach to family history. These studies can be seen as eschewing the large-scale speculation of the 'Sentiments school' while attempting to flesh out in a phenomenological and processual way the statistical skeletons provided by the family demographers. Anderson argues, however, that it is not simply a question of this final 'school' being preferred against the other two. All three, he suggests, can make a contribution to understanding family processes.

There is a 'school' of family historical studies which Anderson does not mention but which might be accorded a separate category. The growth of family history has had a symbiotic, if not necessarily harmonious, relationship with the growth of feminist history and women's history. This, in its turn, may be seen arising out of, and to some extent against, the older traditions of 'people's history', attempts to capture the lives and experiences of the working classes and peasantries in the context of an overall socialist orientation. Whether women's history or feminist history can be described as a particular school of orientation in the sense that Anderson's outlines is perhaps open to question. It can be seen as drawing upon all three or four traditions outlined by Anderson, with perhaps a particular emphasis on the last two. The central emphasis is upon deconstructing the family in order to understand the gender divisions within it, to capture the experiences of women, not simply as family members but as workers and as persons who often have an identity outside the family. The emphasis would normally, although not exclusively, be upon the lives and experiences of working-class women (Kelly-Gadol, 1976).

The main contribution of this orientation will be left to Chapter 9 but it cannot be forgotten in a treatment of historical approaches to the family.

FAMILY HISTORY AND FAMILY SOCIOLOGY

Any discussion of the relationship between family history and family sociology must inevitably be a subset of a wider, and well-rehearsed, debate about the relationships between history and sociology themselves. The question may be focused a little more if we ask ourselves what are the particular contributions that the study of family history may make to our discussion of theoretical approaches to the family, a problem made the more acute by the explosion in studies in family history already mentioned in the chapter. What is the sociologist to make of the overwhelming volume of detailed studies of pre-industrial or peasant family life in small communities throughout Europe and beyond, of the debates and qualifications about the character and composition of the pre-industrial household as well as the growing number of specific studies tracing the changing experiences of families in communities undergoing industrialisation or urbanisation? What is the relationship between the host of specific and relatively small-scale studies on the one hand and the large-scale generalising attempts of a

Shorter or an Ariès to delineate the distinctive features of the modern Western family? 'Yes, but not in the South' may be as effective an underminer of generalisations here as in other areas of scholarly or social life and the sociologist may well be tempted to throw in the towel and retreat to the comparative security of Parsonian or Marxist functionalism or to the social survey.

But this would not only be premature, it would also be fallacious. For one thing the apparent contrast between historical facts and sociological theories implied in the last paragraph does not really stand up to investigation, however comforting it may be to representatives from both parties (Stedman-Jones, 1976). It is fallacious for the same reason that the contrast between facts and theory within sociology itself would be fallacious; facts are thoroughly impregnated with theory; their recognition, evaluation and collection is shaped by theoretical concerns and constructions. In the second place, history and sociology cannot really be understood as separate ways of viewing the world, even if, as disciplines, they have developed different traditions and different methodologies. E.H. Carr's lectures *What is History?* (Carr, 1964) could be rewritten as 'What is Sociology?' with relatively little alteration and Giddens has noted, recently, that there is no logical or methodological distinction to be made between history and the social sciences 'appropriately conceived' (Giddens, 1979, p. 230). From the perspective of the sociologist the point is not one of choosing between history or no history. It is rather one of choosing between implicit and unexamined history and explicit and critically assessed history. This is true even in those studies which might appear to be completely innocent of any historical concerns or understandings, those studies which are based upon some kind of questionnaire survey and which seek to explore some facet of contemporary family living such as marital power or factors contributing to divorce-proneness. In some cases they may use some implicit 'then and now' assumptions, implying some degree of uniqueness or peculiarity about our own times. Alternatively, they may seek to generate or to use law-like propositions that are based upon implicit assumptions that matters have not changed all that much.

A common justification of a more explicit treatment and use of history is to help us understand 'how we got where we are now'.

The implication is often that if we understand our past and the antecedents of our present institutions and problems we may better understand and shape our future. The parallel might be, at the individual level, with psychoanalysis. Current neurosis or phobias may be understood in terms of one's personal history and such an understanding may help us to develop and grow in the future. But the parallel already points out a difficulty with this particular formulation of the use of history. The understanding of the historical antecedents of a contemporary social problem, such as divorce rates, as much as the understanding of the antecedents of an individual problem, such as divorce, are essentially theoretical enterprises. History, whether collective or individual, does not simply and neutrally, 'tell us' anything. It responds to particular questions, particular formulations and understandings. There is not one story that history has to tell us; there are several, depending upon the questions that are directed in her direction. Thus, it makes a difference whether the question 'how did we come to get where we are now?' is being asked by an old-fashioned evolutionist, a Marxist, a feminist or a functionalist.

If we have reason to be sceptical, or at least cautious, about claims that the study of history in any simple way helps us to understand the present, what can we say about another frequently made claim, namely that the study of history provides us with a comparative perspective on the present? To some extent this justification is linked to the previous one: 'It is the task of the historian to show how the seemingly "natural" and enduring forms of family life came into being and how they change over time.' (Mitterauer and Sieder, 1982, p. xiii.) It was statements such as this that led Mount to attempt an 'alternative history of the family'. Mount's argument is that the project being attempted by some sociologists and historians is one of demolition through relativisation and that, ultimately, this project is a political one on the side of all those who have sought to undermine the family in the name of Church or state or ideology. Show that people ordered their families somewhat differently in the past, it is argued, and you undermine the assumptions about the essential nature of love, family feeling and parental affection. Hence the placing of the word 'natural' in quotation marks in the quotation above. Love, parenthood, marriage and childhood become socio-historical constructions.

In the past relativists, advocating free love, referred us to the Trobrianders; now, contemporary relativists refer us to French peasant life in the seventeenth century or to artists' depictions of life at court in pre-industrial Europe.

Mount uses Laslett and a variety of literary sources to argue that, contrary to the claims of some sociologically-inclined historians, the family has not in fact changed all that much, that the 'history of the family' is not so much evolutionary or progressive as a constant, almost cyclical struggle of the family against the intrusions of the state and reformers of all political and religious shades, that the word 'natural' needs no quotation marks. The point may be made more generally and less contentiously by arguing that the use of historical analysis to provide us with comparative spectacles with which to view our own times is not a neutral activity. Goody, for example, warns us of the danger of looking at past families backward, as it were, from the vantage point of the present, an orientation which tends to an over-evaluation of the present in either negative or positive terms (Goody, 1983, p. 2). Thus, there is a tendency to view the present as a time of breakdown and disorganisation as compared with the past, or to see the present as a time of relative freedom, choice and liberation as compared with a past that was locked in tradition. Either way, the tendency is towards a dichotomous view of history, of then and now, us and them (*ibid.*, p. 3). Harris, similarly, warns us againt the 'great divide' approach to historical understandings of the family, indicating some great gulf between the pre-industrial and the industrial or post-industrial families (Harris, 1983).

Indeed, a lot of historical writing on the family would seem to consist of demolishing, or calling into question, earlier assumptions about our past. Thus Mitterauer writes, in terms similar to Laslett, of 'the myth of the large pre-industrial family' (*op. cit.,* pp. 24–47). It is perhaps precisely at this point that the sociologist may be tempted to make an excuse and leave. Laslett and others tended to focus on household composition leading others (including Mount) to make unwarranted inferences from this demographic reconstruction about *family* life in earlier times. Attempts to study the 'mentalities' of past ages suffer from a narrow or unrepresentative range of sources or are open to counter-evidence from other parts of Europe. But our sociologist would be wrong to leave at this point. For one thing, debates about the reliability and validity of evidence, about the range of permissible generalisations are clearly not confined to historians; they are the stuff of methodological and theoretical debates within sociology itself. Only those who seek straightforward or large-scale generalisations should retreat from the field, and if the historical debate tells us anything it is that the notion of the large pre-industrial family and the notion of the unchanging family are both myths in the pejorative sense of the word.

Clearly there are discernible differences between the families of the past and the families of the present although to state the matter in these terms presupposes some continuity of understanding of the central term, 'family', that we are in fact comparing like with like. Consider the following passage:

> In this society, in which widowhood and remarriage were much more frequent than today, it was accepted that the close kinsfolk should intervene to protect orphans from ill-treatment at the hands of stepmothers. (Flandrin, 1979, p. 40)

Accepting the temporal and geographical limitations of this statement we may reasonably view this as a picture of the 'world we have lost'. (Perhaps not entirely – this picture may not be strange to working-class or immigrant communities in many modern industrial cities.) It is not that households were necessarily much larger or contained more than two generations but that wider familial and kinship relationships comprised a fluctuating 'solidarity of honour' (*ibid.*, p. 47) in which one called upon kin 'naturally' for help in times of need and that strangers to a village could guarantee support or protection if they were able to claim kinship with one or more of its members. Or take the expression of popular collective control, the 'charivari'. Doubtless this was not a common feature of everyday life throughout pre-industrial Europe, yet it was also doubtless more prevalent 'then' than it is 'now'. It is not a case of the 'nuclear family' being any different, at least in terms of structure (that could scarcely be the case as a matter of definition) but that the wider family was related to and articulated with the wider society in quite different ways than it is now. This is not a case of the family being more or less 'natural' at one point of time than another but that it is always shaped by

171

institutions and relationships outside it such as kinship, religion, the state and patterned inequality.

Thus, family history may still provide us with some kind of comparative perspective on the present even if we may be required to consider the matter more deeply than might have been the case in the past. But there is one sense in which historical study may clearly provide such a comparative perspective and that is in matters of definition, especially of the key term 'family' itself.[2] The family has a history and the term 'family' also has a history and the relationship between the two is a complex matter. Mitterauer points out that the German language had no word for family as we understand the term (although how do 'we' understand the term?) until the Middle Ages or early modern times (Mitterauer and Sieder, 1982, p. 6). The early part of Flandrin's work is full of a detailed and often bewildering range of definitions and meanings referring to family, household, 'race', 'house' and 'lignage'. Looking at dictionaries in France and England from the sixteenth to the eighteenth centuries he finds two distinct meanings attached to the word 'family'.

(i) As a group of co-residents not necessarily all linked by blood or marriage;
(ii) As a set of kin who did not live together. (Flandrin, *op. cit.,* p. 4)

He concludes:

> The concept of the family . . . as it is most commonly defined today, has only existed in our western culture since a comparatively recent date. (*ibid.,* p. 9)

Williams makes a similar point (Williams, 1983, 2nd end, pp. 131–4). Clearly these observations raise a whole host of further questions about the relationships between dictionary definitions and social practices as well as about the range of definitions and understandings that are present today. But that is perhaps one of the chief virtues of a consideration of the historical debates; that they encourage us to frame new and challenging questions about our present as well as about the past.

This brief discussion of definitions reminds us to be alert to the tensions between dictionary, jural or official definitions and lay, popular or everyday understandings. Bourdieu's discussion of *'habitus'* seeks to emphasise the point that people do not routinely follow rules or laws but rather evolve a set of practices, usages, strategies and understandings which emerge from the particular sets of economic conditions and constraints within which they find themselves (1976, pp. 117–44). Similarly, Goody writes provocatively of a 'dual economy of kinship' that evolved in European society out of the struggle between religious and official definitions of what was to be desired and popular needs and understandings. He notes the emergence of new rules to do with cousin marriage, marriage to affines, adoption and concubinage, and argues that such rules did not have anything to do with Hebrew or Roman law or with the practice and teaching of the early Christian Church. Rather, he argues, as the Church ceased to be a millenialist sect with no thought for the morrow and became a major social and political institution it found it necessary to condemn practices that would deprive it of property. All the outlawed practices would, in various ways, ensure that property would be kept within a relatively restricted kinship group or community rather than passed on or bequeathed to the Church. Goody indicates by the term 'dual economy of kinship' a continuous struggle between Church and laity on these matters leading to these two levels, 'one at the level of rules and one at the level of practice; one open, one hidden' (Goody, 1983, p. 182).

It is not 'history' on its own that has taught us to appreciate the differences between official and popular misunderstandings. Indeed, in the past it was often maintained that historians were much too concerned with official or elite practices and understandings and it is interesting to note that Goody is a social anthropologist while Bourdieu might be more accurately described as a sociologist or a social anthropologist than a historian. Nevertheless, the historical approach to marriage, sexuality and the family has contributed to a much more substantial focus on everyday practices and understandings, an emphasis that is of continuing importance to persons studying contemporary society.

Up to now we have considered the various ways in which historical studies have contributed to our understanding of features of the family in contemporary society through providing some kind of comparative perspective. In many cases family history is not unique in this respect; social anthropology has also provided that kind of perspective. But it may be argued that this contribution is in terms of providing a set of reminders, sharpening our understandings of the ways in which we may be unique and the ways in which we may be similar or alerting us to features and practices in our own society which we may well have failed to recognise. However, what is the distinctive contribution that family history may make to a wider *theoretical* understanding of the family and of family processes? It is here that we must turn our attention more specifically to issues of social change.

There is always something odd about considering social change in a box apart from other areas of sociological analysis, in placing the theory of social change in some kind of analytical ghetto. If we accept the maxim that what we are studying are not things but processes, then the study of social change must be on everyone's agenda. Nevertheless, there does appear to be a built-in tendency to reify and freeze social institutions – classes, families, organisation etc. – and as a consequence social change comes to occupy a box on its own. While regretting this, let us proceed to a more explicit discussion of the particular contribution that family history may make to a study of social change.

To begin with, one issue that has emerged very strongly from the writings of recent family historians is the question of causation, especially insofar as we are considering the relationship between the family and large-scale processes such as urbanisation and industrialisation. The emphasis on the importance of presenting a history from 'below' outlined in earlier paragraphs, has led to a desire not to see families as passive victims in the face of the inexorable march of History. Davis argues that family history may enable us to see social change beginning from below, something that is initiated by and not imposed upon, families (Davis, N.Z., 1978, in Rossi *et al.*, (eds), pp. 87–114). Elder, similarly, argues that the historical approach (or more specifically the 'life course approach') may help us to see 'family and kinship as a causal force in history' (Elder, 1978 in Demos and Boocock, p. 8). Kanter argues that the historical perspective may correct 'a one-sided picture of the family as helpless victims of the forces of industrialisation' (Kanter, 1978, in Demos and Boocock, p. 321).

174

The growing emphasis on strategies (e.g. Bourdieu *op. cit.,* on marriage strategies, underlines the point. Even families with relatively limited resources (or families that have been dealt a relatively bad hand, demographically speaking) have a variety of strategies open to them in coming to terms with unfavourable, novel or threatening environments. Mothers may seek paid employment, making use of grandparents or kin to make this possible, children may be sent out to work or kept off school, lodgers may be taken in and so on. Such approaches challenge the textbook versions of Marx or Weber which place large-scale historical processes on one side as independent variables (capitalism, industrialisation, rationalisation) and people and institutions, especially families, as relatively passive dependent variables in the face of these forces.[3] This is clearly an important emphasis although it is not perhaps as novel as some of the historians seem to be claiming. Anthropologists, turning their attentions to developing towns in Africa, for example (see, e.g. Banton (ed.), 1966; Mitchell (ed.), 1969) came to the same kinds of conclusions. People did not simply carry their tribal pasts with them into the new industrial-based cities neither did they crumble and become atomised or anomic in the face of such new situations. Ties of kinship and tribal or local origin took on new kinds of significance in new circumstances. 'Network' for many of these anthropologists had the same role as 'strategies' does for many contemporary historians.

Moreover, while this is an important emphasis, there is a danger that there may be a confusion between a moral argument ('people matter') with an analytical one about the processes of social change. People are indeed 'resourceful' – certainly more so than many macro-theories might suggest – but the nature and extent of these resources is not, it must be reiterated, purely a matter of their own choosing. Further, to talk of the family as a 'causal force' or as an 'independent variable' is to run the risk of presenting a reified picture of the family, of artificially detaching the family from other sets of relationships and institutions. The point perhaps is not that we need to choose between either the family or industrialisation as causal or independent variables but that the whole attempt to frame the problem in these terms is one fraught with difficulties and should be abandoned. This, perhaps, is the real lesson that we should learn from these historical or anthropological studies.

Themes

If the 'strategies' approach to family history has taught us one thing, it is an appreciation of the variety of responses that are possible in relation to the same 'external' force (Laslett, 1980). Of course, historians working in this field have always emphasised differences and diversity; that has been one of the main problems facing sociologists and others who wish to make generalisations about the 'Western family' or 'the family under capitalism'. Thus Anderson notes important differences in Western family types (Anderson, *op. cit.,* p. 14) and Flandrin emphasises, in his analysis, the differences between the North and the South in pre-industrial family practices in France (Flandrin, *op. cit.,* p. 72). Doubtless even these distinctions might be a little on the gross side. The theoretical point is not that there are differences and that generalisations are difficult if not impossible (scarcely a conclusion of much help or profundity) but that in talking about 'the family' we are dealing with a very protean entity and that these variations and differences are not sources of embarrassment that may be ironed away with higher level generalisations but that, in a variety of ways, they should exist at the heart of the analysis. Reflecting on the character of the family in pre-industrial Europe, Wrigley notes the by now familiar point that it was the chief unit of reproduction, production, consumption and socialisation. However, he emphasises that what constituted the family unit for one purpose was not the family unit for some other purpose and that the concept of family membership was not a stable or an exclusive one. Moreover, in a given life span people experience more than one different 'type' of family. (Wrigley in Rossi, *et al.* (eds), 1978, pp. 71–4). The household might be a somewhat easier unit to handle in this respect but, as we have seen, to focus on this is to exclude or to minimise a whole range of practices and experiences. This appreciation of difference and diversity perhaps comes easier to historians although it is clearly not to be monopolised by them. But the message which sociologists might draw from this is not simply one of caution, of not making generalisations, but of making different kinds of generalisations which are more appreciative of process and variation. Such an emphasis is to be found among those historians and sociologists who are beginning to talk of the 'life course'.

The 'life course' approach, to date, seems to be the main area

176

where the meeting between history and sociology has made some kind of theoretical contribution. Sociologists have, on the whole, been slow to recognise the crucial role of time, process and development in the units of their investigations whether these units be conceived of as individuals (actors, members, etc.) or as collectivities. 'Socialisation' tends to be placed on the borders of social psychology and lumped in with the family while 'old age' tends to be hived off in departments of social administration. Apart from some particular 'careers' (as mental patient, drug user or whatever) there does not seem to be a great deal of process, even in family studies, between leaving school and receiving a pension. The analysis in terms of 'life course', in contrast, places change and development at the heart of the analysis and seeks to explore the inevitable temporal dimension of our lives and experiences. The crucial feature is the articulation of the 'bond between age and time' (Elder, 1978b in Demos and Boocock (eds), p. 23) or the exploration of the differences and relationships between 'family time', 'individual time' and 'historical time' (Hareven in Rossi *et al.* (eds), 1978, p. 61). For example, I was born in 1937. Consequently, between then and now I have had a variety of historical experiences: of the Second World War, of the immediate post-war period, of National Service, of Suez and swinging London, of CND, of the assassination of President Kennedy and so on. During that period I passed through various transitions to do with family, school, work and so on – leaving school, getting married, becoming a father, getting divorced. I experience biological ageing, although these experiences are never simply biological but are always culturally and symbolically mediated. Life course analysis, then, is to do with these complex relationships over time between ageing, between family, education and work careers and between historical experiences.

The idea of the 'life course' is to be distinguished from the older, and probably more familiar, notion of the 'life cycle' or 'family life cycle'. As Elder points out, the fact that models of the family cycle vary from 3 to 24 stages should give us some cause to stop and consider (Elder, 1978a, in Hareven (ed.), p. 46). It is argued that the 'family cycle' tends to deal with a hypothetical nuclear family and fails to give us a sense of the *range* of nuclear (or other) family experiences. The emphasis tends to be on stages of *parenthood* (Elder, *ibid.*) and tends to treat less frequent cases as marginal or deviant (Tilly, G., Foreword to Hareven (ed.), 1978). The life course approach tends to be more individual in its emphasis, more appreciative of differences and variation and, as we have suggested, as concerned with linking historical time with individual biography as with tracing individual progressions through particular typified stages.

What then is the central concern of the life course approach? Elder describes the life course in these terms, as referring to:

> pathways through the age-differentiated life span, to social patterns in the timing, duration, spacing and order of events; the timing of an event may be as consequential for life experience as whether the event occurs and the degree or type of change. (Elder in Hareven (ed.), 1978a, p. 21)

Some of these issues are elaborated by Hareven, who similarly sees the focusing on 'the meshing of individual careers with the family as it changes over time. . . .' (Hareven in Hareven (ed.), 1978, p. 5). She sees three essential features or concerns of the approach. In the first place there is the question of the 'timing and synchronization of transitions'. Here she uses the striking image of a shoal of fish moving through the water with fish breaking free from one little cluster of fish to join another and then to move on to a third, partially composed of previous swimming companions. And all the time the school of fish is moving through the water. The approach is, secondly, concerned with the impact of historical processes (e.g. war or unemployment or migration) on the timing of individual or family transitions. Finally, the approach is concerned with the cumulative impact of earlier transitions on subsequent ones (Hareven, *ibid.*, pp. 5–8). The key word, here, is 'transitions', a word with much more dynamic and purposive connotations than the early 'stage'. Such transitions, although they occur to the individual and the individual is the focus of the analysis are never purely that; any transition has implications for, or reverberations upon, others and is shaped and affected by wider historical change and institutional arrangements. Retirement would be a good example, one shaped by legislation affecting pension rights and so on and one which has wider implications for family, kin and members of one's social networks. Hareven notes that, perhaps contrary to common belief, the timing of family transitions has become more predictable now, than in the past (Hareven, 1978 in Rossi *et al.* (eds), p. 61), in part a reflection of the greater intervention on the part of the state.

The consequence of this orientation for our analysis of the family is, as we have seen, to underline the protean nature of that institution: 'The family unit is portrayed as a set of contingent career lines which vary in synchronization and problems of resource management.' (Elder in Hareven (ed.), 1978a, pp. 55–6.) The point is to emphasise the varying nature of the family not simply in an attempt to remind us of the fact of difference and diversity but also to begin to establish some principles around which and through which this diversity might be understood.

In general this historical approach to the family may show us the interplay between home and work and between the public and the private spheres, thus providing some useful linkages with some feminist concerns (Jordanova, 1981, p. 49). While, in principle, the kinds of orientation that might be included in 'the life course' approach could have come from within sociology, it is likely that historical studies provide a particular emphasis, simply because it is so much easier to be aware of process through a consideration of the past. It is also to be noted that many of these historical studies are of our recent past and hence may be seen as having more of a direct bearing on the under-standing of contemporary situations than may have been the case with other historical studies. However, an approach in terms of a focus on transitions is one which, within sociology, is still in its relative infancy and clearly has a lot to contribute to our understanding of family processes and the articulations between family and other relationships and institutions.

There are, however, two possible dangers with the life course approach. In the first place there is the danger that, as with the case of network analysis, it may become a technique. Since much of the material with which life course analysis deals is so readily quantifiable and amenable to statistical manipulation of quite advanced kinds, there is the danger that method may triumph over meaning. In the second place there is some danger in the relatively uncritical use of the term 'family' in this analysis. While the analysis stresses the variable nature of the family over the life course (itself a considerable advance over more static structural approaches) the assumption would seem to be that the family should be the central and unproblematic focus of attention, the major thread around which other events, careers and transitions are woven. This is, perhaps, related to the methodological point. Family transitions are so readily recorded and have a degree of fixity, being related more firmly to demographic information. However, in principle, there is no necessary reason why the focus of attention need be on families and a life course analysis could focus either on individuals (with no particular priority being given to family events) or on other institutions or groups or collectivities such as factories, schools, informal networks such as artistic groups, movements or political parties.

CONCLUSION

What, therefore, is the use of family history to sociologists? In the first place it is important to stress that history is not simply an academic discipline and that the exchanges and debates that I have noted are not simply of narrow scholarly concern. Take, for example, the report, discussed at some length in the first part of this book, *Marriage Matters*. The first part of the report attempts to place contemporary marriage in its socio-historical context, attempting in other words, to understand how we have got where we are today. The account is a more or less straight-forward evolutionary account, tracing a movement from institution to relationship. It therefore tends to the dichotomous approach castigated by some recent historians and their critics. The aim of having such an introduction is to argue, presumably, that the increase in divorce rates is a sign neither of an increase in individual irresponsibility nor of an impending societal breakdown, but is a change rooted in changes in the character of marriage itself. While there could be several objections to the way in which the account of historical family change has been formulated and perhaps some questioning of the availability or appropriateness of the evidence which might be used to support such an account, there can be no doubt that the *Marriage Matters* account illustrates one prevailing and important use of historical analysis, namely as an antidote again jeremiads. It is after all useful to remind people of the number of broken homes or one-parent families in Victorian times caused by the death of one of the parents and to ask, polemically, whether divorce might not be slightly preferable to death.

These uses will no doubt continue. At a slightly more scholarly level the work of family historians, contrary to what Mount may argue, emphasises variation and hence continually underlines the social character of family living. When we talk of the social construction of various family-based identities – childhood, fatherhood, motherhood, marriage, etc. – we are not simply concerned with the everyday work of maintaining, affirming and constructing these identities (see next chapter) but with the placing of this kind of work in some kind of historical context. Fatherhood, or whatever, has a history. This is not simply to say that it has a past but that the assumptions and evaluations about fatherhood are part of the resources which are used by persons who occupy the status of father (and mother and child) and are shaped by the complex intersections between personal biographies, the overlapping of family careers over generations and wider patterns of socio-historical change. Thus, we are not simply learning about different or strange or even bizarre practices of earlier centuries but are also exploring changes and perceptions of changes, that continue to affect the way in which we live and understand family relationships. Thus, to continue the example, in doing the work of fatherhood, I deploy understandings of what being a father means, not simply from my present generations but from the past, especially that past which is most available to me in terms of my own family of origin and the past that was interpreted and filtered through that source. And such a past is influential not simply in terms of providing role models – which it may well not do – but also providing some kinds of social benchmark, some kind of understanding of differences of the distances we have travelled, of how it is now as compared with how it was, apparently, then. The social construction of family identities, therefore, must be understood historically, not in terms of some kind of abstract history but of histories and biographies that are intimately connected and felt and understood.

At a more theoretical level, family history and the work of family historians is 'good to think with'. In other words, it does not simply provide us with information, to tell us that things were different, or the same, in the past. It provides us with some of the tools to think about these similarities and differences and to work through the consequence of this thought in terms of wider theorising. For example, the sending of child immigrants to Canada during the period of the end of the Victorian era and the early twentieth century (Parr, 1980) does not simply tell a story about a set of practices in our very recent past which now seem alien, perhaps even barbaric. Reflection on these historical events and experiences raises questions about the complexity of ideological definitions of the family for it was evangelically-orientated social workers, strong supporters of the family, who supported and organised this immigration that would appear to be so contrary to family living. The intersections between family, between patterns of social control and ideology become more complex in considering the implications of such a case study, throwing up into sharp relief contradictions and ambiguities which need to be incorporated into, or given full recognition by, subsequent theorising. This is not, let it be emphasised, a simple question of 'the facts' calling into question hitherto accepted theories or understandings; it is the facts called to play through the operation of theoretical speculation and questioning.

Historians will continue, no doubt, to debate particular findings and theses about the family in the past, and the marshalling of evidence and counter-evidence, claims and counter-claims must seem very bewildering to contemporary-minded sociologists who want to know simply what 'really happened'. But this sociologist should not expect to be provided with such 'background' material in order better to continue current investigations or polemical exchanges. To consider historical material is to consider the constant tensions between stability and change, between past and present and the role of historians, professional or lay, in constructing and reflecting upon these tensions and oppositions. As Kanter notes we are dealing with a two-way process:

> If the historian's careful examination of the record is
> a superb corrective to theoretical overgeneralisation, the
> sociologist's attention to concepts and relationships apart
> from their immediate context, can be a corrective to the
> tendency to see only uniqueness and change. (Kanter, 1978,
> in Demos and Boocock, p. 336)

9 Phenomenological approaches

INTRODUCTION

Characterisations of sociological 'schools' are always suspect and prone to refutation, especially from those who are at the receiving end of such categorisations. This is especially true in that still relatively uncharted territory which some label 'phenomenological', others 'existential' and yet others 'ethnomethodological'. Yet others would claim the labels 'interpretativist' or 'humanistic'. It is not Marxist or feminist although, as we shall see, these approaches may sometimes be found to have important affinities with some of the main themes; it is not positivist, although some versions of ethnomethodology would seem to be seeking an analytical rigour and a distancing that would undermine any description in terms of 'subjectivist'. It is clearly not functionalist, in any form, although ethnographers seeking to 'make sense' of their data might at least convey a sense of a whole, of interconnections which might accord with some of the basic assumptions of functionalism.

Recognising, therefore, the real risk of both smoothing over differences and of creating artificial boundaries, I shall in this chapter be referring to a territory which has been partially explored by Weber and Schutz, by Garfinkel and Sacks, by Becker and Goffman and perhaps by Sartre. In terms of studies of the family we are, strictly speaking, dealing with a handful of studies and perhaps, more clearly, a set of potentialities and issues rather than fully realised projects. I shall, therefore, attempt to outline a set of overlapping, although not necessarily intellectual, coherent themes which can very loosely be grouped under the label 'phenomenological'.

Themes

THE MAIN THEMES

1 Taking the actor's point of view

In order to explore these overlapping themes it might be helpful to set up, as a kind of Aunt Sally, a typification of a research project which would clearly *not* be described as 'phenomenological'. Consider, therefore, a study of divorce. Such a study might be concerned with the changing incidence of divorce, over the years and as between different categories, classes, age groups and occupational groupings. It might be concerned with establishing the 'causes of divorce', looking both at changing structural conditions and at biographical antecedents in the marital careers of those who experience divorce. In the light of these findings, such a study may seek to provide advice or make recommendations based on an assessment of those kinds of biographical backgrounds and social circumstances which might lead a person to be more divorce-prone than some other person.

It is in comparison with this kind of characterisation of a more or less 'positivistic' piece of research that we may begin to highlight some of the contrasting issues in phenomenology. In the first place, the phenomenological approach would claim to take the point of view of the actor. This often repeated phrase would, itself, seem to have a variety of strands associated with it which, together, would add up to something like the 'social meaning of divorce'. Firstly, there would be the emotional, expressive or affectual level, the attempt, emphathetically, to get under the skin of someone undergoing divorce, to understand it from 'the inside', to get 'behind' the statistics. This is the object of many journalistic, fictional or media presentations of divorce. Sociologically, this would be best exemplified by Hart's accounts – especially her cases – of individuals reliving their divorce or Goode's account of the difficulties that divorced women encounter after divorce and the pressure to remarry. Both these studies combine more conventional information and methods of enquiry with a desire to get close to the divorce experience itself (Goode, 1956; Hart, 1976). What emerges from these two studies is a sense of divorce as a process or a career, one that does not correspond easily with the various legally defined stages of separation and dissolution. Moreover, such studies do not see divorce simply in terms of personal weak-

184

nesses or incompatibilities or as individual tragedies, while at the same time they seek to avoid a sense of persons undergoing divorce as puppets dancing to the social structure. Divorce, these studies suggest, and the feelings and understandings associated with divorce are to do, in the true interactionist tradition, with the self in relation to others' selves: spouse or ex-spouse, children, kin and in-laws, neighbours and friends.

The orientation to the 'actor's point of view' involves at least two other aspects as well as an attempt to understand from the inside. Meaning is also to be understood in cognitive terms and in moral or evaluative terms. The assumption, still in a lot of writing and discussion about divorce is that it is a personal tragedy as well as, possibly, a wider social problem (see Chapter 5). The use of synonyms such as 'marital breakdown' or 'dissolution' clearly carry these kinds of connotations. Yet, especially as more and more people experience divorce (in the sense of knowing someone who has 'been through' the process or perhaps in seeing situation comedies about divorce and separation), the less likely is it that it will be evaluated in quite the same way. It is also clear that many of the aspects of divorce (e.g. setting up of a separate or different household, division of property or care of children) do not necessarily take place together and that cognitively what 'being divorced' means becomes increasingly problematic. These problems are exacerbated further when we consider the 'break up' of couples not legally married in the first place. The emotional, the cognitive and the evaluative all combine, therefore, to constitute what might be called 'the social meaning of divorce', the complex and often various understandings of what divorce and 'being divorced' actually means to the participants. Further, to ask such questions about the social meaning of divorce is necessarily to question the problematisation of divorce in the first place.

Much of this must now be a commonplace. An almost stereotypical journalistic treatment of divorce is to begin with a summary of recent statistics and then to move to 'the reality behind the statistics' with a personal or blow-by-blow account of one or two particular marital dissolutions. Yet sociological accounts commonly would often claim to be both more and less than this. They would claim to be less in that they would normally claim, at least implicitly, not to be interested in all the details of one particular unique set of experiences. By the same token, they would claim to be doing something more in terms of making some kind of generalisation, even where there may be an avoidance of strictly statistical analysis. The everyday experience of the actor, therefore, is not a simple recording of the verbalised experiences of any concrete individual (although these may be included, used or referred to) but some construction of 'a typical actor' in 'typified situations' or surroundings. Taking the perspective of the actor therefore involves both deconstruction, taking apart the package conventionally labelled 'divorce', and reconstruction, establishing some kind of sociological typifications of actors and social processes. Both 'deconstruction' and 'reconstruction' involve a variety of methodological and theoretical complexities.

2 The concentration on 'how' rather than 'why'

As we have seen, a conventional approach to divorce would seek to draw up some kind of measures of 'divorce-proneness' or, at a more structural level, to seek to outline societal causes of, or pressures towards, divorce. In various ways, therefore, such an approach would seek to answer the question 'why?' In contrast, phenomenological accounts seek to address themselves to the question 'how', or perhaps to 'what?' (see e.g. Benson and Hughes, 1983). Thus Goode's pioneering study could be seen, although he does not use these terms, as much an attempt to describe and understand the processes by which women manage the identity of 'being divorced' as an attempt to explain why they became divorced in the first place (Goode, 1956). Implied here is a methodological orientation, perhaps also an ethical or political orientation as well, which sees social actors as continually being involved in the business of constructing their own world rather than simply responding to external forces or internal drives. This was implied when I suggested that to talk of 'the meaning' of divorce was to talk of more than simply what it 'feels' like from the inside. What is at stake here is not simply the emotional response to a particular situation for that would be simply to reproduce conventional distinctions between subject/object, internal/external or stimulus/response. The emphasis is on how individuals make sense of their own world, how these definitions are shared, how actors, in a sense, create that world. Individuals do not simply respond to something called divorce; they create that 'divorce' and the same is true for other family-based identities such as having a handicapped child (Voysey, 1975), being a grandparent (Cunningham-Burley, 1983) or being a parent (Backett, 1982).

A useful word often used in this context is the word 'work', referring to the everyday work of day-to-day living (Wadel, 1979) rather than to a specialised and paid-for activity. Doing family work, therefore, is not simply a question of fitting behaviour into a preordained set of roles or role expectations but rather routinely going about activities which create, recreate, sustain or perhaps modify these roles, statuses or identities. In terms of the sociological problem chosen as an illustration here, 'doing divorce work' might include talking about a past or impending divorce with others, deciding the occasions on which the public or open acknowledgment of the divorced status might be deemed appropriate and renegotiating one's identity with friends, kin and in-laws.

One particular aspect of this day-to-day divorce work and one which is particularly associated with the ethnomethodological perspective, is the analysis of talk or stories about divorce. Talk (including such academically low status activities as story-telling or gossiping) is the stuff of everyday life. Talk is not simply a set of ordered sounds which might be said to be 'about' something (divorce, marriage, parenthood, problem children, etc.) but may be seen as actually constituting the purported subject. To talk about divorce is, therefore, to construct divorce, to build up and sustain a world in which divorce is an understood category of everyday understanding. Divorce may be seen as an occasion for the production of stories, accounts, for the allocation of blame or the denial of guilt. Talk about divorce may, typically, contain some of the following features:

(a) A reconstructed autobiography which will render the present divorced or about-to-be-divorced status intelligible to the hearer.

(b) An allocation of blame or, where this is not done, a recognition on the conversation or exchange of stories that issues of blame will be attended to unless clearly signalled otherwise.

(c) Some kind of reference to the fact of their being 'more than

one version' of the same set of events, the possibility that
the hearer will address her/himself to the fact of their
being 'two sides' to a marriage (see Cuff, 1980).

It may be expected further that talk about divorce will differ
as between friends, kin and between a 'client' and a counsellor.
Divorce work may include the search for advice, support, help
(Brannen and Collard, 1982) and such activities should be seen
not simply as responses to something which might be defined as
'marital problems' but a constituent part of that problem itself.
Divorce, in the final analysis, may be denied any special status
as a problem by being placed in a more general category of
'problems-to-be-talked-about' or 'problems-requiring-help'.

3 Refusal of the 'taken-for-granted'

Our hypothetical investigator of the factors leading up to
divorce would draw upon, as unexplicated resources, a variety of
categories and terms in everyday use: divorce itself, and
marriage and parenthood, categories such as male/female,
possibly social class or age categories. These terms and
categories would be used in order to construct, let us say, causal
models providing some weighting or ordering of factors likely to
make one kind of marriage more divorce-prone than another.
These categories will often be categories and understandings
used in everyday life and the investigators will adopt the same
attitude towards these categories as lay persons, namely an
acceptance and use that treats these categories as being
essentially unproblematic, as being part of a set of shared
understandings or as part of what 'everybody knows'.

The phenomenological approach would, in contrast, involve a
refusal to treat these categories as unproblematic. Instead of
taking them for granted, of using them as resources to be
deployed in analysis, they would be subjected to critical
examination and treated as topics for investigation in their own
right. Thus the use of the term 'divorce' presupposes a shared
understanding not only of what 'divorce' means but also of what
'marriage' means in the first place as a contrasting term.
A phenomenological approach would include a more critical
examination of the range of meanings that these terms have
and the ways in which these meanings are used in everyday life

and perhaps also an examination of the process by which 'divorce' became problematised in the first place (see Chapter 5; also Brannen and Collard, 1982).

Family life may be particularly relevant in this respect for two reasons. In the first place it would seem that, given the ideological centrality of 'the family' in our society, the terminology that is deployed in family analysis is more likely to be part of what 'everybody knows' than the terminology deployed in, say, urban analysis. We 'all know' what families are, what constitutes a real marriage, what is expected of mothers and fathers and what a child is. In some kind of continuum of everyday to strange or normal to abnormal, family terminology would occupy a place very close to the end at the normal/everyday mark. It is perhaps interesting to note that Wittgenstein used the term 'family resemblances' to serve as a metaphor for general language practices and that ethnomethodologists, in talking about Membership Categorisation Devices, will very often fall back upon familistic terminology for illustration. Harvey Sack's analysis of the 'story', the 'baby cried, the Momma picked it up' occupies a key place in ethnomethodological analysis (see Benson and Hughes, 1983). Thus a phenomenological project that, in part at least, seeks to render strange the categories used in everyday family analysis, categories which fit easily with everyday understandings and usages, would seem to be a very curious undertaking indeed. This is perhaps why phenomenological studies of the family are still relatively thin on the ground and yet why they should prove to be such a fruitful souce of such analysis in the future.

The other reason for the particular appropriateness of family analysis for phenomenological treatment lies in the problem of 'multiple realities'. Cuff, for example, shows how 'marital breakups' provide a particular occasion for the deployment and recognition of multiple realities; there are, he argues, a 'determinate' number of accounts or stories of marital breakups (Cuff, 1980, p. 37). Thus a person listening to a woman talking about her marital problems will routinely be conscious, and may display such consciousness in questioning or interjecting, of there being at least one other version of that particular story. The story-teller too, will be conscious of the possibility of alternative versions or realities and may address herself to this directly in the telling of her tale. A phenomenological approach is not, of course, concerned with adjudicating between these versions or (as may be the case in some more positivistically orientated survey) in using one such version as a resource for causal analysis but with treating such talk as routinely providing occasions for the production of multiple realities and with examining how such versions are attended to by teller and hearer alike.

One set of persons who are particularly interested in the question of multiple realities are family 'experts'. Cuff includes an account of the radio programme 'So You Think You've Got Problems', a programme which often deals with family matters and where the format is usually one or two experts, a chairperson, and a set of family members[1] talking about a particular problem or set of problems such as a son's apparent underachievement at school. Here again, Cuff is not interested in family problems *per se* but the way in which persons designated as experts go about doing 'expert work' and how this involves the attending to and the reproduction of multiple realities within the family. The very format of the programme with the chairperson turning from one family member to another with a linking phrase such as 'now let's see what Lucy has to say about all this', is built upon the presupposition of there being multiple realities and the production of these realities.

We may argue that such a production of multiple versions is part of the business of producing a good radio programme, concerned centrally with conflicts and differences. But this is not the whole story. Different accounts or multiple versions would appear to be the stuff of everyday life. Dorothy Smith attends to the possibility of there being two possible readings of an account of mental illness (Smith, 1978) and Lee raises the possibility of a variety of readings of a newspaper heading (Lee, 1984). However, once again, it is likely that there is a particularly strong association between the question of multiple realities and the business of everyday family living. In other words, within family or marital relationships we are faced with the apparent paradox that a situation which would seem to be particularly favourable for the generation of shared understandings (living under the same roof, an ideology of togetherness and so on) would seem to be especially conducive to the production of multiple versions of the same reality. This is the phenomenon of 'I Remember it Well' (Bernard, 1973, Ch. 1), the stuff of many television situation comedies and at least one panel game. More generally, it would seem that family and marital relationships are, at one and the same time, arenas where taken-for-granted understandings are so deeply rooted and yet also where, at times of stress or conflict in particular, they are so vulnerable to the shock of reality disjuncture. For these reasons, the family should be a rich area for investigations.

4 The concern with everyday life

I tried to demonstrate that the phenomenological approach would entail the adoption of a sceptical approach to the everyday categories and understandings that are deployed both by family experts and by family members, that is an approach which entails examining the routine use of these understandings rather than simply drawing upon them as a resource for further analysis. However, phenomenological analysis does not, therefore, take us away from the everyday. Thus, a phenomenological project would be less likely to take divorce as a point of departure (seeking rather to analyse the everyday patterns of normal family living) or, if it did so, would do so in a way that would refuse or hold in suspension the privileged status of 'social problem' for the topic under investigation. Those few phenomenological studies that we do have tend towards the careful delineation of the routine, the everyday, perhaps even the slightly boring. Backett's study of parents and children deals with 'normal' middle-class families with children who manifest few of the dramatic problems of more traditional family analysis; she is concerned instead with the everyday, routine business of being a parent and the images of children that parents deploy on an everyday basis (Backett, 1982).

Similarly, Cunningham-Burley attends to the everyday business of becoming a grandparent, for the most part concerning herself with relatively undramatic and unproblematic relationships across the generations (Cunningham-Burley, 1983). While Voysey does deal with a dramatic subject – the presence in a family of a handicapped child – her central concern is not with the 'problems' that such a child presents for parents or siblings but rather the ways in which family members, especially parents, address themselves to notions of normal family life in caring for such a child (Voysey, 1975).

Themes

Thus the 'everyday' more often than not refers to everyday families in everyday situations or to the processes by which 'abnormal' situations are routinised. The treatment of the everyday is also manifest, as we have seen, in the use of familiar materials for analysis. The issue is not, therefore, divorce or problem children *per se* but 'talk' about divorce or problem children. The medium is the topic; everyday stories or accounts are not scrutinised, analysed or otherwise treated in order to produce data about something or other (divorce, problem children) but are treated as topics in their own right. Family analysis does not necessarily require a large and expensive research project directed to correct sampling procedures and advanced methods of data analysis; a single transcript may be enough.

5 Reducing the gap between observer and observed

A large number of sociological practices, whatever the differences between them, have as a common feature, their maintenance of a distance between the observer and the observed. This distancing has several distinct features:

(a) There is understood to be a difference between the versions and projects of the observer and those of the observed. In various ways, moreover, the versions of the observed are held to be flawed or partial at least in comparison with the more objective or scientific versions of the observer. Lay versions are typically 'ironicised'; simply by reporting them in a sociological context they are presented as an incomplete, partial or flawed version of the social reality they purport to be about. Their truth value is held into question, perhaps even presented as some kind of 'false-consciousness'.

(b) The feelings, views and values of the observer are not seen to enter into the analysis. In contrast, such feelings and views are seen as problematic, as source of bias and every attempt is made to exorcise them, either through an open acknowledgment or through techniques of analysis that conform to established canons of objectivity. In one sense there is a denial of authorship; it is not 'me' who is writing this report but rather any person who has adopted the correct orientation to the subject matter, anyone who has deployed the same techniques of data collection and analysis.

(c) Style, language and context of presentation serve to emphasise these differences between observer and observed. These may include the scientific paper in the learned journal, the paper delivered at a conference or a seminar, the book (referred by academic colleagues) which is published by a scholarly press. Even where a report may be prepared for a lay public the use of terms such as 'research findings' serve to maintain this separateness of observer and observed.

In the case of the study of divorce, for example, we will not know whether the authors themselves have been divorced or, if we are told, the information about these experiences will be presented in such a way so as not to contaminate the rest of the report. Feelings and values about divorce in general will be separated out from the topic under investigation, even where they may be recognised. Lay versions of divorce in general or particular marital breakdowns may be treated as rationalisations or partial versions in contradistinction to the scientific stance of the observer. Tables, diagrams and chi-squares may further serve to guarantee the scientific character of the research. The extent to which phenomenological accounts may depart from this typification may vary. Some versions of ethnomethodology, conversational analysis, for example, may still preserve the observer/observed distinction even while holding up to critical scrutiny the practices of conventional sociology. Thus there has developed a standardised way of recording on paper the transcriptions of taped conversations, a method which, while undoubtedly rigorous, does not necessarily accord with the way in which such conversations were actually heard by the observer in the first place or by any of the other participants. Participants to conversations may be identified by letters, A, B, C and so on. This is not to criticise the particular project of conversational analysis, merely to indicate that some versions of a phenomenological sociology do not attempt, or possibly seek, to reduce or obliterate the distinction between observer and observed; rather they present a new version of this distinction.

Other versions of phenomenological sociology, on the other hand, may attend crucially to this problem. Stanley and Wise (feminists who are particularly attracted by the ethnomethodological orientation), for example, criticise the conventional socialist-feminist characterisation of 'the family' as the oppressor (Stanley and Wise, 1983, p. 81). This characterisation suggests both an understanding which makes a distinction between individuals and institutions with the latter 'doing things' to the former and edits out the somewhat paradoxical involvement of the author/observer of such statements. If the family is such an oppressive institution, how is it that certain privileged persons (feminists, Marxists, etc.) are able to escape from the family's clutches in order to see 'so clearly' what is going on? There are no points of engagement between the biography of the observer/author and the biographies of those of his/her subjects.

The acknowledgment of the experiences, views, values and feelings of the observer and the way in which these enter into the research project at every point has several different dimensions. There are the feelings that the 'observer' may have about the views or practices of the observed and the possible ethical or political dilemmas that this might involve (Finch, 1984a; Graham, 1983; McKee and O'Brien, 1983). There is the question of the 'Hawthorne effect', the question that the intervention of observer or interviewer creates a new social situation and that it is this new social situation that should be attended to rather than a relatively naive treatment of the responses or observations as data. There is the more subtle interaction between observer and observed in that the former will bring a whole baggage of concepts and understandings derived from different subcultures and orientations and that the research process will be a constant meeting between these and other subcultural understandings. This, for example, has been the dramatic experience of sociologists who set out to study communes (Abrams and McCulloch, 1976). One of the implications of these several and combined strands of the observed/observer problem is the need for a new kind of research report, one where methods and findings are not subject to radical separation but where these are treated as a continuous unity. There would seem to be considerable difficulties involved in this redefinition of the research process (perhaps not least the objections of publishers) although one or two reports approach this (e.g. Cunningham-Burley, 1983; Voysey, 1975).

6 Use of 'soft' methods

Finally, a phenomenological approach would seem to entail the use of so-called 'soft' methods of social investigation.[2] Thus, a phenomenological approach would seem to be particularly associated with observational techniques, open-ended interviews, perhaps the use of life histories, diaries or other documents. While use of such methods does not guarantee a phenomenological approach (Marxists and functionalists might also use such methods as well), it would be difficult to conceive of the more conventional methods of survey analysis being so used, except perhaps in a case where the methods themselves might be held up for scrutiny.

EXAMPLES

(a) A non-phenomenological study

In order to highlight what is at the core of a phenomenological approach, it may be useful to begin with an example of a non-phenomenological study. Hypothetical examples have been provided in the course of this chapter; a real example may present complexities which can be avoided when dealing with non-existent cases. It should be noted that it is not the intention to hold the chosen study up to ridicule, although as will probably be apparent my preference would be for a more phenomenologically-orientated approach.

Thornes and Collard's *Who Divorces?* (1979) may be taken as an example of a study that is clearly non-phenomenological. Arising out of the work of the Marriage Research Centre at the Central Middlesex Hospital, this book aims to begin to gain 'knowledge of the factors which influence marital breakdown' (*ibid.*, p. vii). The main research instrument was a structured interview schedule with some open-ended questions administered to a random sample of divorced persons and a comparable sample of continuing married. There were more or less straight-forward comparisons between the two samples in terms of a wide range of antecedent factors, together with a more sophis-ticated multivariate analysis which produced a typology of marriage. An Eysenck personality questionnaire was also administered to the two samples, although the result of this did not appear to play a major part in the text as a whole.

It is not the intention here to deny that such a survey might have a place in sociological enquiry or that interesting, and possibly important, differences were demonstrated in the carrying out of such a survey. The book is full of interesting comparisons, not only between the divorced and continuing married but also between men and women and between social classes. (Indeed, it could be argued that more analysis might have been conducted to see whether, say, gender or class might in some cases be more important than divorce or marriage *per se*.) Moreover, even if one were to have doubts about various aspects of the enquiry, the use of interview schedules is often 'good to think with'.[3] To contemplate what kinds of factors may be valuable in the analysis of divorce is to ask important questions about family processes, especially, in this case, in the relationships between and across generations.

Nevertheless, from a phenomenological perspective, Thornes and Collard's study does raise some awkward questions that cannot be answered within their framework or methodology. In the first place there is the problem of retrospective accounts. The possibility of 'distortion of recall' is mentioned, in connection with a question about parental opposition to marriage, but is not really explored in depth (*ibid.*, p. 61). Questions about the quality of parents' own marriages, about the courtship phase or about whether there was some degree of parental opposition to the marriage cannot be taken as fixed 'events' with something like status but as personal biographical understandings that are constantly constructed and reconstructed according to present understandings and interpretations. Given that it is reasonable to assume that divorce, like religious or political conversion or suicide attempts, is an occasion where parties are likely to monitor their own constructed autobiographies in order to 'make sense' of the present, that it is, *par excellence*, an occasion for the telling of stories (Askham, 1982; Cuff, 1980) then any differences between divorced and continuing married respondents might be a function of the research process itself and the intervention of the researcher who provides an occasion for the 'telling of stories'. What we have, therefore, is not necessarily a difference in terms of causal factors (which can be used to distinguish the 'divorce-prone' from the 'less divorce-prone') but in terms of frameworks of interpretation which are occasioned by the fact of divorce or non-divorce itself, which in its turn may be located in the way in which divorce may be problematised in contemporary society (see Chapter 5; also Brannen and Collard, 1982, pp. 222–43). Hence such differences may be of interest but not necessarily in quite the way in which the authors intended.

Further difficulties arise, from a phenomenological perspective, in the question of the social meaning of divorce and, for that matter, marriage itself. The authors acknowledge that divorce and marital breakdown cannot be simply equated (Thornes and Collard, 1979, pp. 1–2) although the implications of this observation, i.e. that there exist different understandings of divorce and marriage, are not followed through. Instead, a straightforward legal definition of divorce is adopted. Yet throughout the book there are suggestions that in using the 'external' labels of marriage and divorce we are often classifying together some very disparate circumstances. If the two most 'divorce-prone' social class classifications are classes III (non-manual) and V (*ibid.*, p. 58), does this mean that there are similar sets of factors that may account for this divorce-proneness between two different social groups or does it indicate two different patterns of understanding and interpretation as to the meaning of marriage and divorce between members of these two categories? It would be possible to continue these lines of speculation further. The point here, however, is to underline the belief that such an approach takes certain key variables – marital status, social class, etc. – for granted and then seeks to combine or to link them, assuming a commonality of social meanings across the various classifications devised by the research instrument. One of the ironic end-products of such a kind of investigation is, through the incorporation of taken-for-granted understandings of divorce, etc., that the book may reinforce the problematisation of divorce and hence, indirectly, influence the very understandings that are both being used and investigated.

Themes

(b) A pseudo-phenomenological approach

The often-reprinted essay by Berger and Kellner (1964) has been taken for an example of a phenomenological approach to marriage; indeed, I did so myself in *Social Theory and the Family* (1975). Certainly, there were the references to Schutz and the adoption of a language that seemed to be closer to a phenomenological than a functionalist tradition. In the essay, Berger and Kellner claim to be influenced by Schutz and Merleau-Ponty as well as by the Weberian and Meadian traditions. In line with Berger's other projects, the emphasis is largely theoretical, especially in terms of a long-term interest in the sociology of knowledge. That kind of theoretical interest, no less than an apparent phenomenological orientation, gave the essay a stimulating freshness and certainly achieved one aim of a phenomenological enterprise, that is to make the familiar and everyday strange. Berger was concerned with routine, everyday marriage, not divorce, marital breakdown or any other such 'problems'.

Nevertheless, there are signs in the paper (and elsewhere in Berger's writings for that matter) that 'Marriage and the Construction of Reality' is more of an adaption to an established American social science tradition rather than an indication of a commitment to any new change in theoretical orientation. There may be some parallels here with the ways in which Freud became translated into a relatively optimistic creed at the hands of American therapists. Berger, following here the Weberian tradition, constructs an ideal type of marriage, arguing that it represents a process whereby two relative strangers come together and mutually create or construct a reality, a relatively stable understanding of their own situation and their place in the wider society. As we have seen, central to this 'world-creation' process is the marital conversation through which the partners, over time, establish a strong sense of what the world is about and, over all, a powerful sense of the taken-for-granted such that, on a day-to-day basis, reality does not present itself as problematic, something which has to be built up anew.

The emphasis on the socially constructed character of the human world may itself be seen as a phenomenological orientation, a refusal to accept the social world as given in some quasi-physical sense and an existential recognition of the precariousness of human constructions. Paradoxically, however, Berger and Kellner do themselves take quite a few things for granted. Their ideal-typification, is like Parsons' construction of the family (Morgan, 1975, pp. 39–40), based, it would seem, upon white middle-class urban American couples. Certainly, the notion of the marital conversation would not necessarily seem to accord with research into marriage in other sectors of American society, either as a reality or as an expectation (Komarovsky, 1962). Berger and Kellner, therefore, take for granted that their particular definition and understanding of marriage applies more generally to 'marriage in Western society'. Moreover, they take for granted the idea that this marriage is in fact 'shared' as between husband and wife, social actors who have gender as well as domestic identities. Finally, more in keeping with a functionalist orientation, Berger and Kellner assume a relatively straightforward fit between this form of marriage and the nature of Western industrial society. Against contemporary jeremiads, Berger and Kellner argue for the *adaption* of marriage rather than its decline; thus divorce rates (taken with rates of remarriage) may be taken as signs of the popularity of marriage rather than a flight from it. While Berger would eschew most forms of functionalism, it is nevertheless the case that, stripped of its phenomenological language, 'Marriage and the Construction of Reality' comes closer to a functional analysis than it would seem (Morgan, 1981).

This becomes more apparent in a recent work, written with Brigette Berger, on the 'bourgeois family' (Berger and Berger, 1983). Berger and Berger's defence of the bourgeois family, in which they distance themselves from the conservative fundamentalists, the radical critics and the professionals who have increasingly intervened in the family, is overtly a polemic. They argue that, historically, the nuclear household form antedated the modernisation process and has continued to be dialectically bound up with processes of modernisation. Dialectically, they argue, because the family cannot be seen simply in idealistic terms or, again, simply as a product or a reflection of the needs of a particular social and economic order, the bourgeois family is the chief 'carrier' of the modernisation process (*ibid.*, p. 105). As the institution chiefly involved in the socialisation process, the bourgeois family is intimately bound up with questions of identity, meaning and morality (*ibid.*, p. 148). The defence of the bourgeois family is 'something to be undertaken in defence of human happiness and human dignity in a difficult time' (*ibid.*, p. 167). In particular, this family can be seen as central in maintaining and strengthening the key values of individualism and democracy.

However one may judge this particular argument, it is clear that there is not a great deal left of phenomenology in this most recent work. To be sure there are references to questions of identity and the role of the family in providing a basis for this identity as, in other words, a key element in the social construction of reality. It is true, also, that the use of the term 'bourgeois family' introduces an element of relativism in the whole argument. Nevertheless, the business of identifying this 'bourgeois family' is treated in relatively unproblematic terms, there is little reference to the meanings and understandings that individuals may themselves attach to family and familial relations and, in spite of all the disavowals of functionalism, we are left wih a sense of a family that 'fits' with certain key values, values which can be reasonably described as bourgeois values. From what has been said earlier, it can be suggested the *The War Over the Family* is not some aberration or new direction but an approach that could reasonably be extrapolated from the earlier paper, in spite of its greater use of phenomenological language and references.

(c) A phenomenological study

Whether or not Berger and Kellner's paper may be 'correctly' labelled as a phenomenological study it is certainly the case that the paper had the effect of stimulating research in that direction, a recent example being Backett's *Mothers and Fathers* (1982). From the outset, Backett states her intention of studying the normal and the everyday, in this case the everyday business of parenting among middle-class, two-parent families with two small children. 'Normal' parenthood, she argues, is a process informed by few direct or overt directives from outside and, consequently, it is very much left to the parents themselves to negotiate the reality of their activities on a day-to-day basis. This, Backett argues, is a fruitful extension of Berger and Kellner's idea of the marital conversation (Backett, *op. cit.*, p. 6).

Necessarily, a study of this kind does not follow the structure of the traditional monograph and consequently it is difficult to summarise. However, mention of some of the issues treated may convey something of the value and relative novelty of the study. Backett, for example, considers some of the assumptions that guide family and parental life, assumptions which are revealed in more or less everyday conversations (the unstructured interviews in this case) and called upon as legitimations or interpretative frameworks when required. Thus there are the basic assumptions that family life is a matter of 'trial and error', that it follows certain stages and that marriage and parenthood are matters of 'give and take'. These provide a stock of readily-to-hand assumptions, sufficiently flexible to be deployed whenever occasions demand.

Backett's notion of stages and processes in family life is particularly illuminating. Social scientists have, for some time as we have seen, used notions of 'the family life cycle', developing the idea that individuals, families and households can be understood as passing through a set of stages, elaborated with varying degrees of sophistication. Centrally, the construction of these life cycles are analytical constructions based upon the analysts' assumptions about age and about crucial turning points in family life. Backett, in contrast, seeks to construct an ideal typical construction of family processes based upon the parents' own understanding of their world. Thus, it is not so much the precise delineation of stages that is important but the conveying of the sense that parents have of development and process, a sense that is surely conveyed in the everyday phrase, 'it's just a phase'. Such understandings, coupled with other kinds of images of children and childhood are deployed as everyday frameworks of interpretation or as legitimations for parental or childhood behaviour by the parents themselves and hence, reflexively, contribute to the construction of that reality that these understandings seek to convey.

Another useful feature of Backett's study, and an area where she departs strikingly from Berger and Kellner's original paper, is in her recognition and exploration of the importance of gender differences within parenthood. In spite of the growing attention that has been paid to fatherhood in recent years, there is still an asymmetry that is in danger of being masked by the use of the terms 'parent' and 'parenting'. As her title suggests, Backett seeks, to some extent, to go behind this mask. This is not simply a matter of treating motherhood and fatherhood separately but also of showing how parents cope with the apparent discrepancy between approximately egalitarian assumptions ('give and take') and the reality of the sexual division of labour within the home and between home and work. It is here that Backett elicits some of the sharpest comments from mothers and provides a useful illustration of the way in which feminist sympathies can provide new insights and new knowledge, especially when coupled with the flexibility of a phenomenologically-based study.

SOME DIFFICULTIES

It must be stressed that, in talking about a phenomenological approach, we are not talking about a unitary phenomenon. Approaches which may come under this broad umbrella may possess one or more of the characteristics listed in the earlier part of this chapter. Hence any attempt to discuss the difficulties associated with this kind of approach must also be seen as dealing with tendencies rather than absolutes.

1 One set of difficulties may be seen in the relative lack of attention to structural or historical factors. The emphasis on 'how' rather than 'why' seeks to demonstrate the processes by which members create their own sense of reality and by which they render their activities accountable and reasonable, rather than to ask questions about the social material with which persons construct their marriages, children, sexuality or whatever. The emphasis on members' versions suspends judgement on the correctness of one version as against another and turns away from the difficult question as to whether certain understandings of the world may be systematically distorted through their particular sets of locations in the social structure. Berger and Kellner's paper on marriage and the construction of reality does at least attempt, perhaps somewhat crudely, to locate the marriage they are talking about in some kind of social-structured context.

This absence may be illustrated in Backett's *Mothers and Fathers*. Parents, as she demonstrates, have a variety of notions about children and about the business of doing parenthood and they deploy these notions in the everyday work of rendering children's actions accountable, in negotiating and in legitimating. The point is made that parents in contemporary society have a considerable degree of lee-way in constructing and interpreting their roles. Yet, if that be the case, it may be asked why or how it is that they come to relatively similar sets of understandings or interpretations? The very idea of the construction of parenthood implies some materials with which to carry out this day-to-day work of construction and it is possible to speculate on the source of these materials. At a perhaps more remote level we may instance scientific theories about children and child-rearing as filtered through newspapers and popular magazines or television programmes. At another level, we may instance a whole range of professionals and semi-professionals with whom the parents might be expected to come in contact in the course of carrying out their parent work: doctors, nurses, health visitors and teachers. At the most immediate level we may indicate social networks of kin, neighbours, workmates and friends, a set of contracts ranging from relatively casual conversations at supermarkets or in waiting rooms to sustained and more purposeful interaction with relatives or other couples. Parentwork and a sense of parenthood is conveyed not merely between the parents themselves but between different sets of parents and across generations. The marital or parental conversation often includes persons other than the marriage partners or the parents themselves.

An imaginary, although not impossible, illustration may make this point clear. At the time of writing, the newspapers were full of accounts of a Conservative minister and the child that he was about to have by his secretary. Such newspapers and television reports are undoubtedly subjects of discussion at meal tables, in pubs, on commuter trains and elsewhere. Such events provide the occasion for the deployment, the 'airing' as it were, of notions of marriage, of fidelity, of responsibility, of sexuality, of gender and of countless other topics. In such conversational occasions, stories may be matched with stories, theories tested against experience and links made between the public events and more immediate private beliefs and practices. What we have is a very complex set of interactions between the social-structural, the ideological and the historical, on the one hand, and the immediate, the experienced and the day-to-day on

203

the other. To paraphrase Lockwood and Goldthorpe's well-known aphorism about attitudes to work and factory behaviour, we cannot let our analysis stop at the domestic walls.

A work that attempts to relate the structural and the phenomenological is Voysey's *A Constant Burden* (1975). Voysey's concern to present a phenomenological project is apparent in the early pages. There have been a variety of studies of parents with handicapped children. Many of these earlier studies, she argues, have started with the assumption of some kind of pathological or difficult situation and have examined how parents cope with or come to terms with these difficulties, or look at the impact of these problems on the family as a system. In contrast, Voysey aims, using an interpretative paradigm, to see how parents invoke notions of normality in going about their day-to-day business of parentwork. She is examining a particular instance of the methods people use in constructing their social reality, the attempts that these parents make to get others to regard their family as a more or less conventional one (*op. cit.,* p. 146). Under such circumstances parents operate, as far as possible, with notions of what 'any' parent might do under such circumstances (*ibid.,* p. 156).

But Voysey is not content to carry out this micro-analysis, important and revealing though it is. She argues that, in drawing upon everyday understandings of normal family practices, parents of handicapped childred are drawing upon ideological prescriptions. That is, these everyday understandings and legitimations are not created out of nothing. The construction of the normal family is an historical process involving the Church, the state, professionals, the mass media, as well as the countless everyday conversations of parents and children. While there is, perhaps necessarily, something of a leap between her use and interpretations of open-ended interview data with a relatively small number of parents and her more theoretical speculations about the nature of working of ideology, Voysey is clearly aware that both levels have to be used and that ideology is not something that is located 'out there' but something much closer to home, at the level of the common sense:

> As Geertz argues, the construction and use of an ideology is
> 'an occurrence not in the head' but in that public world

where 'people talk together, name things, make assertions and, to a degree, understand each other. (*ibid.*, p. 195)

2 A second difficulty revolves around what might be described as a tension between reportage or description on the one hand, and interpretation on the other. Phenomenologists often acknowledge a distinction between first and second order constructs (e.g. McLain and Weigert, 1979, p. 170). First order constructs are those constructs which are developed by social actors or members as they attempt to make sense and use of their everyday world. They are part of their taken-for-granted world. Second order constructs are those made by the sociologist in an attempt to comprehend these social worlds, these everyday understandings, and to convey them to others who are not part of that world. In Weberian terms these are the 'ideal types', those abstractions from reality which continue, nevertheless, to attempt to incorporate the meanings of social actors. An example of this process may be found when Cuff uses the word 'version' (Cuff, 1980, p. 19). He is talking about accounts members provide (in this case, in recalled stages of a marital breakdown in more or less routine conversational exchanges). In using the word 'version', Cuff is both being faithful to the members' perspective in that he seeks to record it faithfully without interpretation or explanation and yet, at the same time undercuts the members' claim that this is in some way 'what really happened'. To use the word 'version' is to relativise, to open up the possibility that other versions are possible, even likely. While members sometimes do present their accounts in this kind of way – 'Well, of course, I know I could be biased' – in many cases they seek to persuade others of the truthfulness and accuracy of their accounts. To use the word 'version', therefore, is to be engaged in the business of constructing a 'second order' concept.

The central paradox is this: to get at an actor's own world, it is necessary to rearrange that world, to edit it, perhaps to reformulate it in different terms. The reason for this is simple. The sociologist, even with the most open of interviewing or observational techniques, has a different kind of involvement in the situation under investigation. The sociological project is different from the married project, the teaching project or the watching football project, although, in other contexts, the sociologist may be involved in all of these. Centrally, the sociologist is involved not simply in recording data but in recording data *for some others*. These others may be potential critics who will scrutinise the account for flaws or logical inconsistencies or readers, who it is assumed, might wish to have some kind of social insight or, yet again, might wish to bring about changes or reforms in the light of the information so collected. This is not to argue that the sociologist is in some way incapable of understanding the situation under investigation, as a somewhat loose use of the phrase 'finite provinces of meaning' might suggest. Society is not a set of isolated, encapsulated units but rather a set of overlapping circles, whose boundaries are defined with varying degrees of firmness. Thus, as I suggested, sociologists are also teachers, spouses, football fans and so on, and cultural meetings and understandings are possible. The argument here is rather different, namely to emphasise the fact that the difference between the sociologist and the 'member' is one of project, of those 'others' to whom and for whom the everyday work is being undertaken. To this extent a sociologist interviewing a married couple is not the same as a sociologist living a married life.

CONCLUSION

In a recent book on feminist methodology, Stanley and Wise refer to the 'egalitarian impetus' within ethnomethodology (Stanley and Wise, 1983, p. 111). At a first glance the identification of a feminist approach with the ethnomethodological perspective might seem a little strange, although it can be argued that the way had already been opened up by Dorothy Smith. The language of most ethnomethodological texts is as 'strange' and distancing as the language of most other sociological paradigms, and the attention paid to conversational practices may, on the surface, seem some distance from the concerns of feminism. The marriage between feminism and Marxism, although 'unhappy', may at least seem more natural.

Nevertheless, I hope that this chapter has shown that there is considerable critical potential within the phenomenological perspective and, indeed, within the ethnomethodological approach. When Stanley and Wise use the word 'egalitarian' they are referring to the tendency (perhaps not always realised) to take the subjects of research seriously, to seek to understand their worlds without, as far as possible, reducing them to puppets manipulated by an analytical puppet master and without forcing them into preordained theoretical categories. At the same time, the awareness of the failings of much conventional sociological practice, whether positivist, functionalist or Marxist, leads to a continuing and critical awareness of the sociologists' own role in creating the subjects and situations under investigation. To study the family is, in a sense, to create the family. Prior to such a study there are definitions, implicit or explicit, and these definitions derive either from the sociologist's own common-sense and taken-for-granted understandings of his or her own world or, less directly, from a particular theoretical tradition or orientation. Consequently, to call into question or to hold up to critical awareness the everyday practices and assumptions of sociologists is to call into question the everyday assumptions that inform daily life. This is both more humanistic, since there is a constant striving towards, if never fully realised, a reduction of the distance between sociologist and lay person, and more critical, since the everyday assumptions and practices of both are rendered strange, new and uncertain.

It can be seen that these strengths of the phenomenological orientation have a particular relevance in the study of the family and related matters since it is here that so much is taken for granted and, as we have seen, it is here where so many taken-for-granted assumptions are carried over into sociological models and applied analysis and practice. A phenomenological orientation may, for example, call into question many of the taken-for-granted assumptions in the area of the study of gender (Kessler and McKenna, 1978; Matthews, 1982; Morgan, 1985). Hence the achievements of a phenomenological perspective on the family are considerable, given the relatively small number of texts and studies which are available. Yet there are unresolved tensions within the approach which are perhaps both unresolvable and also shared with other orientations. The extent to which such an orientation can be combined, realistically, with other approaches is a question that will be deferred until the Conclusion.

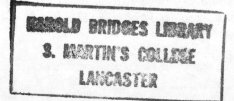

10 Critical perspectives

INTRODUCTION

If the term 'phenomenological' appears to cover a range of divergent and even contradictory approaches, the word 'critical' would seem to be even more hopelessly imprecise. Moreover, the further difficulty arises that it would appear that there is an attempt here to divide theoretical sheep from goats, 'goodies' from 'baddies'. The social sciences are not simply divided, with Marxist or feminist perspectives on one side and bourgeois or patriarchal ideologies on the other. There are contradictions within and overlaps between both sides.

Nevertheless, it should be possible to point to a clustering of perspectives that could be described as 'critical' in spite of the differences between them and in spite of the fact that other clusterings of perspectives, the phenomenological being a major example, might be seen as having strong critical elements within them. Included under this general label would be Marxist and feminist perspectives, radical psychoanalysis and the actual 'critical' sociology associated with the Frankfurt school. In attempting to see what all these streams have in common the following points would seem to be of relevance:

(a) A critical stance towards the dominant model of scientific enquiry in Western society. This model includes notions of objectivity and rationality, opposes science to ideology and sees scientific progress in largely cumulative terms. In sociology, this model of science is taken as a model of 'the social sciences' (of which sociology is seen as a part) and identified with the troublesome word 'positivism'. The social world is seen as

presenting certain 'difficulties' to the straightforward application of scientific methods but it is usually assumed that these
difficulties might be reduced by more rigorous model or theory
building or the application of more scientific methods of social
enquiry. There is a strong emphasis, therefore, on the more
quantitative methods.

Critical theories, on the other hand, question this model of
scientific progress in general and its specific application to the
social sciences. Scientific enquiry of all kinds is seen as being
socially located and its practitioners seen as directly or indirectly
contributing to the maintenance of a particular social or
economic order. Science, far from being a detached and disinterested activity, is seen as being very much rooted in the
interests of the age. In some cases, even the very notion of
scientific enquiry itself, as distinct from its particular uses or
applications, may be seen as having social roots.

Here we meet a couple of important divergences within the
critical perspective. In the first place there is the debate over the
use of the word 'science' itself. On one side there may be the
tendency to reverse the positivistic distinction between science
and ideology and to apply the latter term to science itself as
currently practised, reserving the former for certain kinds of
Marxist orientation. On the other hand, there are others who
would be cautious, to say the least, about the use of the term
'science', as a general accolade or as a description of their own
practices. Another division would be that between feminists
who would argue that the gender order and gender inequalities
are the most fundamental distinctions within society and those
who would see such divisions as part of a more general system of
exploitation and inequality. Whatever these divisions, and they
are often deep, there would seem to be agreement about the
socially located character of dominant scientific practice and the
way in which scientific statements, in such a social order, often
mask ideological positions.

(b) It need hardly be added that this critical orientation to the
prevailing understanding of scientific practice is linked to a
critique of the wider structure and set of institutions within
which these practices are located. These structures may be
variously described: 'patriarchal', 'capitalist', 'industrial' and so
on and the differences in emphasis between and within the

deployment of these descriptive labels may vary considerably. However, these structures or systems are seen as being in various ways oppressive or exploitative, as presenting limits to human potential or as distorting the possibility for the realisation of human commonality. In most cases, these structures are seen as especially constraining for particular groupings in society – the working class, women – or in some fewer cases they are seen as being oppressive in a much more general sense (Marcuse's *One Dimensional Man*, 1964, for example).

(c) 'He who desires, but acts not, breeds pestilence'. People working within the areas broadly classified as 'critical' are not simply content to provide a critique of Western science and of the oppressive structures that are located in Western or patriarchal formations. Following from the awareness of the location of scientific practice in structures that may be described as oppressive or exploitative comes the realisation that true science, in this case social science, can and should take on a liberatory role. The analysis of the oppressive structures of contemporary society is coupled with the belief or understanding that such structures can be reformed or overthrown. This beneficial process of purposeful social change can be assisted by social scientists working on behalf of, or through, or in alliance with, the more exploited groups in present day society.

Thus, critical social science contains a critique of current notions of science and scientific practice, a critique of prevailing social institutions and some guidance as to the prospects for social and individual liberation. In the particular case of the family, this can be seen as working out at all three levels. Conventional 'sociologies of the family' almost by definition take a commonsensical understanding of 'the family' for granted. The tendency is towards some kind of biologism or functionalism, one which sees the family, with all kinds of qualifications, as a 'given' in social science. The aim is seen as describing or analysing these familial structures, of providing deeper, more firmly based, theoretical understanding and of coping with the problems that arise out of pathological family structures. Critical theory, on the other hand, would see definitions and understandings of the family as being socially located and historically determined. Such theorists would also see the family, again in various ways, as being an oppressive institution, and as being linked to wider oppressive structures. Thus the family may be seen as a key institution in the reproduction of capitalist or patriarchal structures. Finally, there will be some kind of emphasis upon the possibilities for change.

It will be seen that, in outlining these three elements in a critical approach to the family, the divisions between my characterisation of critical sociology and other forms of sociological practice do highlight certain overlaps. Phenomenological approaches, in particular, may be equally critical of prevailing models of scientific practice or, specifically, of studies of the family. There are plenty of examples of more conventional social science being aware of divisions in terms of class and gender both within the family and between different families. The differences are often sharpest in the case of the third heading. While it is not the case that more orthodox social scientists are unconcerned with questions of change or liberation it is less likely that they will be found unequivocally identifying themselves with particular exploited groups in society. Nevertheless, the overlaps between critical social science and 'the rest' (however that may be characterised) are often considerable.

If there are overlaps between critical and conventional sociology in the treatment of the family, so too are there considerable differences within the critical camp, differences which have been smoothed over in this ideal typification. It is now time to explore some of these differences and to examine four sub-categories of critical theorists. These are classified as Marxists, feminists, radical psychoanalysts, and the 'critical sociology' in its more limited sense.

STRANDS IN CRITICAL THEORIES

1 *Marxism*

The critical stance taken by the Marxist tradition is indicated by the use of the term 'bourgeois social science'. This troublesome phrase (see Williams, 1983, pp. 45–8) conveys a variety of overlapping arguments. It encapsulates the argument that social science is not a neutral, independent activity but one which directly and indirectly serves the interests of the capitalist ruling class. It suggests that the practitioners of social science, both in terms of familial and educational background and in terms of current social status, form a class fraction which limits their vision and capability of understanding the world. And, finally, the use of the qualifier, 'bourgeois', continues to carry with it an unmistakable whiff of the pejorative, with a hint of the safe, the respectable, the narrow-minded. (Strictly, quite unbourgeois in fact, as Marx would have recognised.)

Implied also in the Marxist critique of prevailing social science practice is the distinction between ideology and science. Unlike other critical strands, the term 'science' still carries a plus sign in most streams of Marxist thinking. Its difference from the ideological, and thereby incomplete, bourgeois social science is in terms of its appreciation of the totality of thought and action within a social formation and within history and to the extent that it is allied to the task of the emancipation of the working class. Scientific practice is, therefore, allied with political practice. Bourgeois social science, on the other hand, while it has many recognisable achievements, is necessarily incomplete and limited.

In what respects would conventional sociology of the family be held wanting in the light of a Marxist critique? In general terms – and this might apply to several other strands of critical thought as well – the very term 'sociology of the family' would be held to be defective, a product of the tendencies within bourgeois academic institutions and practices towards splitting, specialisation and reification. To talk of the 'sociology of the family' implies both some kind of object of study (the family) and some kind of specialised discipline which is applied to it. At one and the same time to talk of 'the sociology of the family' is to fix the concept of 'family' and to isolate it from other practices within society, particularly the economic.

To talk of 'the family' in conventional sociological analysis is to talk, it is argued, of an entity which is understood in naturalistic, static and individualistic terms. At some stage or another, and despite some important differences, bourgeois sociology will take the family for granted, treating it as a cultural universal or as necessary for the fulfilment of fundamental human needs both individual and societal. It follows from this that conventional sociological versions of the family are also criticised for their static quality. A universal family is also a family without history. Conventional sociology, further, has a tendency towards methodological individualism, treating the individual as a basic unit of analysis. In the case of the family this tendency does, to some extent, run counter to what I call 'methodological familism', a tendency to treat the family as the basic unit of society. In practice this is resolved at a theoretical level by positing more or less universal psychological or biological needs whose site of origin may be said to be 'the individual' and at the level of actual sociological practice by the use of questionnaires and other individually centred research techniques. It is possible, indeed, to indicate a tension or contradiction within conventional sociological practice at this point between the treatment of the family in holistic terms and the adoption of largely individualistically based research techniques.[1] On the whole, however, the individualistic emphasis within bourgeois social science, as a whole, is reinforced rather than substantially undermined by routine sociological practice in the study of the family.

Thus, within a Marxist framework, conventional sociological approaches to the family may be held up as being defective, in terms of their being essentialistic, static and individualistic. In contrast, the Marxist approach may be seen as one which, firstly, is committed to the notion of the family as a changing entity. Just as change and process are built into Marxist understandings of society and classes, so too the family is seen as a changing entity, changing in broad historical ways within the structure of society itself. The dialectics of class struggle were themselves dialectically linked to evolutionary understandings of the development of the family (Morgan, 1975, pp. 136–40; Coward, 1983, pp. 130–3). The early ethnographic studies that Marx and Engels followed were used for a variety of arguments: that, indeed, the family did have a history; that patriarchal control was linked to the institution of private property and that the family would change as the structure of society itself was changed through political or revolutionary struggle. The bourgeois family, in other words, was simply one stage in the history of the family and was neither its apotheosis nor a simple reflection of universal tendencies.

To see the family as an institution changing and evolving as other institutions change and evolve is to see the family as being crucially related to other institutions in society. It is to be noted that the full title of Engels's book is *The Origin of the Family, Private Property and the State.* This grouping is clearly not intended to be arbitrary or random; the process of growth and development of the one is closely bound up with the growth and development of the other two. This is clearly a strength in the Marxist perspective since it provides a powerful safeguard against the reification of the family through the arbitrary separating of that institution. Yet, it may also be seen as a weakness, particularly in the eyes of some feminist critics, in that it fails to pay attention to the specificities of the family and patriarchal domination within it (e.g. Coward, *op. cit.*).

When we are talking, in Marxist terms, about the relationships between the family and other institutions in society we are, of course, talking specifically about the economic dimensions of family living. As I have attempted to show in my discussion of much of the recent applied family literature there is a current tendency to assume that the family and marriage have no economic aspects at all. In traditional Marxist theory, on the other hand, this was seen particularly in terms of an understanding of the crucial role of private property in shaping the development of the family and in underlining patriarchal authority. The institution of primogeniture provides a clear link between the family and the societal institution of private property. The family becomes an institution within which there is a whole nexus of inter-related interests and processes: the familial control over property within a generation and its passing on between generations; the concern to produce legitimate male offspring; patriarchal control over women and children; the desire to establish profitable (or at least not loss-making) alliances and so on. Thus too we have links and continuities between the 'natural' family of married couples and legitimate offspring and a class society; the family becomes a central institution in the reproduction of class inequalities (*ibid.*, pp. 137–8). The family becomes a central unit in the continuity of classes over generations, the maintenance and expansion of class privilege and the establishment of methods of social closure. The family as an institution ensures the continuity of the havenots as well as entrenching the power and privilege of the haves.

But the economic aspects of the family are not simply in terms of its role in the wider economic system. The family is also an economic system in its own right (again, something which tends to be ignored in much current writing stressing the emotional or the relational aspect), and there are complex relationships between the internal domestic economy and the role of the family in the wider economy. As Fitz and Hood-Williams note:

> It is seldom observed that in the midst of capitalism we have an entrenched system of distribution which is not capitalist but upon which capitalism relies. (Fitz and Hood-Williams, 1982, p. 66)

Marxists have, on the whole, been more successful in drawing attention to and analysing the 'external' economic relationships and less so, as feminists have noted, in exploring the dynamics of economic activity and control within the household where gender differentiation plays a significant and, to some extent, an independent role. Certainly, Engels noted that within the family the woman was the proletariat while the man was the bourgeois thus emphasising the presence of sexual antagonism within the family but, at the same time, the metaphorical use of the class terms does suggest that sexual antagonism was regarded as being of somewhat secondary importance and, to a large extent, dependent upon economic class struggles.

Clearly, Marxism would aim to go a little further than simply providing a critique of the methods and assumptions involved in family research. In place of the emphasis in conventional social science on the relatively harmonious fit or adjustment between family and society, the Marxist approach would emphasise contradictions in this relationship. In place of the dominant assumption of a long-term shift towards equality within the domestic unit, the Marxist perspective would seek to underline the persistence of sexual inequality and antagonism within the family and marriage although here, feminists would argue, the argument was never taken very far. Thus, the bourgeois family, rather than being taken for granted as *the* family form is shown to be a form which has its own particular history and role, a role which, among other things, serves to perpetuate class and gender inequalities.

There is, in the English language, a certain ambiguity about the words, 'critical', 'critique' and 'criticism'. At one level, the terms may simply refer to a particular kind of stance vis-à-vis the objects of investigation, a relationship of detachment, perhaps, or a perspective which, by virtue of its location from the point of view of the more oppressed or deprived elements in society, seeks to cut through the justifications and mystifications that surround dominant ideological constructions. Nevertheless, the other more popular sense cannot help creeping in as well, that is of a holding up to some kind of moral evaluation. Now, whether or not Marxism can be said to constitute a moral critique of existing institutions is a matter for considerable debate. On the one hand, there would be the argument that Marxism is a science and that morality, by referring to timeless or essential qualities of 'humanity' or 'human values' represents a pre-scientific and probably ideological way of thinking. At the same time, the vigorous language that was used and which continues to be used in Marxist writing cannot be simply written off as mere rhetoric. In the case of the family and family matters, it is difficult not to sense an abhorrence of the more hypocritical features of the Victorian family (the symbiotic relationship between respectable marriage and prostitution, for example) while also having an equally Victorian concern with true family values. Both the bourgeois and the proletarian families were seen as being in some way distorted by the relationships of capitalism, the former through the unholy alliance between 'sex-love' and property, the latter through the processes which resulted in conditions within which anything like free and warm family and marital relationships were impossible.

Thus, potentially at least, Marxism presents a critique of bourgeois modes of studying the family and of the working of that family under capitalism. It should follow, therefore, that Marxism should also be committed to change in family and marital relationships. Yet here, the picture is far from straightforward and the Marxist commitment to change in domestic arrangements often seems far from being wholehearted. The famous passage in the *Communist Manifesto* where Marx and Engels satirise the bourgeois obsession with the apparent communist demand for the abolition of the family has an ambiguity. At one level they seem to be saying that they are indeed seeking to abolish the bourgeois family, a family form which is corrupted through its association with property. Yet, at another level, they appear to be satirising the bourgeois *fear* of a communist overthrow of the family. As in more recent political debates the early communists seem to be claiming to be the party of the family.

There are a variety of reasons for this hesitancy. In the first place, as has often been remarked, there is a strong streak of puritanism in the Marxist and socialist traditions, a tradition that persists to this day. Sexual licence and experimentation were features of a corrupt bourgeois way of life; indeed prostitution and adultery could be taken as apt and pointed symbols of that way of life. Socialists, on the other hand, should commit themselves to values of love and fidelity (Morgan, 1975, pp. 171–200; Reiche, 1970). But there are more theoretical and political reasons for this hesitancy. The Marxist analysis of the family showed it to be, largely, a dependent variable, as an institution that drew its character in each epoch from the other institutions with which it was connected: kinship, property, state and class. Thus, to seek to change the family would be to seek to change a part while leaving the whole relatively untouched – a fruitless project. The family, in this line of argument, was therefore in more or less the same position as religion where, too, Marxists castigated freethinkers and others whose whole focus was on attacking religion and its works. There was, however, an important difference. In the case of the family it would seem to be a case, in at least some versions, of releasing the 'true' family from the corruption and constraints that surrounded it in a pre-communist society.

Politically, the argument paralleled the theoretical. The central struggle was the class struggle. Here class interests had, for the time being at least, to be seen as paramount over individual interests. Moreover, since the proletarian family was characterised as embodying, however imperfectly, genuine family feeling, for others to claim identification with the working class but to persist with 'irregular' sexual relationships would be both an affront to the workers and their families and a diversion from the real struggle. Hence also, the uncertain relationship between the Marxist tradition and homosexuality, an uncertainty that persists in communist societies. Workerism and economism allies with and reinforces a kind of Marxist machismo. One wider consequence of this was, as Coward has suggested, the too easy subsumption of the 'woman question'

Themes

under the more general heading of 'the family' (Coward, *op. cit.,* p. 186). It was this, and other defects, that led to the feminist critique which saw patriarchal continuities between bourgeois thought and socialist thought.

2 Feminism

The feminist movement from the late 1960s to the present day has constituted a thoroughgoing and wide-ranging critique of sociological practice. While it would be beyond the scope of this book to explore all the ways in which this critique has had an impact on sociology it is important to stress that the critique has not simply been of sociological theories. It has been, more profoundly, a critique of the main assumptions that have guided sociological research and theorising, of the male-dominated institutions within which such work was and continues to be carried out, and of the relationships of the men in these institutions with their colleagues, with their wives and lovers and with the secretaries and interviewers who have served male sociologists. The attack has not simply been concentrated on the sociology of the family but also on the sociologies of work, leisure, stratification, politics, deviance and numerous other subdisciplines and categorisations.

Up to a point, the critique of family sociologising has paralleled the attack that has come from Marxists. Conventionally, the sociology of the family has operated with tunnel vision, narrowly concentrating on a particular small set of relationships to the exclusion of wider considerations of history or social structure. The development of family history is a movement that has been influenced by this feminist critique and the realisation that the family must be seen as a changing body, intimately bound up with changes in the wider society. Conventionally, also, family sociology has operated with a relatively optimist model of the family in contemporary society or, where it has been more pessimistic, has worked on the assumption of a more or less universal set of needs which are or should be met by the family. Feminists, like Marxists, have provided a critique of this institution, and particularly of its more optimistic version. However, they have gone further in focusing attention on the family and its relationship to the wider society.

218

If Marxists have criticised orthodox sociological practice for its tendency to present bourgeois ideology as if it were social science, feminists have substituted the word 'patriarchal' for the word 'bourgeois'. In other words, they have noted the obvious (but often unremarked) fact of the male dominance of the sociological profession and have drawn the conclusion that this dominance has not simply shaped the direction of research and theorising in such a way as to often render women as either invisible or as deviating from some male-defined standard, but has also operated in such a way as to maintain, to reinforce or to legitimate this dominance. As in the case of bourgeois ideology, this effect is not always direct or blatant; nevertheless, it remains all pervasive. Indeed the very fact that it was and still is difficult for many people to think or talk of male dominance or male interests shows the pervasiveness of this domination for it derives its daily legitimation through its identification with the natural order of things.

Feminist theory, therefore, involves a radical and thorough-going critic of sociological practice: 'Woman's perspective . . . discredits sociology's claim to constitute an objective knowledge independent of the sociologists situation.' (Smith, 1974, p. 11.) As the 'symbolic modes which are the *general currency* of thought' (Smith, 1978a) are produced or controlled by men, the feminist critique of sociology cannot simply be content with documenting those cases where women have been ignored or distorted (in stratification studies for example) but must go further, to consider the higher levels of theory and the assumptions about theorising itself, to consider the methods deployed in sociological investigation and even such questions as style and modes of presentation and the distribution of sociological knowledge. Women, in short, are not simply something to be added to conventional sociology.

One area where this has been particularly important has been in the use of experience. Dorothy Smith argues that a woman finds herself alienated from her own experience in sociological writing and that therefore the reformulation of sociological work must begin with this fact of an awareness of a disjuncture between theory and lived experience. Keohane *et al.* note that feminist theory 'is fundamentally experiential' (Keohane *et al.*, 1982, p. vii) and Stanley and Wise seek to transcend and to oppose the convention distinction between science and the personal (Stanley and Wise, 1983). This has led to a reassessment of the conventionally labelled 'softer' methods of sociological enquiry and a critique of the masculinist bias often inherent in many methodologies.

An important feature of feminist approaches to the family is that their critique of orthodox sociology also includes a critique of Marxism. In part, and perhaps most important in the initial stages, feminism provided a critique of conventional practice within Marxist or socialist parties and movements where women found themselves as marginalised as they had found themselves marginalised in more orthodox parties. But, it was argued, this marginalisation was no incidental feature of Marxism in practice but something built into the movement from its inception. Workerism operated with a more or less straightforward model of the male breadwinner and 'the family wage', and economism located the central sphere of activity in the public economic sphere, putting to the margin questions of the family, household and sexuality. Since this private sphere was seen as the location of women, then 'the woman question' tended to be something that was added on to mainstream Marxism:

> Most Marxist analyses of women's position take as their question the relationship of women to the economic system, rather than that of women to men, apparently assuming the latter will be explained in the discussion of the former.
> (Hartmann in Sargent (ed.) 1981, pp. 3–4)

Hartmann, and other feminist critics of the Marxist position, argue that these difficulties were built into the original writings of Marx and Engels and the early history of the socialist movement rather than being a later deviation. Engels, by calling his work *The Origins of the Family, Private Property and the State*, while in some ways a merit over more essentialist accounts of the family, tended to see discussions of the family and the domestic sphere as one part, and a small part, of the wider more comprehensive analysis of different social formations. The specificity of family relationships and, in particular, of the relationships of men and women was lost; the 'historic defeat of the female sex' was described as a fact but was not analysed (Coward, *op. cit.*, p. 153).

Feminists differ in the extent to which they regard Marxism

as redeemable. While some might argue that Marxism, like orthodox sociology, must be rejected almost *in toto* (Stanley and Wise approach this position) most would argue that it is a question of building upon and incorporating the insights of Marxism rather than an outright rejection. There may be an argument in favour of a continuing, if often 'unhappy', marriage between the two or, more likely, a related but separate movement, holding open the option of some fuller integration in the future. For the time being, Eisenstein's term 'capitalist-patriarchy' (Eisenstein, 1979) understood in dialectical terms would seem to represent the main orientation of feminist thought, with some emphasising the one more than the other.

In turning more specifically to the ways in which feminism provided a critique of the actual institution of the family we find a variety of strands. In the first place there is a critique of a whole range of assumptions that inform everyday under-standings and practices as well as sociological, and often Marxist, analysis. The package of assumptions that go to make up the model of 'the family' include the following: the assumption of a relatively unchanging and naturally-based unit; the assumption of a conventional sexual division of labour and the separation of home and work; the assumption of relative equality and cooperation between partners and so on. All these, and many other assumptions, have been subjected to critical attention through the work of feminist historians, sociologists and anthropologists and through a focus on the way in which the family actually works in contemporary society.

This demystifying of the family goes beyond simply showing that prevailing assumptions about that institution are incorrect or misleading. Feminism has attempted to distinguish between the 'family' as an ideological construction and the actual experiences of women and men living in a whole range of domestic arrangements (see, in particular, Barrett and McIntosh, 1982). There is an examination of the processes by which, and the institutions through which, this ideological construction is achieved and maintained and of the inter-connections between the ideological constructions and actual experiences. Further, feminism has sought to deconstruct the family and marriage, in particular, to explore the differences in terms of gender, age and generation within the family and household and the ways in which these are structured and

221

provide for different ways of viewing and understanding the family (see, especially, Thorne and Yalom, 1982).

Secondly, therefore, the feminist analysis of the family has concentrated on gender differentiations within the family. These are seen not simply as a particular case of domestic divisions but as the central and core division. While there are many ways in which these divisions may be understood – in terms of power, of the differential capacity for physical violence and so on – the key focus of attention is usually on the economic aspect. This provides both a critique of much prevailing socio-logical analysis, which seems almost to focus exclusively on the interpersonal to the exclusion of the economic, and of Marxism which focused on societal class divisions and tended to stop at the door of the household. The emphasis, within the feminist analysis, is upon the division of resources within the household and the way in which the household relates to and contributes to the wider sexual division of labour. Thus, Maureen Mackintosh argues that it is not enough to say that women's work benefits capital. Rather, it is important to show the ways in which capital has made use of existing social and sexual divisions, divisions which are themselves not simply to be seen as the product of capitalism (in Young *et al.*, 1981, p. 5). She, in common with many other feminists, argues that much of the domestic labour debate took the sexual division of labour for granted (see also Burman (ed.), 1979, pp. 173–91).

The complexities of the domestic labour debate do not concern us at this point. While some of the arguments might, with hindsight, seem like an attempt on the part of mainstream Marxism to take over some of the strands of the feminist critique, the significance of the debate should not be lost. The family was seen as having a place in the mainstream of social and economic analysis, and there was a recognition that economic work was performed within the household and from which the wider system benefited. The debate led to a much more integrated attack on the problems of the sexual division of labour seeing it as an inter-related set of three divisions: between women and men in the labour market or markets; between women and men in the home and between the home and the work, seeing this last relationship in terms of a continuity rather than a radical separation. Thus, Barrett and McIntosh emphasise the point that men benefit more from housework than women benefit from the variable and conditional support that they gain from men in 'return'. They point to the differences in power between men and women in the household, especially over the distribution of resources operating under ideological assumptions of 'shared' consumption (Barrett and McIntosh, *op. cit.*, p. 65). Thus, in dealing with economic relationships within the household, this is not simply seen as a division of roles and responsibilities but as a complex relationship of structured inequality.

Linked to this analysis of the relationships between the household and the sexual division of labour is the analysis of the particular role of women in reproduction. Earlier statements by Engels about the 'production and reproduction of immediate life' were seen as dangerously vague (Coward, *op. cit.*, pp. 141–2) and liable to slide back to biologism or essentialism or to postulate an unhelpful distinction between the biological and the social. Feminism sought to explore in much greater depth the sets of overlapping meanings around the word 'reproduction' and the ways in which these relate to women's unequal place within the household and society as a whole.

Moreover, the feminist critique explored another relatively unheralded feature of women's activities within the home. This was to look at women as consumers. In popular and ideological construction, the housewife and the consumer are often synonymous. However, the trivialisation of the term 'consumer' in political and commercial rhetoric should not blind us to the vital function of 'consumption work' within the household. This is defined by Weinbam and Bridges as 'part of the attempt to reconcile production for profit with socially determined needs' (in Eisenstein (ed.), 1979, p. 194). The social and historical construction of 'the consumer' and the processes by which this function has been mapped upon that of the housewife have yet to be explored in detail.

Feminism, of course, is not simply concerned with divisions of labour and distinctions of function. It is concerned with the oppression of women. Consequently, the family is not simply analysed in terms of its relationship to the wider society or in terms of the ways in which various functions are distributed within the household but also as a particular and crucial site of women's oppression. While theories of women's oppression are numerous (for a very useful summary see Randall, 1982,

223

pp. 12–24), increasingly the central role of the family and household in this oppression is being recognised (see Mary McIntosh in Burman, *op. cit.*, p. 154; Young *et al.*, *op. cit.*, p. ix).

If there continue to be important differences between Marxists and feminists, there would seem to be agreement on at least one point. That is that it is not enough to provide detailed theoretical, critical and empirical analysis of capitalism or patriarchy. Both are committed to changing these systems and this commitment provides the rationale for the analysis in the first place. There is, therefore, an attempt to strive for some kind of unity of theory and practice or, in feminist terms, between the personal, the experiential and the political. Indeed, the commitment amongst feminists may well be stronger than amongst current Marxists, the latter often being safely installed in male-dominated academies, from which women still tend, in effect if not in intention or policy, to be excluded. Thus feminism is not content to analyse the family but also to strive for, and to live, alternatives.

3 Radical psychoanalytical

Of the two remaining critical perspectives, relatively little needs to be said. The perspective which was once referred to in shorthand terms as 'Laingian' would seem to be appearing less and less in the works that could be described as 'critical' in the broad sense used here. That the approaches of people like Laing and Cooper could have been so described is hardly in doubt (Morgan, 1975, pp. 103–33). In the first place, these workers were clearly critical of prevailing social scientific, or more accurately social psychological and psychiatric, practice. This was condemned for its scientism or positivism and as being anti-humanistic in both its theory and its application. The political dimension of psychiatric interventions into individuals or families was either ignored or denied. In place of these dominant practices, Laing and others offered a methodology and a therapy that was closer to individual experience and that sought to minimise the gap between therapist and patient. Although Freud continued to be a major influence, this was complemented by reference to more existential or phenomenological writers, especially Sartre.

Further, these texts were clearly critical of the institution of the family itself. The relatively bland models of the family that appeared, especially in more sociologically-orientated texts, were replaced by a focus on the strains, tensions and potentialities for violence of both a psychic and a physical kind that characterised normal family living. Reference was made to the 'politics' of everyday family living, the inequalities and exercises of power, the processes of scapegoating, blaming and rejecting that could be seen in almost all everyday family living. The paradigmatic case was the daughter labelled as schizophrenic: the processes by which she became so labelled and the pathological family situation, in terms of which many of her utterances could be seen as intelligible, were carefully documented. Such cases were seen, it appeared, not as deviations but as slightly highlighted examples of everyday family life. While this was the main focus of their critique of the family there was also, especially in the writings of Cooper, a critique of the processes (usually blandly described as 'socialisation') by which individuals were prepared to accept living in a capitalist, imperialist and fundamentally violent society.

When we turn to the solutions posed for these issues, the discussion becomes more blurred. While Laing and Cooper (together with people like Jules Henry) were loosely associated with the New Left, the way in which these insights could be translated into political practice was left somewhat vague. Apart from the mere fact of raising levels of political awareness – itself important in an area relatively unpoliticised – and the elaboration of a kind of radical therapy, the vision provided by these theorists was more often of a tragic or perhaps mystical and quietistic rather than a revolutionary kind.

It was, perhaps, the apparent lack of political solutions that contributed to the diminishing interest in the works of Laing and Cooper and was the basis of a variety of criticisms from the left (Sedgwick, 1982). Moreover, the lack of any systematic treatment of issues of gender differentiation in these 'radical' works could only be seen as a major flaw in a context where feminist theory was beginning to make a much more substantial impact. Collier's defence of Laing, that his critique of contemporary family situations is not opposed to feminism but distinct from it, is true but probably beside the point (Collier, 1977, p. 136). Finally, and paradoxically, it might be suggested that some of the more substantial features of the Laingian approach – the critique of orthodox and individualistic psychiatry and the analysis of the dynamics, contradiction and paradoxes of everyday family living – became incorporated into the mainstream of family and marital therapy. Perhaps, as Collier suggests, Laing's departure from Freud was less radical than might at first have appeared (*ibid.*). This tendency, although not marked, could only confirm some of the suspicions of the earlier critics of Laing.

Nevertheless, it would be wrong to dismiss Laing and Cooper as gurus whose times have passed. If radical approaches have moved from the interiors of family life to the complexities of the relationships between the family and economic life, both internally and externally, this trend may tell us more about trends in the wider economy than the correctness or otherwise of these analyses of family processes. Much of what Laing and Cooper argued has now been incorporated by more recent critics (e.g. Barrett and McIntosh, 1982, p. 51) and the critique of at least a certain kind of family pattern – relatively isolated, closed in on itself, oppressive – is still as relevant today as it was in the 1960s and early 1970s.

4 The Frankfurt School

While I have considered a variety of perspectives under the label 'critical', the term, in a more narrow sense, can be seen as applying in particular to the cluster of approaches and theories that emerged from what was described as 'The Frankfurt School'. First and foremost, this 'school' can be seen as a critique of dominant modes of thought in the social sciences. As with the other approaches we have noted, this could be seen, broadly, as an attack on positivism in the social sciences, on the assumption that prevailing understandings of the natural sciences could provide a model for social enquiry, on the adoption of methods of enquiry that seemed to imply a scientistic or technocratic model of human beings and, more generally, a critique of the dominant culture of instrumental rationality (Connerton, 1976, p. 27). In such a culture, science is used as an instrument of domination rather than as a human means of serving human beings and human needs. Weberian and Marxist themes merge in this critique of the growing dominance of instrumental rationality, not simply in mature capitalist societies but also in industrial socialist societies such as the USSR.

An important strand in this critique was the attack on systems and the idea of system, emphasised in Adorno's often quoted aphorism, 'The whole is unreal'. The idea of a system was subjected to criticism at all levels from the critique of over systematised or reificatory modes of thought to the increasingly systematised and rational patterns of conduct and subordination required in advanced industrial societies. One important corollary of this was the extension of this critique to Marxism itself. Attempts were made to preserve the critical core of the Marxist tradition while rejecting and criticising the reificatory tendencies within that same tradition. We may also note the similar attempt to do the same with Freud and the Freudian tradititition.

Clearly, prevailing models of family theorising would come under the same kind of critique. Thus we have a critique of the ways in which the idea of the family is reified in contemporary social theory, the way in which it tends to be treated as a quasi-naturalistic thing, outside history. The very attempt to establish subdisciplines as 'the sociology of the family' would implicitly come under the terms of this kind of critique since it implied that the family had something like reality and that its study could be detached from the study of other processes in society as a whole.

It can also be seen that this critique of established or dominant modes of thought also extended, as with the previous cases, to a critique of the society in which such modes of thought were dominant. Writing in the shadow of Nazism, the central concerns were with patterns of domination, totalitarianism, oppression and repression and institutionalised terror. Even where the domination was less stark and the terror less physically tangible, the tendencies towards a total domination of thought and practices were delineated and subjected to critical examination. Adorno's *Minima Moralia*, for example, is surely one of the bleakest studies of patterns of domination in contemporary society, of the all pervasiveness of one-dimensional modes of thought and human practice, a picture of a huge psychic prison in which even the escape tunnels invariably fail to take the escapees beyond the prison walls. Marx rewritten by Kafka. Our most human acts, such as the giving of gifts, become

227

tainted by the logic of instrumental rationality appropriate to an advanced industrial society. Music, the arts and culture in general are eaten by the acid of the 'culture industry' within which they are inevitably caught up.

The family has a complex and shifting relationship to the examination of changing patterns of domination. In the classic bourgeois society, the family could be understood in more or less straightforward functional terms. The patterns of repression within the authoritarian and patriarchal family could be seen as functional in maintaining both patterns of domination and subordination within the wider capitalist society but also in producing men of independence and initiative who, strengthened through the struggle of the ego in the family of origin, came to occupy positions which demand such skills. Nevertheless, this classic bourgeois family becomes eroded by the wider processes and contradictions within bourgeois society. Capitalism becomes dominated by large oligopolistic bureaucracies, often directly or indirectly assisted by state intervention. The power and authority of the father becomes eroded as his power and authority in the increasingly organisation-dominated society becomes weakened. The traditional rationale of the family becomes weakened, and it is no longer the site of classical oedipal struggles, serving to strengthen the ego. But this weakening of the family does not mean liberation. Denied the inner strengths that the classic bourgeois family provided for the individual, he (sic) now becomes prey to the dominating and totalitarian tendencies within the wider society, the dominance of demogogues of 'irrational' movements, of the mass media, of the organisation. The position of the family in advanced society, is essentially contradictory: 'The tendencies which threaten the family seem at the same time to strengthen it. . . .' (Frankfurt Institute for Social Research, 1973 (1956), p. 130.) The family increasingly becomes eroded by the totalitarian or dominating forces within the wider society. If it seems stronger in some ways it is because it has turned in on itself as a defence against these self-same destructive forces. The apparent success of the family in this respect would seem to be only temporary. As in Poe's story of the Masque of the Red Death, the plague is already within the apparently impregnable walls of the family.

What is to be done? Here the critique provided by the Frankfurt School would seem to falter. Clearly, there is no going back to the certainties of an earlier age. Clearly also, the traditional Marxist agent of liberation, the proletariat, can no longer be relied upon in any straightforward sense. For one thing, the very term 'the proletariat' may be seen as a piece of mystificatory holism. More significantly, the working classes themselves have become too thoroughly incorporated into advanced capitalist society for them to be seen as an unambiguously liberating force. Attempts by people like Marcuse to locate signs of hope in student revolts in Europe and the United States now seem, perhaps unjustly, as quaint as 'flower power' and the more mystical pronouncements of the alternative drug culture. In its extremities the approaches of the Frankfurt School would seem to provide only the bitter comfort of an intellectual elite, tortured by painful insights into the world about them, stoically awaiting the night.

Yet again, it would seem that the Frankfurt School continues to be influential, even if the writings of its key members are less likely to be quoted than might have formerly been the case. The critique of positivist methodology continues to find its resonance in the feminist critiques of patriarchal methods, although the earlier and parallel critiques are rarely cited. The critique of 'the culture industry' has perhaps been all too successful, and 'the media' has now taken on a kind of holistic and reified quality that would probably be anathema to writers within the Frankfurt School. But perhaps the abiding legacy is a suspicion of systems and systematising modes of thought, a suspicion that extends to Marxism itself.

CRITICAL THEMES

It can be seen, therefore, that the term 'critical' covers an extraordinary range of perspectives, of contradictory and cross-cutting strands. Marxism and feminism are united in their commitment to change, to a unity of theory and practice; the Laingian perspective and feminism are linked through their sensitivity to the micro-politics of everyday life; feminism and the writings of the Frankfurt School may be linked in terms of their suspicion of holistic systems and so on. If there be some kind of unity here, it is a unity of contradictions.

The distinctive contribution of this set of perspectives may be seen by taking a range of issues and contrasting the approaches implied within the critical method to more conventional socio-logical ones. This enterprise runs all the dangers of further reification although it may bring us closer to an understanding of some of the key critical issues. I shall not, further, attempt to give equal weight to all the critical perspectives in each case. If I were asked to choose as to which of the subperspectives included under the general heading of 'critical' was the most important I should choose the feminist, since it is the more comprehensive.

(i) Conflict and contradiction

Conventional social science is not unaware of conflict within marriage and the family. Divorce, after all, is a central issue in contemporary marital research and strained relationships between parents and adolescents cannot come far afterwards. Nevertheless, these approaches may be found 'wanting' in a variety of respects. Firstly, they tend to be individualistic in that the focus tends to be upon the individual personality as the site of the conflict and that, very often, the solution is seen in terms of individual action or therapy. Methodologically, this entails (as in Thornes and Collard's study of divorce) a com-mitment to survey-type research based upon the summation and aggregation of a series of individual responses. Where a social dimension is provided this is normally stated in terms of external trends, changes in the climate of opinion or in attitudes (permissiveness, trends towards egalitarianism between men and women and so on) or, at its strongest, strains introduced by external pressures or circumstances. In the case of some more recent approaches to therapy, the family or marriage is treated as yet another strand in the growth of methodological familism.

To think, in contrast, in terms of contradictions, is to move towards an understanding where such conflicts are not simply things that may or may not happen within a relationship or a family but which are, to some extent, built into that relation-ship. Indeed, there may be contradictions in a relationship or institution without there being any overt manifestations of conflict, strain or hostility at all. Moreover, such contradictions are not built into the relationship or institution and treated as isolated entities but are seen as structural in origin, that is the origins at one level lie 'outside' in terms of social space and time. It follows from this that such contradictions cannot simply be resolved through individual or lower level social responses but require some more fundamental change in the way in which society is organised.

Examples of contradictions abound in the critical literature. Mention has already been made of the approach of the Frankfurt School which understands the contemporary nuclear family situation in terms of some kind of vicious circle. The growth of late capitalist-industrial enterprises and of large-scale systems of social domination has both meant the erosion of the traditional bases and sources of strength of the patriarchal family, while at the same time rendering the nuclear family more essential as a kind of refuge from this self-same world of dominating impersonality. A further version of this is presented by Harris. If there are trends towards egalitarian marriage, it is in terms of the erosion of some of the more traditional sources of male authority and of the ideology which legitimated male dominance in the home. Nevertheless, the occupational system and the sexual division of labour continues to be premised upon assumptions about the more traditional sexual division of labour. The prosperity of the group is still seen to depend upon the activity of the man; whether the woman seeks paid employment or not, the male occupation is still the dominant theme in the home. This may lead to tension within the home – a tension between the pressures of the occupational system and the premise of egalitarian relational marriage – and here it will be the wife who will be called upon, in true Parsonian fashion, to manage these tensions:

> The price paid by the wife to pursue occupational success is guilt, anxiety, disorientation and anomie, resulting from a combination of adult responsibility without the correlative degree of autonomy. (Harris, 1983, p. 230)

It is clear in Harris's arguments that the question is not one of *either* individual strain *or* structural pressures but a dialectical combination of both, such that the wider structural tensions reach into, shape and condition the individual responses, which in their turn structure and shape the domestic situation further. It is unlikely, therefore, that any amount of therapy or counselling will resolve the problem. Indeed, they may well exacerbate it by diverting attention away from the structural sources of individual discontents.

Themes

Most of the writings within the 'critical school' would not simply concern themselves with contradictions in some abstract or generalised sense but with the working out, at all kinds of levels, of some master contradiction or hierarchy of contradictions. Within capitalism this may be the contradiction between socialised production and individual profit or between classes; within patriarchy this may be a built-in contradiction between men and women and so on. In short it is not enough to talk, in some essentialist fashion, about a contradiction between the individual and society. This rather abstract formulation has to be filled and located in a wider system of structured inequality between classes or genders.

(ii) Socialisation or reproduction

Conventional sociological texts and treatments of the family will typically include, often as a central theme, a section on socialisation. Such accounts will often make a distinction between primary and secondary socialisation, the site of the former being located chiefly, if not exclusively, within the family household. The descriptions of the socialisation process, often overlapping considerably with social psychology or psychology at this point, will outline the complex processes and patterns of interaction between parents and children which at one and the same time turn the child from a bundle of instincts, biologically determined responses and dependences into a fully social human being, while, at the same time, training that child to fit into a whole array of specific roles and statuses in the society within which the child is being reared. These roles may be as general as sex (or gender) roles or somewhat more specific roles associated with class or occupational positions. Generally speaking, the more specific the role, the more likely is the task of socialisation to be allocated to agencies outside the immediate nuclear family. Within the process of primary socialisation, the 'work' of socialisation is often less deliberate, less programmed and more a matter arising out of sustained and/or repeated interactions between parents (or other adults or elder children) and the child.

One central concern of the analysis of socialisation has been with sex-role socialisation, the processes by which, in a given society, a child becomes a gendered individual. Here the analysis has to take account, perhaps even the greater account, of the informal, unrecognised and taken-for-granted inter- actional features of parent-child relationships. While there may be direct admonishments – 'that's not ladylike' – the emphasis would seem to be increasingly upon the much less overt and taken for granted elements in that interaction, from the way in which the parent relates to, punishes or reprimands the child, the toys and the clothes that are given to the child, the character of the linguistic interchanges between parent and child and the role models presented in story books. Increasingly, the emphasis is more and more upon the subtle daily interactional cues rather than the more overt, and openly criticised, aspects such as 'blue for a boy, pink for a girl' or 'Action Man vs the Barbie Doll'. One crucial feature of the taken-for-granted aspect of the socialis- ation process is that, especially where we are concerned with infant socialisation, for 'parent' we should read 'mother' in most cases.

As Barrett and McIntosh note, academic social research has tended to be more receptive to the idea of sex-role socialisation (*op. cit.,* p. 106). Indeed, a considerable body of research material of all kinds and theory has been elaborated around sex-role socialisation and it is clearly a topic that presents many fasci- nating problems of analysis and elaboration. Nevertheless, a variety of inadequacies have been noted in relation to this whole, overall conceptionalisation of the research problem and, by implication, to the approach in terms of socialisation as a whole. At one level it can be argued that sex-role studies, by stressing the learned and constructed aspect of gender, consti- tuted a considerable advance on more overtly biological or deterministic models. However, it may also be argued that such approaches tend to replace a biological determinism by a socio- logical determinism. Society is seen in terms of a structure (often very complex) of roles of varying degrees of salience and centrality; probably the most central is that of sex-role. The research problem, therefore, is one of explaining the process by which infants are, firstly, assigned to one of two gender cate- gories and how the 'boy' or 'girl' learns and internalises the appropriate sets of behaviour patterns, norms and values, relevant to their assigned gender. The roles are presented as givens: the issues are how people are socialised into occupying such roles. Thus studies of sex-role specialisation may tell us quite a bit about the way in which gender relationships and expectations are perpetuated from generation to generation but hardly anything about the processes by which these roles are structured in the first place.

Theories of socialisation, therefore, may be very effective and skilful in telling us how individuals are socialised within their families into filling particular societal, in this case gender, roles. While such theories may also provide accounts of how some individuals are 'inadequately' socialised and therefore later find difficulties in living up to the expectations surrounding male and female identities in society as a whole, they would seem to be less satisfactory in explaining how individuals might come to challenge, question or seek to change these prescribed roles. Further, most versions of socialisation theories seem to presuppose a relatively homogeneous 'wider society' where there is considerable amount of consensus about role expectations and consequently relatively little strain, ambiguity, contradiction or pressure towards change. Moreover, as has been pointed out on several previous occasions, the theatrical metaphor which informs role socialisation theory focuses chiefly upon the performance and tends not to ask questions about authorship or, in other words, questions of power and inequality. In short, a critique of theories of socialisation would seek to argue that roles are not simply or neutrally 'given' but are, in a variety of ways, 'imposed' upon individuals or collectivities by other individuals or collectivities. In the case of gender roles these processes are undeniably complex and often appear to be given and inevitable; nevertheless, it may be argued that such role definitions are of particular benefit to one group, men, rather than simply fitting into some set of functional needs for society as a whole.

This critique of sex-role specialisation can, in many respects, be applied more generally to socialisation theories as a whole. To what extent does the use of the term 'reproduction' in place of socialisation overcome any or some of these difficulties? The use of the term 'reproduction' in critical theories of the family has a variety of overlapping meanings. Very briefly, we may talk firstly about social or cultural reproduction, the concern here being with the ways in which a social system or formation continues over time. In the second place, we may talk about 'reproduction of the labour force', here adopting a specifically

Marxist orientation and distinguishing within this the question of the reproduction of a labour force on a day-to-day basis and the reproduction of a labour force over time. Thirdly, we may talk about 'biological' reproduction (Edholm, Harris and Young, 1977; Morgan, 1979). These are some of the strands which are distinguished in discussions about 'reproduction'.

In concentrating on issues of reproduction we are concentrating on issues of continuity both on a day-to-day basis and on a generation-to-generation basis. It is therefore a somewhat broader concept than socialisation which tends to focus on generational continuity. Moreover, while there are differences in emphasis in various approaches to reproduction, there would seem to be a general focus on the reproduction of relationships of inequality, of patterns of exploitation and oppression. These are to do with structure of class and gender inequalities. In the case of gender we are concentrating on a complex and even paradoxical situation since the individuals most immediately associated with the work of reproduction in all its dimensions are also themselves reproduced in the process as women in the context of a patriarchal society.

Thus, to talk of reproduction in place of socialisation provides a strikingly different emphasis. In the first place, discussion in terms of reproduction has a much more distinct societal, indeed historical, emphasis, pointing much more directly to questions of origin or at least to the wider processes and structures within society that shape gender and class inequalities in the first place. Given the origins of the concept of reproduction in Marxist and feminist thought this shift of emphasis is not surprising. Moreover, the model of society to which our attention is directed is strikingly different from the model of society to which our attention is directed in socialisation theory. It is a society structured around fundamental relationships of inequality of class and gender and how such relationships maintain themselves over time.

Nevertheless, there are some similarities between the two approaches. Both approaches share the difficulty of assuming a relatively unproblematic passage from society (however that society might be conceived) through the socialising or reproducing institutions to the socialisee. The flow, in both cases, tends to be from society to the individual and in both cases, the outcome would appear to be relatively unproblematic and

235

successful. Socialisation (at least in its more recent, more phenomenological versions) might be a little less defective in this respect since it does allow for some degree of interaction between socialising agencies and socialisee. Indeed, socialisation approaches tend to begin with the processes of socialisation, often analysed in fine detail, and to assume society and societal processes while reproduction theories tend to start from society and assume relatively unproblematic responses on the part of individuals.

One attempt that does, to some extent, try to combine approaches derived from a micro, largely psychological social-isation approach with elements from a structural, feminist approach dealing with reproduction, is that of Chodorow. She focuses upon the fact that it is women who are normally entrusted with socialisation/reproduction and that, therefore, they are doubly implicated in the process. In reproducing small children, women are reproducing themselves. Chodorow starts from the premise that women, almost universally, are entrusted with the care and responsibility of small children, both male and female: men with full adult status do not 'routinely care for small children, especially for infants' (Chodorow in Eisenstein, 1979, pp. 86–7). Using a combination of Freudian and objects-relations theories she goes on to analyse the consequences of this for gender divisions in society, for example the processes by which girls learn to identify with their mothers while boys have much greater difficulty in effecting the transition from close and enjoyable dependence upon a woman, who is also a mother, to full adult male status. This loss of, and apparent rejection by, a female figure contributes to the development of the typical male character type; resentful or suspicious of 'softness', more at ease in the company of men than in (save in an often aggressive sexual relationship) the company of women, and in some cases often hostile to the point of violence towards these female figures (Chodorow, 1978; Easlea, 1981).

Chodorow's work has been accused of 'universalism, deter-minism, latent celebration of difference, and voluntarism. . . .' (Sayers, 1982, p. 92). Nevertheless, it does attempt to deal with some problems that may be all too readily by-passed in dis-cussions of reproduction. Discussions of reproduction, quite correctly, emphasise that they are not dealing simply with biological reproduction. One consequence of this is that they may end up in not talking about the 'biological' at all. If by 'biological' we mean not a notion of unchanging and deterministic processes (which is probably not a notion that appeals to many contemporary biologists anyway) but rather an area of overlap between physiological, psychological and sociological processes – a complex, dynamic and often changing area – then this is properly an area to be considered in the analysis of the processes of reproduction. It is not falling into crude determinism to argue that women do tend to experience birth in a more immediate way and that it may be possible to talk about 'reproductive consciousness' (O'Brien in Keohane *et al.*, 1982, pp. 104–5). At the very least, Chodorow, in common with some socialisation theorists, reminds us that in talking about the processes of reproduction we cannot remain simply at the societal or structural level.

(iii) Social construction or ideology?

As I have shown (Chapter 9), the notion of reality as socially constructed has become a useful and central theme in sociological analysis. Within the context of the family the 'work' involved in the daily social construction of parenthood, childhood, marriage and the family is being examined in some fine detail. As such, these accounts serve a valuable function in counteracting the tendencies towards biologism, essentialism and functionalism which continue to represent real dangers in the analysis of the family.

These tendencies towards biologism and essentialism have also been detected within some feminist and Marxist arguments (see Coward, *op. cit.*; Harris in Young *et al.*, 1981, p. 50). As against this there has been a variety of attempts to explore the processes whereby the family and marriage are ideologically constructed while, as some analysts might further argue, themselves contributing to the ideological reproduction of a social formation. These studies range from the more theoretical expositions to the more historically-based analyses. For example, the frequent confusion between the household and the family may be seen as being not simply a logical or linguistic mistake but an ideologically shaped processes of misrecognition (Harris in Young *et al.*, *ibid.*, p. 51). This means (a) that the confusion of the two is systematic and that it has its origins in

237

certain structural processes which are wider than the simple 'error' itself and that (b) this misrecognition has further consequences in terms of the maintenance of a patriarchal or capitalist order. What we have is the prioritisation of a particular structure of domestic relations (parents and children) as against other forms of household and against other kinds of domestic relations. For example, the exclusion of the elderly grandparents from this ideological model of the nuclear-family-based household both derives from and has the further consequence of the marginalisation of the elderly in our society (Phillipson, 1983). Conversely, such a model is in keeping with a notion of a society as 'forward looking', gearing to change and 'creative destruction' and which identifies youth with the future. Hence this confusion of household with family (and a certain section of family at that) both derives from a complex set of social and historical processes and contributes to the continuation and reproduction of those processes.

However, to say that something is ideological is to say something more than this. It is to point to specific processes and practices which are to do with the symbolic and the ideational but which are not of themselves purely ideal. Barrett and McIntosh make a useful distinction between 'familism and familisation' on the one hand, and 'familialism and familialisation' on the other (Barrett and McIntosh, *op. cit.,* p. 26 fn.). The first set of terms deal with sets of values, ideas and images which are themselves pro-family. Here one might include many overt statements in favour of the family to come from religious or political leaders, the pro-family right in Britain and the United States, for example (David, 1983). The latter couple of terms deal with something more interesting and deeply embedded, that is the more everyday and taken-for-granted prioritisation of family and family-like values. In other words, we are dealing here not simply with positive and overt evaluations of the family but the wider importance and resonances that these ideas have in everyday language and understandings. A crude example might be the stereotypical managing director's phrase, 'we are just one big happy family here', a phrase which undoubtedly is intended to do work in relation to particular formulations of industrial relations but also, and less obviously, does work in reinforcing this process of the centralisation of familial relations. Barrett and McIntosh also provide another interesting example: an anti-nuclear weapons poster which relates family expenditure to expenditure on nuclear weapons and which features missiles in a supermarket trolley. What is interesting in this, and in other images in everyday speech, is the relatively effortless character of such work; the family images readily and 'naturally' come to mind. Ideology is as much, perhaps more, to deal with these processes as it is with the more overt messages of political or religious leaders, and the work of feminists or Marxists in the criticism of these processes lies in the questioning, exposing and isolating of such 'natural' images (much in the same way as Roland Barthes does with a whole variety of everyday visual representations in *Mythologies*) and in beginning to tease out the complex historical and structural antecedents of these processes.

What is the difference between such work of 'unmasking' ideological practices and the discussion of the social construction of everyday domestic activities mentioned earlier? Generally speaking, the difference parallels the differences between socialisation and reproduction and the cluster of ideas of practices that have grown up around these two words. Analysis of the 'social construction' of reality concentrates on the *how*, the day-to-day routine activities of members as they go about their regular work as parents, spouses and children. Such processes, as we have seen, are less concerned with the antecedents of such activities. Moreover, the formulation of social practices in terms of the 'social construction' formulation may have the effect of according too great a leeway or autonomy to the human agencies naturally engaged in these day-to-day practices. To talk of 'the social construction' is to talk of the how without necessarily asking questions about the materials, the origins and limitations of these materials, with which this work is carried out (see Emmett, 1983). A shift to the examination of ideology, on the other hand, does begin to ask questions about the origins of these processes and, indeed, their consequences for the wider social formation within which these practices take place. Both approaches work against a simply naturalistic or biologistic interpretation of family processes, although the approach from the perspective of ideology seeks to ask questions beyond and behind the particular practices under investigation. Yet, insofar as there is often a tendency towards a kind of functionalism in Marxist or feminist analysis, it is not a

239

Themes

question of the 'ideological' approach replacing the 'social construction' approach but rather of the former incorporating the latter in order to provide for a richer, and more critical, understanding.

(iv) Sex roles or patriarchy?

Until fairly recently the study of gender differences in society was typically conducted in terms of a discussion about *sex-roles*. Sex-roles were seen as being among the most fundamental and all pervasive ('basic', 'ascribed') roles into which children were socialised. In terms of research orientations, the critical questions were the processes whereby individuals acquired these roles; the ways in which these roles were manifested and sustained in a variety of settings and contexts such as home, work, the media and religion, and the ways in which these roles might be understood to be changing. In relation to this last question, considerable attention was paid to the interlocking factors of growing female participation in the labour force, trends to smaller families and more democratic family structures and changing legislation affecting both of these spheres.

As elsewhere, the emphasis on sex-roles, while representing a considerable advance over more biologistic explanations, still often carried with it strong traces of functionalism with the image of individuals fitting into more or less preordained roles and still tended to by-pass questions of origin or causation. Where the theatrical metaphor was used more overtly, the concentration still tended to be on the players rather than the script and its mysterious author.

This is not to say that the sex-role approach excluded questions of social change. Indeed, books, courses, weekend schools and lectures on 'the changing roles of women and men' have become a regular feature of the pedagogic landscape. Again, however, the hand of functionalism was often to be detected. The 'changing roles' were largely seen as roles which were changing in response to outside forces: two world wars, changing legislation, changes in the structure of the economy and the labour markets and so on. The struggles, collectively and individually, of women (and sometimes men) themselves were often minimised. Moreover, such an emphasis on change tended to assume too

240

optimistically a tendency to increasing democratisation in the home and equality within the labour market. Feminist writers, on the other hand, continued to draw attention to persisting and deep-rooted inequalities within both spheres as well as exploring areas of society which had been largely ignored in the 'sex-role' discussions but which were part of the everyday experiences of most women, that is the fact or the threat of male violence in the home or on the street, sexual harassment at work and porno-graphic representations of women in the media and advertising. The continuing, deep-rooted and pervasive character of sexual inequality seemed to deserve a title which more accurately reflected the reality than the rather bland 'sex-roles' with its hidden theme of relative equality. There was clearly a need for a term which introduced to the forefront of the discussion questions of power between men and women; such a term was 'patriarchy'.

Patriarchy, then, could be seen as introducing all kinds of themes which were absent or muted in the more conventional discussions of sex-roles: questions of sexual politics, questions of pervasive inequalities and questions of wider and deeper struc-tural and historical origins. But the term has never been universally accepted, even within the feminist movement. It has always been seen that the term, whatever its uses as critical rhetoric, did present a variety of difficulties and that even among those who regularly used it there were a variety of important and contested issues.

(a) The origins of patriarchy Hartmann defines patriarchy in these terms:

> I define patriarchy as a set of social relations which has a
> material base and in which there are hierarchical relations
> between men, and solidarity among them, which enables
> them to control women. Patriarchy is thus a system of male
> oppression of women. (Hartmann in Eisenstein, 1979, p. 232)

The definition as a whole is controversial, but the final sentence – 'Patriarchy is thus a system of male oppression of women' – would, however, be taken as some kind of minimal starting point.

The use of the term patriarchy does underline the fact that systematic gender inequalities are both all pervasive and widespread in time and in place. Anthropological and historical research at the very least shows this to be the case (Morgan, 1984; Reiter, 1975; Rosaldo and Lamphere, 1974) although such research also reveals considerable diversity in the ways in which these inequalities are elaborated. Given the all pervasive character of systematic gender inequality, or systems of male oppression of women, what are the origins of patriarchy? The very terms in which the debate is recast would seem to exclude simple biological explanations, although biological may enter into the accounts to some degree. Thus, explanations may lay some emphasis on the unique and special character of women's role in child-bearing and rearing although would go on to stress the importance of the ways in which these roles are treated in particular societies. Other explanations, again usually only in part, might lay some stress on the relative physical weakness of women, placing women at a more or less permanent dis-advantage in the battle of the sexes, especially in societies where male strength, agressiveness and warfare are stressed. Nevertheless, primarily biological explanations would seem to be excluded.

Even more certainly, it would seem, are straightforward functional explanations to be excluded. Arguments about the ways in which society might benefit from the gender division of labour would seem to be ruled out in advance by any account which lays stress on the male oppression of women. It is not society which benefits but men, and that is what needs to be explained.

The term 'origins' is, in any event, obscure. One set of meanings to be attached to the word would refer to a source located somewhere in a concept of human nature, that is in terms of either the needs of the biological organism or of human society. As we have seen, these kinds of explanations, taken alone, are ruled out in advance. At the very least they are seen as being modified by historical explanations, using the word 'origin' here to refer to antecedents in the past. Here, while the explanations do serve to modify and to relativise purely biological/functionalist explanations, they also raise further problems to do with the extent to which we can or are able to understand fully the earliest human societies and the problem of how it is that such patterns persisted into quite different societies. This leads us to another set of explanations which refer more directly to questions of how such patterns of oppression persist over time, how they are reproduced. These would include socialisation theory and some psychoanalytical accounts. And against or apart from – but also related to – all these kinds of explanations there are certain kinds of explanation which would be described as materialist.

The desire to seek out materialist explanations of women's oppression stems from the continuing debate between Marxism and feminism. Feminists found straightforward Marxist explanations focusing on relationships within capitalist society as being too narrow in focus. Nevertheless, they sought to provide an explanation – or perhaps an overall orientation – which preserved some of the strengths of materialist explanations and did not fall into idealism. The early attempt of Firestone to apply Marx's method while shifting the focus to the sexual class struggle as the most fundamental struggle of all was seen as a useful point of departure but too single-stranded and ultimately too biologistic.

Hartmann argued that the material basis of patriarchy is: 'all the social structures that enable men to control women's labor' (Hartmann in Sargent (ed.), 1981, p. 16). Delphy, similarly, lays stress on men's appropriation of the labour power of women (Delphy, 1977; Barrett and McIntosh, 1979, p. 96). Delphy lays particular focus on the marital relationship, simultaneously looking inward to the particular patterns of appropriation and control that exist within the relationship, and outward to the wider structures of laws and practices that support, sustain and benefit from these patterns of oppression within marriage. Hartmann, similarly, has a twofold orientation, pointing to the processes whereby women are excluded from access, or full access, to economic activities and to the patterns of control and restriction over women's sexuality. It should be noted that both these, and other more recent 'materialist' accounts of women's oppression, seek to avoid a single-stranded or monocausal examination. The materialist points to sets of relationships and practices which have material consequences and which are fundamentally related to the economic framework of society but this may be seen as representing a general orientation rather than a once-and-for-all explanation. It is a guide to historical understanding rather than a substitute for it; it seeks to allow for the diversity of practices within a variety of social formations and to enable the exploration of this diversity through social and historical research. To this extent the feminist materialist explanations of female oppression remain faithful to Marxism.

It is not intended here to adjudicate between different explanations of female oppression or to distinguish carefully between the writings of different schools of feminism and Marxism. The general emphasis should, I feel, be given to the overall orientations provided by recent feminist materialist accounts since they are, potentially at least, the more inclusive. However, all sorts of questions about the origins and reproduction of gender oppression will continue to be asked and it would be wise neither to foreclose on any particular line of enquiry nor to focus on one to the exclusion of the others.

(b) The role/rule of the father It has been noted on more than one occasion that the current feminist usage of the term 'patriarchy' departs from the traditional use of the term. Originally it clearly meant 'rule of the father'; under feminist usages this sense has been lost, or at least submerged, under the more general notion of male oppression of women. The question at issue is whether this original and literal use has any part to play in feminist usages.

While some feminists explicitly state that there should be little or no place for the older usage (Walby, 1983), suggesting that it is but one instance of the wider set of practices, other approaches at least would seem to include some reference to fathers and to include it as a part of the analysis. The quotation from Hartmann (p. 241) would suggest as much, pointing to relations of hierarchy between men as well as solidarities between them. In the myth of the primal horde, of course, the hierarchal relationship would be that between father and sons and the solidarity relationship would be between siblings, and while that model is clearly of limited applicability to contemporary society it serves as an illustration of the kinds of relationships that Hartmann might be talking about.

More generally, the older usage of the term 'patriarchy' might be felt relevant in a variety of interconnected ways:

(i) The structural similarities between the father/child and the male/female relationships, especially within the family. In both sets of relationships there are notions of legal obligation and compulsion on the part of the two groups. These obligations and compulsions may differ in degree and kind as between different societies although they are often significantly linked as, for example, in the notion of 'dependants' which brackets both the wife and the children. In both cases the relationships are of a personalistic and particularistic kind. In both cases we get, to some degree, the appropriation of unwaged work. While, in our own society, we are more familiar with the appropriation of the work of the housewife, the appropriation of the work of children is often also of some importance. In both cases we get a system of control which is based upon a combination (varying between and within societies) of emotional power and physical force. All this, as Fitz and Hood-Williams point out, leads to sets of contradictory status within the household. A son is both a male and a child, both dominant and subordinate. A mother is both parent and woman. There are sets of similarities and differences between women and children although, in the present analysis, it is the similarities that should impress themselves upon us (Fitz and Hood-Williams, 1982, pp. 72–3).

It should be said that these similarities are not simply parallels. I am not simply arguing that one set of relationships is *like* the other. It is also being argued that the two sets of relationships are systematically connected. It is probably true to say that the greater the sway of familial and kinship relations over social relationships as a whole, the greater the importance of the role of the father: nevertheless, its importance persists in those societies where the formal importance of kinship may have declined.

(ii) We may elaborate these linked parallels further. One important area of linkage is in the area of property. While the original story of Engels, as Coward has noted (Coward, 1983) begs too many questions, it does seek to explore the linkages between questions of the control over property and inheritance and the control over women.

(iii) We are also led into the complex area of the relationships between psychoanalysis and feminism (Mitchell, 1975;

Rose, 1983). Whether or not we should accept in detail the relevance of the application of Freud's theories to feminism is still an open and hotly debated question. What is clear is that it does draw our attention to the actual complexities involved in the processes of reproduction, going beyond the more or less superficial positivist accounts of socialisation into exploring the unconscious and emotional basis of the reproduction of gender identities through familial relationships. If attention to questions of legal power, inheritance and property throws light on the material linkages between the two usages of patriarchy, psychoanalysis highlights the emotional and unconscious linkages. Taken together, the material and the psychic, we have a powerful argument for the retention of the older usage of the term 'patriarchy' and its systematic incorporation into analysis.

The case against this would seem to rest on an understanding of the character of modern society and the dominance of relationships other than kinship within the social order as a whole. Here Parsons's use of the 'pattern variables' to differentiate between particular social orders, while open to considerable question and modification, does point to the kinds of differences that might be important. Patriarchy, it will be argued, is to do with the relationships within the market-place and the political orders, arenas not now primarily dominated by considerations of kinship. This is true but it does not eliminate the case for considering the psychic structuring of such an order and the continuing importance of family and patriarchy in the old sense as part of this. Similarly, the continuing importance of property in the reproduction of inequality continues to be documented (Chapter 4; Harbury and Hitchens, 1979), suggesting that paternal power, although modified in many ways, does continue to exercise a significant influence at least in some sectors of society. What the confrontation between the two usages of the term 'patriarchy' does suggest is that there is a need to talk about 'patriarchies' in the plural, using the different ways in which the two usages might be articulated as the lynchpin of the analysis.

(c) One or many? One of the chief arguments against the concept of patriarchy is that it is much too all-inclusive. A concept which embraces a whole range of societies – possibly almost all known societies past and present – would seem to have little explanatory value. In the context of this argument there are three possible responses: to argue the case for patriarchy more closely; to abandon the concept altogether; or to argue for a plurality of patriarchies.

If it is decided to abandon the concept of patriarchy, then there would appear to be a variety of terms waiting to take its place. The 'sexual division of labour' is a widely used term (for one definition see Whitehead in Young *et al.*, 1981, p. 90) although it does not immediately suggest the idea of subordination and gender relationships as political relationships. 'Gender subordination' might be another candidate, seeing this as a material as well as a system of ideas and values (Elson and Pearson in Young *et al.*, 1981, pp. 151–2). Perhaps the leading candidate for an alternative is Rubin's 'sex-gender system'. Rubin is against the use of the term 'patriarchy', preferring to reserve that usage for its more traditional one, as referring, for example, to the kinds of relationships described in the New Testament.

Rubin describes the 'sex-gender system' in these terms:

A . . . set of arrangements by which a society transforms biological sexuality into products of human activity, and in which these transformed sexual needs are satisfied. (Rubin, 1975, p. 159)

The use of the couplet 'sex-gender' (as opposed to simply 'sex' or 'gender') follows on from the conventional distinction between sex and gender and suggests that we are dealing with both the biological and the social but seeing the two as essentially in relationship. To focus on either one to the exclusion of the other would be a distortion. The focus on sexuality might, at a first glance, seem to be a little narrow, yet it performs a useful service in focusing on the fact that we are dealing with the social meanings attached to the differences between men and women and the approved ·sets of relationships between the sexes, products of the interaction between biology and culture. The reason why societies continue to make and to stress differences between men and women and to place these differences among the most important distinctions that societies can make is, ultimately, to do with sexuality in the widest and deepest sense of the word. Rubin then goes on to deploy the insight of Lévi-Strauss (particularly his linking of the values of reciprocity with the incest taboo) and Freud (seeing psychoanalysis as a 'theory about the reproduction of kinship', *ibid.*, p. 183) to explore the deep structure of sexual oppression (*ibid.*, p. 198). To focus on questions of sexuality is to focus on to questions of the exchange of and the control over women and on to the way in which the gender hierarchy is reproduced at the unconscious as well as at the more conscious or overt levels. Only this kind of focus can direct us to confront the deep-rooted character of gender divisions while still retaining a sociological, as opposed to a simple, biologistic, understanding of gender relationships and oppressions.

Rubin's approach, while like Mitchell and Chodorow among others, seeks to deploy anthropological and psychological insights in the understanding of gender oppression and is certainly impressive. Moreover, it is not a static system: it is subject to 'historical change and development' (Chodorow, in Eisenstein, 1979, p. 85). Nevertheless, there is a question about the extent to which this model can be usefully applied to all societies. Rubin herself argues that kinship is no longer the basis of society and that it has been 'stripped of its functions' (*ibid.*, p. 199). While it is possible to argue about the details of this argument in relation to kinship it can be recognised that kinship is not the sole or the central organising principle in society today. Under such circumstances it may be argued that the fundamental links which might have once been established between sexuality and the sexual division of labour have been weakened, if not severed, much in the same way as, more recently, Illich has contrasted a regime of 'vernacular gender' with the much more limiting exploitation of 'economic sex' in industrial society (Illich, 1983). We are here approaching some kind of notion of a great divide which was, after all, one of the central concerns of the classic sociological tradition. By-passing the complexities of this debate, the question can be raised as to whether Rubin's 'sex-gender' system more properly applies to one, earlier, side of the divide leaving open the question of what we are to call more historically recent patterns of relationships.

Consideration of Rubin's argument on behalf of the 'sex-gender' system leads us to make one kind of distinction around the much debated 'great divide' notion. Yet even this distinction may be only a point of departure, blurring over, for example, the variety of patterns of gender relations on both sides of the divide. Sanday, for example, analyses in considerable detail the variety of patterns of gender relationships in societies, looking at the extent of the sexual division of labour in terms of the numbers and kinds of task which are felt to be appropriate for one gender or another, the degree of separation or overlap of power and decision making between men and women, the extent of ritual or symbolic segregation and the degrees of violence and hostility shown by men towards women. Fundamentally, she argues, societies vary in the way in which they handle gender scripts and these variations can, very generally, be related to the economies and histories of the societies and the extent to which, as a result of these, the societies have a fundamentally cooperative or antagonistic view towards nature and the outside world. Where these relationships are seen to be more or less in harmonious or unthreatening terms, then such societies will tend towards much greater gender equality and cooperation (Sanday, 1981).

In the light of this discussion, where does this leave the notion of patriarchy? Positively, the concept does serve as a sensitising orientation to the widespread character of gender domination and to the essentially political character of this domination. Gender subordination is not, therefore, the same as the sexual division of labour, although this is an important part of it. The idea of patriarchy (or possibly the sex-gender system, although this would seem to be limited to certain kinds of societies) would seem to be necessary in order to preserve some sense of gender inequalities which were separate from and not reducible to regimes or social formations that might be characterised in other ways, such as feudal societies, tribal societies, capitalist societies and so on. To simplify a great deal we may argue that almost all societies are patriarchal although few, if any, are ever *simply* patriarchal.

However, while it would seem to be necessary to preserve the idea of patriarchy, it would also seem to be important to go beyond it, to begin to analyse the variety of themes which may be elaborated within an overall patriarchal framework. A start, indeed, may be made by reintroducing the older usage of the term, 'rule of the father', and to distinguish those societies where there are strong and direct links between rule of the father and the rule of men and those societies where these linkages, although not entirely lost, are severely attenuated. It might also be useful to distinguish those societies where patriarchy is, as it were, written into the formal charter of rules, constitutions, myths and symbolic representations, and those where it is not and where, indeed, the formal constitution might be deemed in many respects at least to be anti-patriarchal, although patriarchy may be found to persist in all its strength on an informal basis. Whatever the kinds of distinctions that are to be made, it would seem that, short of abandoning the concept altogether, the way forward is towards exploring variations and the sources of these variations, to analyse patriarchies rather than patriarchy.

(d) Capitalism and patriarchy A central debate stimulated by the growth of the feminist movement has been the nature of the relationship between capitalism and patriarchy. As has already been suggested, contemporary feminist thought developed in full recognition of the weaknesses in traditional Marxist theorising which tended to see capitalism and class relationships as very much the dominant partner with gender subordination, if mentioned at all, as a somewhat secondary and relatively untheorised feature of capitalist society. Even where theorised, class relationships and the needs of capitalism remained the prime consideration. Clearly the debate has moved beyond this kind of position, just as it has moved beyond the position (most usually associated with Firestone) which tended to see patriarchy and the politics of sex as the central consideration with capitalism and class relationships as either subordinate to, or derivative from, these wide and deeper patterns of gender subordination. There would seem to be some kind of consensus emerging that both class and gender relationships need to be considered in relation to each other but this still leaves considerable space for debate about the nature of the relationship and the relative autonomy of the two main elements.

A starting point might be the recognition that, within capitalist society, gender seems to show a remarkable resilience in the context of a more fluid class structure. For one thing, capitalist society does allow for a degree of social mobility; it is possible for an individual to move out of 'his' class. For another thing, the class structure of advanced capitalist societies can be seen as undergoing change with the development of a middle class. However this development might be conceptualised in Marxist terms, it did, experientially at least, mean the opening up of opportunities and work situations that were less immediately oppressive even if the fundamental class relationships remained the same. For another thing, the working *man* was permitted some kind of release from the rigours of his class position in his home and in his leisure, a release which, however distorted or incomplete, was denied to his wife, whether she were in paid employment or not. Looking further afield, the actual practice of socialism and socialist parties within capitalist societies did not hold out a clear and unambiguous promise for a release from gender oppression. There can, indeed, be few more powerful pictures of patriarchy than the line of Soviet leaders and officials on the annual May Day parade.

However, the continuing deep and all pervasive character of gender oppression does not in itself justify a concentration on gender and patriarchy at the expense of class and capitalism. Class continues to represent a significant source of difference between the experiences of women. Class differences between men, similarly, have their consequences for women; the notion of the 'family wage', for example, may be understood as being patriarchal in its origins and/or consequences but it can only be rendered fully intelligible in the context of a class-divided society and the elaboration of particular notions of class solidarities and the relationships of trades unions and the labour movement to these solidarities.

While, at a certain stage of the analysis, it might seem to be important to analyse the workings out of class and gender inequalities separately, this can only be a preliminary methodological or conceptual stage. The full significance of class and gender can only be understood by analysing them in their interaction; this is expressed in Eisenstein's adoption of the couplet, 'capitalist-patriarchy', a term which preserves both the sense of distinctness of the two components while seeking to explore the

251

dialectic between them (Eisenstein, 1979). Examples of the fruitfulness of this approach abound from the awareness that gender does indeed make a difference to the class structure (Gamarnikow *et al.*, 1983a; Wright and Perrone, 1977; Wright *et al.*, 1982), with women constantly coming out at the bottom of a combined class-gender hierarchy, to the exploration of the working out of the labour market in class and gender terms. Hartmann argues, and seeks to demonstrate using a variety of historical evidence, that the crucial link between capitalism and patriarchy lies in the sexual segregation of jobs and the position of women within the labour market (Hartmann in Eisenstein (ed.), 1981). Such processes cannot be understood by examining the logic of capitalism in isolation for in formal terms it could be argued that capitalism as a system is 'gender-blind'. Given the nature of work in late capitalist society (where there is much less stress on sheer physical labour, for example) there are no strictly economic reasons why women should be allocated primary responsibilities for housework or why they should be concentrated in a relatively narrow range of occupations, largely segregated from their working-class male partners.

To call for the analysis of the relationship between capitalism and patriarchy is not necessarily to argue for an equality of influence in each and every instance. Clearly, in certain contexts, there will be a case for according the greater priority to gender or to patriarchal relationships; this would be true in cases to do with the whole area of violence towards women and the study of sexuality. In other cases, class would seem to be the dominant influence; the study of housing might be a possible example although it must be admitted that it is more difficult to find examples of 'pure' class or capitalist relationships than it is to find examples of 'pure' gender or patriarchal relationships. What the inclusion of class into the analysis does suggest is the importance, already underlined in the previous section, of breaking down the monolithic notion of patriarchy and in exploring the varied and different ways in which it interacts with class and other variables. Age and ethnicity would be two very important further variables. The particular model of paternal patriarchy described by Lown in her study of a nineteenth-century silk mill (Lown in Gamarnikow *et al.*, 1983a) is different from the working out of patriarchy among a group of dinner ladies or a group of female tobacco workers in our own time (Cunnison and Pollert in Gamarnikow *et al.*, 1983a).

(e) Patriarchy begins at home? While there might be considerable debates around the origins of patriarchy, there is little doubt about the continuing centrality of the family in ensuring its reproduction. The familistic reference in the term is not, therefore, simply metaphorical. The continuing emphasis on housework and domestic labour bears witness to this even if it has progressed beyond the somewhat rarefied debate within largely Marxist theoretical terms of some years ago.

The earlier terms of the debate concentrated on whether domestic labour produced value, and if so what kind of value, and the way in which a domestic mode of production, if such could be identified, was articulated with the wider capitalist mode of production. The emphasis came to be placed upon the idea of reproduction. What was missing from some of the earlier statements were any clear explanations as to why it was that it was women who ended up with the prime responsibility for domestic labour, whether or not they themselves were also involved in paid employment. It might also be argued, further, that one of the important distinctions is to be made between housework on the one hand, and the care of and responsibility for children on the other, the latter proving to be more intractable to change than the former. (For a useful summary of the domestic labour debate see Finch, 1983, p. 79.)

Consideration of the role of the family within a wider patriarchal system often leads to some bewildering spirals of action and interaction. Why are women at a disadvantage in the labour market? Managers, trades unionists and many social scientists argued that this is to do with the fact that the woman's prime responsibility is seen in the home. However others, Hartmann and Walby, for example, argue that these are often rationalisations and the important factors are the discriminatory and exclusionist practices of male workers, both in the past and continuing into the present despite legislation formally outlawing such practices (Hartmann, in Eisenstein (ed.), 1979; Walby, 1983). Yet why do men adopt such discriminatory practices? In part this may be due to the character of male groups; in part it may be due to the particular experiences of class; and in part it may be due to the widespread and all pervasive character of the traditional ideology locating the woman's prime responsibility in the home. The circling around market-place, home, class and ideology is perhaps a sign of intellectual confusion or perhaps impressive witness to the systemic nature of these interconnections.

The family would, therefore, seem to be crucial, although not uniquely so, in the understanding of the working of patriarchy. It is the site of the extraction of a whole range of unpaid but significant (to society and to male individuals) services largely from women. It is, therefore, an important location of a whole set of privileges that men enjoy and which they would be reluctant to relinquish; this may be especially the case for men workers with relatively few alternative sources of privilege in society. It provides, just as it is shaped by, a set of powerful and pervasive images through which we come to understand our society and the place of the gender order within it. As the main institution within which children are brought up, the family household is not simply an arena within which ideological reproduction takes place but is also the arena where, crucially, the reproduction of motherhood occurs. Ideologically and economically, the family household is crucial to the understanding of the working of patriarchy, the point to which, however labyrinthine, the paths always return.

QUESTIONS ABOUT CRITICAL THEORIES OF THE FAMILY

There is no one single unified critical theory. For the most part I have concentrated on Marxist and feminist approaches to the family although, as has been shown on a variety of occasions, these approaches themselves cannot be characterised as unified orientations. Indeed, some of the sharpest debates in the study of the family have come between and within the various approaches described as Marxist and/or feminist. At a more general level there would seem to be three sets of problems with a wide range of applicability which may be explored here: the question of Marxist functionalism; the issue of the nature and significance of gender; and the problem of the persistence of the family.

(a) 'Marxist functionalism'

In the course of the debate between feminists and Marxists, the term 'Marxist functionalism' has sometimes been used. The phrase refers either to a particular strand of Marxist writing or, more generally, to a tendency which is thought to be inherent in Marxist thinking. The use of the term 'functionalist' as a stick with which to beat Marxists is not necessarily new nor is it confined to feminist writers: 'Parsons' actors are cultural dopes, but Althusser's agents are structural dopes of even more stunning mediocrity.' (Giddens, 1979, p. 52.) Earlier Marxists were often accused of being 'mechanistic', all too prone to emphasise the System or History at the expense of any sense of human agency. In more recent times, some versions of feminism or sexual politics may come in for similar kinds of criticism. Stanley and Wise, as we have seen, are critical of approaches within the feminist or gay movements which see an institution such as the family as something that is seen as *doing things* to people, the people being viewed as relatively passive recipients of external institutional pressures (Stanley and Wise, 1983, pp. 72–3). We are, in fact, dealing with a debate which has a long pedigree and which appears in a variety of guises.

As an example of what we might mean by 'Marxist functionalism' let us take a passage in a recent paper by Navarro (Navarro, 1982; see also Barrett and McIntosh, 1982, pp. 85–92). In the course of a discussion relating certain issues in welfare provision to the international capitalist crisis, Navarro writes:

> In summary, capital uses all forms of ideological codes and messages, including those generated from cultures of protest, to avoid the creation of a political consciousness capable of going beyond the capitalist system. We find, then, a long list of movements – from 'counterculture' to 'holistic medicine' (among many others) – that are presented as anti-establishment but all of which share the same road to political unconsciousness. . . . These movements become components in the process of restructuring bourgeois

ideology, a restructuring that is needed to retain its
dominance. (*op. cit.*, p. 47)

Here we find many of the features associated with Marxist
functionalism: a sense of a self-regulating system which allows
little scope for human agency; a tendency to see individual
actors or movements at the receiving end of the workings out
of such a system; and a marked unwillingness to explore
ambiguity. 'Holistic medicine' may well be narcissistic, individualistic and middle class; but it may also contain within it
the potentiality for a critique of commercialised medicine and
medical bureaucracies.

Within the broad critical tradition, indeed within Marxism
itself, there are forces working against these versions of Marxist
functionalism. From the Frankfurt School there is the abiding
and persistent warning against reification, and from within the
feminist movement there is a long-standing suspicion of male
systems and established formulae. Indeed, so widespread is the
notion of Marxist functionalism as a beast to be avoided that
there is a danger that some of its potential strengths may be
forgotten. It is likely that there will always be a need for some
kind of systematic approach which will have some elements of
functionalism. This is certainly the case if we are to preserve a
sense of a society in which there are connections which need to
be taken into account if we are to understand fully any one part
of it. Thus to say that we cannot fully understand the institution
of the family or relationships within it without taking into
account factors 'outside' the family such as work, ideology,
politics and so on is to make some steps into a territory traditionally marked out by functionalists. The same is true if we
draw attention to societal constraints upon individual courses of
action. Perhaps we would be better in withdrawing the label
'functionalist', Marxist or otherwise, with all its pejorative
connotations, and concentrate on problems which concern many
shades of social thinkers.

(b) A question of gender

Among the critical streams which we have outlined in this
chapter, feminism has been most influential in bringing
questions of gender to the fore in the analysis of society.

Sociological practice, including that influenced by Marxism, was held to be defective in that: (i) it ignored questions of gender in many cases; (ii) that where gender was considered it was often in terms of conventional or distorted images, especially of women; (iii) that the social world was generally seen through male spectacles; and that (iv) women tended to be treated as a problem whereby the status of men was taken for granted. In place of this, feminism sought to restore questions of gender to the front of sociological analysis; to introduce a sense and an understanding of women's experience, so long either suppressed or mediated through male interpreters; and to see gender as a main axis of sociological enquiry. For grand macro-theory, operating often at the more abstract, formal or systemic level, gender might represent something incidental, an untidy remnant of the empirical world that should have been swept up in the higher levels of theoretical work. For feminist theorists, however, gender was at the heart of the analysis, the very subject of social enquiry.

Within sociology, and certainly within most areas of the sociology of the family, at least lip service is now paid to the importance of gender. In many respects it may often mean simply adding another lecture or chapter with the heading '. . . and gender'. The areas of concern may become too readily ghettoised within sociological practice. It might, therefore, seem to be an unlikely question to ask whether the subject of gender has not been a little overplayed. Surely the topic is still in its relative infancy, often having to fight for attention and recognition? The question would seem to be ruled out of court at the outset. Nevertheless, there does seem to be a growing movement to cast critical attention on the use or over-use of the gender categories in sociological analysis. Some of this critique comes from within feminism (Eichler, 1979; Matthews, 1982; for a summary of some of the issues see Morgan, 1985). Others seem explicitly to be influenced by an ethnomethodological or phenomenological orientation (Kessler and McKenna, 1978).

The point of issue is as follows. In spite of the routine recognitions of the distinctions between biological sex and cultural gender, gender still seems to be understood in terms of a dichotomous variable, either female or male.[2] Taken-for-granted assumptions about the 'nature' of women and men, largely understood in dichotomous terms, are carried over into the

257

heart of sociological enquiry itself. To 'break down by sex' an array of questionnaire responses is to make a set of assumptions about femaleness or maleness that makes this a meaningful operation in the first place. Dichotomous gender categories are reified and common-sense assumptions about female and male natures are reproduced. Further, the taken-for-granted assumption is that gender, seen in this straightforward way, matters in each and every instance and this assumption too may have the consequence of perpetuating stereotypical notions about women and men in society.

It may be that, behind much of this growing debate and unease about the use of gender, together with the equally growing sense that gender is important, lie important differences within feminist thought which are not captured by simple distinctions between liberals, radical, Marxists and so on. Glennon's ideal types of feminist responses may take the argument further. She is reluctant to perpetuate taken-for-granted notions of men and women and so adopts the Parsonian poles of instrumentalism and expressivism, recognising that in our culture, men will tend to approach the former and women the latter. Feminist responses, then, are:

1 *Instrumentalism.* Seeking advancement and progress for women in the world of careers and work as a key to the advance of women generally.
2 *Expressivism.* Seeking to cultivate and to encourage expressive 'feminine' values of care, concern, emotion and so on: encouraging men to be more expressive.
3 *Synthesism.* Seeking an amalgam of expressive and instrumental values, with neither being more highly valued than the other. Other writers might refer to the androgynous principle.
4 *Polarism.* This, she claims, is rare but is gaining attention. It might be seen as a kind of separate but equal policy, a recognition of the importance of gender oppositions in society as a whole on a kind of yin/yang principle (Glennon, 1979).

In the context of this discussion, it would seem that the third orientation, synthesism, might be most sympathetic to the questioning of taken-for-granted gender assumptions that is taking place in some areas of, largely American, sociology. The first two and the fourth responses, in different ways, persist with certain assumptions about men and women and seek either to encourage or to surpress them.

What are we to make of this? Since cases where gender is either ignored or marginalised continue to be fairly obvious and come to the attention on a day-to-day basis, a call to abandon or to depart from analysis in terms of gender might seem to be a little premature. On the other hand, to conclude that we should continue to explore gender themes but to be careful would seem to be a little limp. We can, however, say a little more. Where we are concerned with questions of 'gender inequality' (in terms of resources, power status) the analysis should continue, the only qualification being that we should be alert to the ways in which gender inequalities relate to other bases of inequality such as age, ethnicity or class. More generally, we should perhaps adopt the principle that was suggested in relation to the study of patriarchy. There are few if any situations where gender might be deemed irrelevant; there are few if any situations where gender might be deemed to be the sole factor of relevance. If it is impracticable for us to adopt the policy of, allegedly, some North American tribes, and think in terms of more than two genders, we might at least see the way in which gender occurs in different mixes, along with ethnicity, age, class and a host of other factors and variables. In short, we might move towards a decomposition of gender.

(c) The persistence of the family

Socialists have to deal with the problem of the persistence of capitalism, in the face of many predictions of impending crisis. They also have to confront the fact that the capitalist system is accepted, sometimes passively, sometimes almost enthusiastically, by those who would seem to be among its chief victims. Feminists (and other theorists, critical of the family) similarly have to confront the fact that the family, however understood, still persists and, moreover, continues to be welcomed as a source of pleasure and identification, a life interest certainly more central than work for a large section of the population. Indeed the issue is much starker in the case of the family; a Conservative prime minister may be able to maintain that capitalism has an 'unacceptable face' in a way which would be impossible if one were to substitute the word 'family' for 'capitalism'.

This question of confronting the apparent widespread support for (or at least reluctance to attack) the family is not short of proposed explanations; the apparent 'natural' basis of the family, the lack of feasible or visible alternatives, the far-reaching and wide-ranging work of ideology and so on. All these explanations are pertinent The question is not so much one of finding an explanation but of formulating a response. Here the parallel issue may be not so much capitalism as religion. Marxists, traditionally, have been able to voice their objections to religion and to provide reasons for its continuance. However, in the main, such Marxists have not spent a great deal of time attacking religion since it was thought bound to disappear with the advent of socialism and, tactically, to attack religion would unnecessarily antagonise those whose support the movement was anxious to gain or sustain.

In recent years, therefore, there has been some debate within feminism as to whether the attack on the family with which feminism has been identified was tactically wise or even desirable. At one level it might be argued that the family does indeed have widespread support and that a direct attack on it would be harmful to other struggles, especially the struggles of working-class women in the workplace and ethnic minorities. The more publicised alternatives to the family, communes and other forms of shared living arrangement, were all too readily identified with disaffected sections of the middle class and hence the overall critique of the family could be effectively marginalised.

Indeed, some have gone further and have argued that the family does have some positive things to be said in its favour. This has been associated with a questioning of the highly individualistic approach characteristic, at least in the United States, of the early feminist movement, still carrying echoes of the hippy, flower-power rebellion even where reacting against many of its manifestations. The family, on the other hand, could be seen as standing for altruistic, collective values, values to do with caring and responsibility. What is at issue is the tragic way in which the family becomes distorted under capitalist and patriarchal regimes. The continuation of an individualistic, do-your-own-thing ethic with strong anti-familial overtones was, in fact, to endorse some of the central values of a late capitalist society, hedonistic, fragmented and narcissistic. Many familistic values – especially those to do with parenthood – came up for more positive re-evaluation (see Friedan, 1981 and Elshtain, 1981 for an elaboration of some of these views; Thorne and Yalom, 1982 for a discussion of the general dilemma).

Critical approaches to the family cannot ignore these arguments or simply label them as manifestations of the more general rise of the 'moral majority' or 'new right'. Indeed, some sections of critical thinking have never been unambiguously opposed to the family, the Frankfurt School or some versions of Marxism, for examples. It has to be realised that what is at issue here is not simply a question of tactics but also a question of theoretical understanding about the place of the family in contemporary society. Solutions to the dilemma are not likely to be easy but two points may be relevant here in what is largely a theoretical discussion. In the first place it needs to be realised that to call for 'the abolition of the family' is, paradoxically, to support the *idea* of the family since such a call presupposes that there is a clearly identified entity which may be abolished in the first place. It is to fall into the traps of reification and functionalism already discussed. Secondly, while critical (in the broadest sense of the word) studies of the family must continue, the more positive emphasis should be in terms of those values which are allegedly identified with the family: caring, tolerance and mutual respect, closeness and so on. An exploration of the way in which these values may be more fully realised in a society which continually strives to push them to the margin or to ghettoise them in a relatively narrow ideologically constructed unit is a major political and theoretical task.

11 Conclusion

There are at least two possible, and not necessarily alternative, ways of understanding what has been happening to marriage and the family in the period from the early 1970s to the present day. One version would be to see it in terms of a retreat from the humanistic optimism of the 1960s, a time when the institutions of marriage and the family not only came under critical scrutiny but also when alternatives were suggested, tried and publicised. From the early 1970s, however, things began to go into reverse and neo-Conservatism began to gain ground in a whole variety of areas such as economic theory and practice, a growing critique of the welfare state and, towards the end of this period, a reassertion of nationalistic or patriotic values. In the area of the family there was the growing influence of born-again Christians and the 'moral majority' in the United States (David, 1983) where there were also signs of a positive re-evaluation of the family on the part of feminists (Friedan, 1981) and socialists (Epstein and Ellis, 1983). Conservative thinking in Britain included a reassertion of familistic values (Scruton, 1980; Mount, 1982), values which were to be heard repeated in various forms in a variety of public speeches and pronouncements.

The other version would be to argue that this period saw the re-entry of questions to do with marriage and the family into the public arena. These areas became the increasing focus of public and political concern, the subject of government or privately funded research and discussion and of the increasing pressure for some kind of family dimension to discussions of issues of social policy. While this politicisation of the family was often linked, as in the case of the book by Mount, to the reassertion of conservative values, the debate took place across a much wider spectrum of perspectives. Labour politicians, for example, were to be heard arguing the case for 'family impact statements' and the elaboration of a family perspective on social policy.

Both these sets of understandings would seem to be flawed although they are important not so much as indications of what 'really' has been happening but as signs of the ways in which certain sets of people are thinking about family matters. The first version (yet another variation on the 'swing of the pendulum' theme) seems to be flawed in that, firstly, it exaggerates the extent and impact of liberationary talk about the family in the 1960s and early 1970s and secondly, and consequently, overstates the degree of retreat since then. In spite of some public pronouncements, women are not yet retreating from the labour market into the home in large numbers, divorce rates are not going into reverse and feminism continues to publish and to provide sustained critiques of public and private practices. Throughout this period, the majority of people appeared to expect to get married and to have children and continued to value marriage and family life as expected and actual sources of happiness. It would be as dangerous to assert that nothing has changed as it would be to argue for major shifts in family values;[1] for the time being perhaps all that can be said is that marriage and the family remain central life interests for a large part of the population while, at the same time, feminism has proved to be much more than a passing craze.

The notion of the increasing politicisation of the family in the later 1970s has perhaps more to be said in its favour, although this too must be treated with some caution. Firstly, it must be qualified by stating that the family has never really been 'out' of politics; at the very least models of the family provided background understandings for the enactment and implementation of social policy. The family has always been a political unit and has often been recognised as such; what happened in the late 1970s was a particular conjunction of circumstances that lead to the re-recognition and the redefinition of this fact. And again, as I argued in Chapter 5, the notion of a 'public debate' about marriage and the family is a little misleading; 'public' today actually refers to a relatively small subset of politicians and professionals with particular kinds of involvements or investments in family matters.

Themes

Nevertheless, the theme of an increasing politicisation of the family in Britain in the 1980s is a useful point of departure and constituted the focus of the first part of the book. One central focus of this politicisation was on the rising divorce rates, seen by various parties as an index of other interpersonal, social and economic problems, or as a major barometer of wider patterns of social change, sometimes evaluated positively, in other cases seen as a symptom of more malignant social forces. In this first section I focused on the publication *Marriage Matters* as an example of this wider social and political concern, seeing it in terms not simply of an illustration of one kind of state intervention but also as a sign of a growing medicalisation of family and interpersonal life. I also examined the way in which this publication, the debate around it and similar publications, tended to cut out or obscure questions to do with inequalities in family life, inequalities stated in terms of class or of gender or both. The debate about divorce and its causes and consequences was seen as being socially constructed. This is not to say that the concern is somehow insincere or cynically manipulative, simply that it has particular social, economic and historical roots which cannot be explained simply in terms of some kind of automatic or natural response to the problems attendant upon the rise of divorce. The first part was, therefore, the examination of the construction of a public issue, the way in which a variety of family themes were woven together to produce one particular story, one particular set of understandings about our society and the place of one key institution within it.

The second part of this book would seem to be of a different order. Here I examine a variety of family themes as woven this time by academics or, at least, persons partially or wholly working within academic contexts. There was the relatively optimistic model of the changing patterns of marriage and the family presented by the Rapoports. There were the theoretical understandings, often derived from the clinical practice of therapists, to be found in systems theorising, understandings particularly focused on the family as a system in relation to its wider environment. There were the growing, if often hotly debated and controversial, contributions from family history of various kinds. There were the relatively new contributions from a set of perspectives which might be largely labelled as phenomenological and, finally, there were the range of perspectives,

264

under the critical label, largely Marxist and feminist.

What are the links between these two sections, the first dealing with the themes elaborated by practitioners and politicians, the latter dealing with the elaboration of theoretical themes within largely academic contexts? In the first place, it is possible to place some fairly direct links such as those between the committee that produced *Marriage Matters*, the Tavistock Institute, the Marital Research Unit, the Study Commission on the Family and the work of the Rapoports, the last link being particularly strong. Indeed, the Rapoports would have no hesitation in seeing their work as being one of essentially practical and applied importance. Family and marital therapy, in theory and practice, also influenced some parts of the general approach outlined in *Marriage Matters* and here too, the role of the Tavistock Institute may, in Britain at least, be of particular significance. Within family and marital therapy, systems theory may be seen as an important and growing influence. As far as the historical contribution to the political debate has been concerned, this may be somewhat less direct and twofold. A general historical understanding of a fairly diffuse kind (the main source would appear to be *The Symmetrical Family*) informs the opening section of *Marriage Matters* in its attempt to chart the shift in marriage from institution to relationship. And the subsequent debate around family issues has been increasingly, and often sharply, informed by historical material. The apparent relativising effect of much recent family history, the attempts to see marriage, family, sexuality and childhood as socio-historical constructions, was challenged by Ferdinand Mount in his *Subversive Family*, while a call by Margaret Thatcher for a return to 'Victorian values' was countered by attempts to show just what such values meant in terms of family and gender relationships (Davidoff and Hall, 1982). Family history is not always a disinterested, detached and scholarly enterprise.

While feminist works are scarcely mentioned in *Marriage Matters*, it is clear that the feminist critique of the family forms part of the backcloth against which much of the contemporary debate has taken place. The unspoken understanding went something like this: feminists have challenged the institutions of marriage and the family and this challenge has become increasingly influential. It is therefore necessary to make some

265

kind of a stand against these, and other, negative approaches to the family. Moreover, feminism has been, at least in part, responsible for the rising divorce rates. In a more moderate version, feminism might not be seen as a challenge to be resisted but certainly a force to be taken into account and a major causal factor in current confusions about marriage and the family.

Perhaps the joker in the theoretical pack is the phenomenological approach since, at its best, it seems capable of casting an ironic eye not simply on the everyday understandings deployed by family practitioners and associated political spokespersons but also on the understandings deployed by other theoretical schools or approaches. To have a debate, even a heated and sharply divided debate, about a particular issue is one thing; to call the very terms of reference of the debate into question is quite another.

Family theorising does not then take place in a social or economic vacuum. Some theoretical approaches derive directly and indirectly from actual practice (systems theory and some of the key notions of the Rapoports) while some therapeutic and political practices have, as we have seen, been influenced by theoretical themes. The themes which I shall attempt to explore in the remaining part of this book derive from points of interaction between theoretical and public concerns and also, at times, from more experiential considerations.

Before proceeding, it is worthwhile pausing to consider two preliminary issues. The first is to do with the relationships between the various themes and approaches that have been outlined in the second section. It should be stressed that what I have presented here are not paradigms in any strict sense of the word. This might be true of systems theorising but scarcely applies to the others. The Rapoports, while certain consistent thematic concerns emerge from their work, draw upon a variety of theoretical and research traditions. Family history encompasses a variety of theoretical perspectives, articulated or otherwise and, in common with the phenomenological and critical approaches, represents a broad clustering of themes rather than a distinctive paradigm. In other words, the boundaries of the approaches outlined here are already fairly indistinct and overlap is not simply possible but is already implied.

Nevertheless, it would be wrong to assume, simply because

these boundaries are already indistinct, that some grand synthesis is already possible or desirable. Arguments for such syntheses usually proceed from the metaphor of a set of unrelated persons attempting to describe some topographical feature such as a mountain or a large building from their own vantage points. (Or of a set of blind persons attempting to describe an elephant by feeling various parts of the body). The assumption is, clearly, that a combination of all these accounts would be more truthful than any one account taken singly. The metaphor falls down, however, in its assumption of a radical disjuncture between the set of describers and the object being described. Thus, although different people located at different parts around the Houses of Parliament would provide different descriptions of that building, the assumption is that it is the descriptions that are partial and that the building remains more or less the same and that any two observers occupying the same place would provide approximately the same description.[2] Things are far from being so simple when we move from the Houses of Parliament or Mount Everest to an institution such as 'the family', or 'social class'. Here, the persons viewing the institution do not simply have partial visions of the same object but also constitute that object through their particular perspectives.

A systems theorist and a feminist are not simply providing different accounts of the same object; they are also constituting such an object through their elaboration of their distinctive accounts. Indeed, in the case of some kinds of phenomenological perspectives, it is this business of constructing and constituting the family as a social institution that may be the central topic of enquiry and not the 'institution itself'. Thus any notion of synthesising or combining of accounts becomes, at the very least, a much more problematic operation.

It is for this reason that I find certain approaches to the family more helpful than others in that they do regard the object under investigation as having a problematic status, as being essentially socially constructed. Thus, I would prefer certain phenomenological, feminist and historical accounts to certain Marxist, positivist or systems-functionalist accounts. Yet, I should stress that I find all these accounts and perspectives to be of value. Not that they can be combined in any simple way but that a consideration of these different perspectives, a consideration that respects and maintains these differences rather than attempting to submerge them into one grand synthesis, enables a variety of questions about the family to emerge in sharper relief. Thus, a consideration of the systems and the phenomenological perspectives finds both these orientations wanting in their relatively scant appreciation of history and processes of change. The response to this is not, in any simple way, to 'add in' history or change but to consider, at least as a preliminary stage, what it means to ask that the family be considered in some historical perspective. Similarly some Marxist accounts may be found wanting in their scant appreciation of the experiential or the interpersonal interaction within the family. Again, these features cannot be simply added to a Marxist account; rather the whole issue of the relationships between the interior and the structural have to be considered in more detail. It is not, therefore, a question of submerging different perspectives in some wider whole but rather of considering the points of interaction and conflict between them, while retaining the distinctive, and often irreconcilable, character of these approaches.

The second question is one which has already been touched upon and is to do with the relationship between the extended and elaborated case study presented in the first section and the theoretical debates of the second section. It has already been suggested that there is considerable overlap between the two, that the 'public debate' outlined in the former was informed to some extent and in ways direct and indirect by the theoretical debates in the latter, and that the theoretical discussions arose and became elaborated within a particular political and economic context. The distinction between pure and applied scarcely holds here if indeed it holds anywhere. Nevertheless, the *rhetoric* of the pure/applied distinction holds considerable sway, with one side eschewing abstract speculation in favour of tackling real problems while the other side views the applied as involving compromise and incorporation and being politically or morally suspect. Rhetorically, the applied/pure distinction has considerable power, particularly in relation to the topic of the family. 'Practical' men and women seek to claim that they are speaking the language of ordinary people, that they are addressing themselves to everyday issues and to popular and widespread concerns, that they are articulating what everybody already knows since the family is a natural institution, part of all our everyday experiences. Feminists, Marxists, sociologists of various persuasion, academics and intellectuals can, in this context, be seen as reflecting a minority perspective, seeking to mystify what should be plain, to undermine what should be, if not sacred, at least central and fundamental.

The concept of ideology, troublesome though it is, does remind us that the articulations of practical men and women are as much theoretical constructions as are the articulations of academic specialists. The concept of ideology, in other words, tends to muddy the distinction between pure and applied, seeing them both as being two sides of the same discourse. For the time being it will be maintained that not only are there discernible and obvious links between the public debate and the various academic enterprises but that the affinities and overlaps exist at some deeper levels as well.

(I) QUESTIONS OF DEFINITION

Weber has been taken to task by some of his commentators for arguing that a definition (in this case of religion) should appear at the end or as a result of a process of enquiry rather than at its beginning (e.g. Robertson, 1969). How, it was asked, was it possible to embark on an enquiry if the object and boundaries of the enquiry were unknown at the outset? Yet if we regard definitions as indicating the range of uses to which a particular word is put in a particular society, if we regard these linguistic uses as not merely reflecting an underlying social reality but, in a sense, constituting that reality, then Weber was surely correct. To deploy the well-known distinction used in ethno-methodological writings, definitions should be topics of, rather than resources for, enquiry; or, at the very least, the two should be accorded equal importance.

This is not, of course, to say that we are thrashing about in the dark. We know (although how we come to know this may be itself an object of social enquiry) that the word 'family' has something to do with marriage and parenthood and that these two terms themselves have something to do with, respectively, the relationships between adults and the relationships between adults and children, these two sets of relationships being focused on something that may be called a home or a household.

In short, we know enough at the outset to direct us towards domestic and interpersonal relationships rather than, say, towards a relationship between professionals and clients.

We also know that this knowledge is, to some degree, shared with those who may be said to be belonging to the same society as ourselves, that words such as 'marriage' and 'family' are widely used by such persons and are used effortlessly, that is on the easy assumption that both hearer and speaker know what is being spoken about. Moreover, persons are commonly capable of a range of uses and may slip from one usage to another without having to warn the hearer of the shift:

'I've just got one of those family-sized packets of cornflakes. Well I thought we needed it since we've got the wife's family coming over for the Bank Holiday.'

Thus, in a particular society, we would expect to find a range of uses of these key terms and one of the tasks of the sociologist must be to make a systematic exploration of these usages. For example, we may adopt at the outset of our enquiry, the following definition of the family as a kind of signpost: 'a group of two or more persons related by blood, marriage or adoption and residing together' (US Dept of Commerce, 1973). We note that this is an official definition and we need, therefore, to enquire into the uses made of such an official definition and the reasons as to why it was thought necessary to provide such a definition. Later in our enquiry we might note a usage such as the following: 'We shall judge our policies by one simple test: do they make life better for the individuals and their families? (Mrs M. Thatcher, quoted in *The Guardian*, 31/12/83).[3] Clearly, the word is being used in a slightly different way here. The emphasis would seem to be on something that individuals have rather than on some kind of residence which is shared according to certain principles. There is, here, also a suggestion of the idea that there is some kind of distinction between individuals and families and that those persons subsumed under the latter term are in some sense not individuals. Any investigation into the usages of words, particular words such as 'family' and 'marriage' may expect to find such puzzles along the way.

I shall return to the question of definition, in true Weberian fashion, towards the conclusion of this enquiry. However, a couple of further points need to be stressed. One is to underline the fact that the word is mostly used without definition and in such a way as to imply that no such definition is required. It is part of 'what everybody knows'. Secondly, it would appear that there is a distinction between abstract and explicit uses of the word (where definitions may sometimes be felt to be required) and concrete, specific and implied uses of the word. For the most part again, the latter sets of uses are preferred or more common than the former; people are more inclined to talk about 'my family' or 'the family' than 'The Family'. Nevertheless, we would expect to find some interesting and complex connections between the two sets of usages.

(II) VARIETIES AND TYPES OF FAMILIES

Sociologists are increasingly likely to give recognition to the variety of patterns of family living to be found within a society such as contemporary Britain. Yet theoretical writings may still talk of 'the family in capitalist society' or 'the family in industrial society' and historical studies may still seek or claim to study the 'rise of the modern family'. Certainly, it would seem to be possible to add all kinds of qualifiers to the word family in order to stress differences and variety: working-class, extended, one-parent, Sikh, problem, poor, large and so on, and each of these subdivisions may be further divided to provide a bewildering variety of types. It is clear that this kind of enterprise (best illustrated in the collection edited by Rapoport, Fogarty and Rapoport, *Families in Britain*, 1982) is of a descriptive rather than a theoretical nature and that the aim is not to provide some particularly rigorous taxonomy. For one thing, many of the bases of classification may overlap, to provide, perhaps, further subdivisions; thus poor families are usually also working-class families and may sometimes, although not always, be large families. Others may adopt more theoretical distinctions, distinctions which may be based upon the author's own understandings and practices. For example, Jordan, speaking as a social worker, elaborates a distinction between two types of family, the integrative and the centrifugal (Jordan, 1972, pp. 23–54). A more complex classification, but along the same lines, is provided by Kantor and Lehr (see Chapter 7).

The differences between those who see diversity and those who see unity may be accounted for in a variety of ways. Firstly, it may be argued that it is a question of the point of view of the observer and the distance of the observer from the observed. Seen close up, the 'family in Britain' may dissolve into a bewildering variety of types so that there is no such thing as the British family (see Laslett in Rapoport *et al.*, 1982, p. xii). Yet others, standing back a little further and taking a broader historical or comparative sweep may talk about the distinctive features of the British (or European, or Western) family in which even the apparent variety may be seen as one of its distinctive features. Yet others, standing back even further, may see even the Western family as but a slight variation on a much more general family theme.

We may, therefore, suggest that the differences may be in terms of the project of the investigator. The difference may be likened to the town-dweller who sees a field of brown and white cows and the farmer who, it is alleged, knows each one by name. Yet, there is more at stake than this. Particular kinds of theoretical project would seem to imply a strain towards emphasising the similarities and in minimising the differences. Freudians may differ among themselves as to the role that may be attributed to culture in their understanding of the family, but would all tend towards seeking to unravel a variety of family themes and processes which are relatively, if not absolutely, culture-free. The same would be true, by implication at least, of systems theorists, who may again be aware of differences (as in Kantor and Lehr) but would tend not to see such differences as being historically or culturally constructed. Marxists and some feminists would tend towards emphasising the distinctive features of the family within a particular social formation, relating such variation of family types as may be discovered to different historical epochs.

In the widest sense, these differences in perspective are also political. It has been suggested that the pluralism of the Rapoports and of most of the productions of the Study Commission on the Family reflects a general liberal political stance, one associated with notions of freedom of choice, self-determination and so on. In this they would be joined by some feminists with the central qualification that this variety of types (or modes of domestic and personal living) has yet to be fully realised, that it constitutes a goal to be sought after rather than something that is actually achieved. Conservatives and some Marxists would argue for a more unified understanding of the family, although from radically different viewpoints.

What can be said about these two quite distinctive ways of seeing the family in contemporary society, the one emphasising variety and difference, the other emphasising similarities and structural unities? Again, it would not be desirable to strive for some facile synthesis. In the first place, it may be possible to discover that the two kinds of approaches are not talking about the same thing; a theoretical object is not the same thing as an empirical object and the relationships between them are often complex and sometimes obscure. Or, more simply, the differences may hinge around something fairly straightforward such as the distinction between household and family. The distinctions made by the Rapoports *et al.* tend to be more to do with the former while Freudians, say, may be more concerned with familial relationships, that is relationships that may often straddle different households. Or, yet again, the differences may be to do with the differences between a range of actually living practices on the one hand, and ideological or popular constructions on the other. Clearly, part of the task of the sociologist would be to attempt to unravel these distinctive and various ways of understanding the family to discover what, if any, principles lie behind these differences.

It may be noted that most of these differences about the nature of the family and the range of possible variations are differences between sociologists or others professionally involved in the study of the family. Little has been said, or indeed is known, about the range of understandings that people as a whole have of the family. Since, to the best of my knowledge, this kind of undertaking has not yet been conducted, I can only speculate on some of the differences that such an investigation might reveal:

(a) It is likely that people will make some kinds of distinctions upon the basis of generation, between then and now. These distinctions may approximate to sociological distinctions between extended and nucleated, often with some kind of positive moral evaluation in favour of the former. Other kinds of lay distinctions, focusing largely upon generations, may point to differences between 'authoritarian' and 'domestic' although here with a more uncertain and ambiguous moral evaluation.

(b) It is possible that people may use distinctions based upon class or region. It is certain that they will use some kind of variation upon the 'rough' and 'respectable' theme where it is interesting to note that the evaluation is often of families as a whole rather than of individuals. 'Rough' families (with close kinship with 'problem families') tend not to be able to keep their children under control, tend to quarrel noisily among themselves, tend to show all the outward signs of lack of care and so on. Bearing in mind that these distinctions often have their mythological character ('rough' families are always elsewhere, in another estate or on the other side of the street), these are distinctions which are routinely used but which also have some affinities with more professional classifications.

Generally, one may expect to find a considerable desire to stress uniqueness and individuality in family living. Families, it would seem, often like to describe themselves as slightly 'mad', as not quite like other people. Not rough, certainly, but not quite respectable either. At another level, however, the same people will probably see underlying unities and similarities. It is highly likely that the two sets of images, one of diversity and one of similarity and unity, may roughly be equally available to people, to be deployed in different ways as circumstances demand. But, as yet, we do not know this, neither do we know much about the way in which people use these different understandings.

It should be noted, in conclusion, that there is a two-way relationship between this discussion about variety versus unity and the questions of definition. This is inevitable. To substitute the term 'families' for 'family' (as in *Families in Britain*) is still to maintain some, perhaps changed or expanded, notion of what 'family' is, of what all these different varieties have in common. Recognition of, and publicity for, the varieties of patterns of domestic living have an effect on the process of definitions (consider the growing recognition of co-habitation for the definition of marriage) just as definitions seek to put limits around the range of activities that can reasonably be described as 'family' or 'familistic'.

(III) THE PERSONAL AND THE STRUCTURAL

One of the key issues of sociological theory is the establishment of relationships between various levels of analysis, specifically the relationships between the personal and/or interpersonal at one level and the social/structural at the other. The problem has been formulated in a variety of ways, some of which will be explored later in this section, but it can be seen that this debate has a particular applicability with relation to the family. Indeed, it may be argued that the family is not only an interesting or special case in the attempts to relate the interpersonal and the structural but that it is the institution in society which is centrally concerned with these interconnections.

In order to approach this question more closely, I shall attempt to analyse it in the form of a set of questions, somewhat in the style of Merton's treatment of functionalism (Merton, 1957, pp. 19–84). Such a project, while it may not necessarily provide any firm conclusions, at least draws attention to some of the ambiguities in existing formulations.

A What is being related?

1 The macro and the micro The distinction between the macro and the micro is one that runs through a variety of branches of the social sciences, but particularly economics and sociology. In the latter, under the heading of the 'macro' we would include comparative analyses of societies, studies of social change and studies of organisations. Under the latter would be included social psychological studies of small groups, studies of interpersonal interaction and conversations. In part the distinction is related to methods of study. Macro-sociology would seem to be more amenable to large-scale surveys, to historical analysis and to the use of official statistics. Micro-sociology would seem to be the sphere of small group experiments, various kinds of observation and in-depth interviewing. There is not a clear fit between methods of study and the macro/micro distinction, however; there can be historical investigations of the personal and the interpersonal (a recent and important development) while there may be in-depth surveys about large-scale issues. In any event, the boundaries between the macro and the micro tend to be unclear and the study of the family is not alone in

275

falling into either or both of these camps; the studies of deviance and of religion, for example, may be similarly understood.

Moreover, there is a certain ambiguity in the macro/micro distinction in that it can be either based upon numerical size or upon some kind of distinction that draws upon the difference between compound and simple. Macro structures may be large and/or compound while micro structures may be small and/or simple. ('Small' and 'large' are, of course, themselves highly variable categories although we may be on slightly firmer ground if we confine the former term to all those structures which have the formal properties of 'small groups' as understood by social psychologists.) Households, therefore, would be small but most likely also compound structures since there are major lines of cleavage on the basis of age and gender. Families may be large or small and also compound. This underlines the point that 'families' do not fit easily into the macro-micro distinction.

2 *Society and the individual* The distinction between the macro and the micro indicates two different spheres and perhaps kinds of social enquiry but both these kinds of enquiry attend to the distinction between the society and the individual. As Lukes and others have shown (Lukes, 1968) the nature of this distinction is far from clear and it must be stressed that this is a theoretical distinction not one that is unambiguously rooted in common-sense understandings of the world. To start with the individual, this is apparently the simpler of the two elements of the opposition but a little reflection may show that this is not so. This individual may be understood as a system of biological processes, of psychological processes, as a moral entity or as the sum total of a complex set of interactions with other individuals. How we understand the other term in the opposition, 'society', depends very much on how we understand the term 'individual'. If we understand individuals in biological or psychological terms, then society will be seen as a collectivity arising out of the attempts by individuals to realise biologically or psychologically based needs. The more specifically sociological approach, however, would tend to see the individual and the society as two sides of the same coin or as two moments in a single process. Society and social processes arise out of the interaction of individuals; individuals arise out of social processes and their goals, desires, feelings and values are the

product of the society in which they live and have been socialised. Neither should be seen as prior; the relationship is understood to be a dialectical one of mutual influence and causation.

Sociologically, therefore, the term 'individual' at one level is relatively straightforward and accords with, in our society, common-sense understandings of the term. Individuals are more or less those individuals that we see and know: me, you, the person next door, the person delivering the milk, the line of persons at the bus stop. Sociology may depart from the common sense when it comes to explain or understand these individuals but the entities so designated are roughly the same in both cases. Society, however, is a much more problematic designation. When I use the phrase 'in our society', as I did above, I am referring to a whole range of overlapping entities: a political unit variously described as Great Britain, the British Isles, the United Kingdom and so on; societies similar in terms of economy, political system and so on to the United Kingdom; societies where the main language is English; a society which I share with those who are my assumed readers and so on. Generally speaking, the term 'society' is a theoretical abstraction but one which is normally taken to indicate the nation state in which the enquiry is located unless the author takes pains to say otherwise.[4]

If the answer to the question 'what are being related?' is 'the individual and the society' therefore, then the way in which these entities are understood as well as the relationships between them will depend upon whether the approach being adopted is primarily psychological, socio-biological, sociological, political or moral. Both terms carry a considerable degree of complexity and have a particularly complex and tortuous history. If we are concerned with locating the family within this kind of distinction, then we would put it somewhere 'in between', although the exploration of what this may actually mean will be deferred until later.

3 The institutional and the personal This opposition is similar to the last one, although it raises further issues. To take the first term, the institutional might possibly be replaced by the term 'the structural' although they are not strictly equivalent. However, what the terms seek to convey are similar: something that is larger, less immediate, often less physically tangible

277

than the personal and yet something that persists over time, something that may indeed outlast the personal. Institutions may refer to particular and identifiable organisational structures such as the DHSS or the TUC or they may be more theoretical abstractions such as 'the working class' or 'the family'.

The personal, on the other hand, deals with the immediate experiential world of individuals. Raw experience, if there be such a thing, is a small part of this; the experience we are concerned with here is mediated, thought over, interpreted by the individual actor concerned. We are, therefore, not so much concerned with individual feelings of physical pain but with more complex feelings of alienation, attachment, identification and hostility. These experiences, although located in individuals, may be shared and may, indeed, derive their status as experience through their being shared. (This might be seen as one of the functions of consciousness-raising.) The personal is, therefore, located in individuals; it is more immediate and experiential.

Note that the definitions of these terms and of the relationships between them is very much bound up with a moral and political critique. The personal is often seen in opposition to the institutional, sometimes to the detriment of the former when the latter is identified with rationality and objectivity but more often to the detriment of the latter when it is identified with alienation, lack of praxis, remoteness and bad faith. The institutional, in short, is often seen to stand *against* the personal and much of the politics of recent years may be seen as an attempt to upgrade the personal, to deny rationality's attempt to place it at the margins. Nevertheless, a moral evaluation need not be a central part of an analytical use of these terms since institutions or structures may be seen as a necessary part of the human project, only becoming alienated under certain sets of circumstances. The family, again, may come on either side of the divide. In conventional sociological terminology, the family is a social institution in that it outlives particular sets of experiences and can be understood, theoretically at least, as apart or distinct from any individual manifestations. Yet the family is also experienced and in some ways may be seen to be the particular location of the personal. This identification of the family with the personal is, as we have seen, the outcome of a complex set of social and historical processes. Moreover, the family as an institution, as a structured set of expectations, roles, practices and statuses, may be seen as standing against the experiences located in the personal. This is a way in which the family is seen within various critical traditions. Hence, the location of the family within this particular opposition is again ambiguous and depends upon a set of prior choices and orientations.

4 Public issues and private troubles This particular opposition, of course, derives from one author, C.W. Mills (1959). As an opposition and as a statement of the sociological project it has been particularly influential and consequently deserves a separate mention. The example that Mills provides stems in part from Durkheim's distinction between the suicide rate and individual acts of suicide. In Mills's case he chooses unemployment and divorce as his illustrations. In all three cases there are distinctions to be made between suicide, unemployment and divorce as sets of statistics which may vary from year to year or between societies and as issues that are the subject of public debate and the actual experience of the suicide of a friend, of one's own experience of being made redundant and one's own divorce. Mills sees the distinction between the two as itself a social and historical construction and regards the sociological task as one of restoring a sense of a flow of understanding between the two levels.

Mills already provides an example of one family-based process – divorce – and shows that it can appear on either side of the divide. We can speak of divorce as a set of statistics, as a prognostication (one in three marriages will end in divorce) or as a problem with all kinds of social and economic consequences. We may also view it experientially, as my divorce or the divorce of my friend, my sense of loss and separation, my problems of readjustment and reorientation. Family and family matters are, therefore, in Mills's terms, both public issues and private troubles.

There are, no doubt, various other similar oppositions that can be made. Nevertheless, the oppositions, although different, do have something in common, in that at the very least, the second term is included in the first term and that, metaphorically and sometimes actually speaking, it is 'smaller' than the first term. While not seeking to obscure the real differences between these oppositions nor the contradictions and ambiguities involved in the use of any one of them we may continue with the analysis by taking them all together. Since we see all the terms as being some aspect of the social, let us assign the capital S to all the terms on the left-hand side and the small s to the other terms on the right-hand side:

S	s
Macro	Micro
Society	Individual
Institutional	Personal
Public Issues	Private Troubles

B How are they related?

1 S determines s Determines, as Williams has noted (Williams, 1980, pp. 31–2) is an ambiguous term, conveying both the idea of setting limits and the idea of causing. Nevertheless, one set of ways in which these two groups of terms are related is to see s as dependent upon, secondary to, derivative from S. This may be qualified in all kinds of ways, 'in the last instance', 'ultimately', 'in the final analysis' and so on, but the direction of the relationship is from S to s. We may see this in some versions of Marxism and feminism, most versions of systems theorising and in the traditional version of functionalism.

2 S arises out of s This is both a moral and a methodological claim. Here, priority is given to all the items on the right-hand side, the s's, and S is seen in various ways as deriving from them. In practice, some versions of phenomenological sociology, some recent historical approaches, together with some versions of feminist analysis would seem to locate themselves in this area. In terms of the family the emphasis would be on family members' continuous work in constructing their family worlds, in processes of elaboration and innovation in family and domestic living and upon the varieties of family living that are possible and that exist. This would be opposed to analyses in the first category which would emphasise features such as the family and marriage as institutions, ideology and ideological apparatuses and other kinds of economic or social constraints.

3 S and s are mutually related The main direction of socio-logical analysis, it would seem, would be towards giving priority to neither side but to emphasise the continuous and dialectical relationship between them. The clearest statements of this process would be found in the various writings of Berger but the idea of a dialectic between the two is more or less a sociological commonplace. This can only strictly apply to the last three elements, since the macro-micro distinction does tend to be of a somewhat different order. In terms of family living, then, the emphasis would be to see both the constraints and the strategies that family members adopt in dealing with these constraints and, in so doing, in elaborating new or personal styles of family living.

4 S and s are two sides of the same coin

(a) Any aspect of social life may be examined from either side, the one emphasising the macro, the structural, the public and so on with the other emphasising the micro, the individual and the personal. Thus, the family may be seen as a set of experiences, as a collection of interacting individuals or as a source of private troubles; or it may be seen as an institution, socially and historically structured, and as a public issue. The choice is one of theoretical orientation or perhaps of moral or political choice.

(b) A version of this is the Russian dolls model, In Parsonian structuralism and systems theorising, systems may be seen as nesting inside each other. In the case of the family it is, again, a matter of choice whether you seek to emphasise the relationships between the family as a subsystem of some wider system or whether you move into its interior and see the family as being composed of a set of personality subsystems. A full analysis should, of course, proceed in both directions.

C Where does the family stand?

In terms of the distinctions already made, the family may be located at various theoretical positions.

1 At S The family may be seen as a social institution and may be understood in institutional or structural terms. Clearly, this can only apply for some of the oppositions listed, particularly the institutional and/or the public.

2 *At s* The family may be located on the right-hand side, closer to the personal and the experiential, if not exactly the same as the individual. It may clearly, at least in one sense, be seen as a micro-social structure.

3 *The family may be seen as a mediator between S and s; more actually it may be located somewhere between them* Again, this applies most fully with reference to the second of our distinctions, that between the individual and society, or it may also apply to some versions of the macro/micro distinction.

4 *The family belongs to both sides* The family can be seen as looking both ways, at society and at the individual, at the institutional and the structural and at the personal and the private. To anticipate later discussions, the family may be seen as uniquely or specially placed in this respect.

Of these last two positionings of the family within society as a whole, it is the former which has the more established theoretical pedigree. The notion of the family as being in some way placed betwen the macro and the micro, the societal and the individual, the institutional and the personal and between the public and the private is an idea that runs through, with varying degrees of explicitness, a variety of theoretical traditions. In Parsonian functionalism, the family looks outward to the wider social system and inward to the individual personality systems, a picture largely reinforced to some degree by more recent systems theorising. In a variety of accounts, the family/household is seen as the major agency of social placement, the link between the individual and the system of social stratification. In more explicitly Marxist accounts, the family stands between the subject and the wider social formation. Althusser's notion of the family as an ideological state apparatus, working hand in hand with either the Church or the school may serve as an example here (Althusser, 1971).

Perhaps the most common term that is used to place the family in this kind of discussion is to describe the family as a 'mediator'. This term implies that not only does the family stand at some point between the spheres indicated by S and s but that it also does some active work in this location. Thus, to return to the most common opposition, that between the individual and society, the family may be seen not simply in terms of preparing individuals to take their place in society but also, to some extent, of shaping, or organising, that very society in which these individuals are to take their place. Socialisation, in other words, is not simply a question of preparing individuals to fit certain available slots in the 'outside world' but also of presenting that outside world to the individual, of telling the individual what that world is about. This may happen when a mother switches off the television set prior to the broadcasting of some unsuitable material or when parents seek to limit their children's set of friends, perhaps upon some implicit set of understandings about the rough and the respectable. It happens in relation to gender, and the gender order in society, when a daughter finds more stringent expectations being applied to her domestic responsibilities than is the case with her brother, a sense that is reinforced when she finds similar differences in relation to time keeping and staying out late.

The notion of the family as occupying an active space between the individual and society (etc.) is a useful one and one that may give rise to a whole range of possible metaphors: the family as amplifier, the family as transformer and so on. Any of these metaphors at least takes us away from the notion of the family as a relatively passive dependent variable, doing the tasks that society assigns to it. The family is accorded some relative autonomy and some importance as, in some respects, an independent variable in its own right. It points to a need, as some systems theorists have reminded us, to look at the complex internal processes of the family system not simply as something that is of interest in its own right and not simply as something that may help us understand individual psychologies but as something that must be understood in order to understand wider social processes. Thus, it is commonplace that unemployment or disablement do not simply affect an individual but have reverberations throughout the family and household of which that individual may be a part. Moreover, the nature of these repercussions are not ones that automatically follow from a reduction of income but are shaped by the structure of relationships (roles, statuses, expectations, etc.) that already exist within the family or household. Thus, we need to ask not simply what is the effect of unemployment upon the family but what is the effect of the family on unemployment.

Associated with this is the idea of the family as a linking or connecting mechanism, as an institution that brings together a variety of unrelated themes and issues and transmutes them in a variety of complex ways. A writer on family and ethics in the beginning of this century wrote: 'Every pressing social problem is seen to be conditioned by the family, and to act and react on the family. . . .' (Lofthouse, 1912, p. 2.) It was, of course, considerations such as these that have led more recent commentators to call for a family dimension to social policy. If we are still considering the social topographical location of the family it may not be enough, therefore, to see the family as being located on some vertical dimension between the individual and society but we also need to place that family on some horizontal or lateral space, between different institutions, problem areas or whatever.

This emphasis, whatever the chosen metaphor, on the active role of the family is surely to be welcomed. However, the attempt to locate the family in this way – as in some way being 'between' various points – has its own difficulties. For one thing it has the effect of reifying or fixing the various oppositions already mentioned, especially perhaps that between the individual and the society. The spatial metaphor, while useful in some respects, may also – as is the danger with all such metaphors – serve to obscure our understanding. Thus, we might be confronted by a sharp opposition posited between the individual and the society with the family located, as some thing-like object, somewhere between these two points. The same might also be said for some of the other oppositions that have been considered.

In the second place, these modes of thought do tend towards the adoption of a largely male-orientated perspective on social processes. The functions that the family might be said to perform (in a Marxist or more traditionally functionalist version), the effects that the family might be said to have are all, to a very large extent, the effects upon men. The use of another implied distinction in this discussion between 'inner' and 'outer' underlines this; in a wide range of psychological, anthropological and sociological writings, women are allocated to the inner sphere where men are to be seen as occupying the outer sphere. Put another way, the individual in the individual/society opposition more often than not turns out to be of the male gender. This male moves through and to and from the family in society (outer, public) while the woman remains in the inner, private sphere of the family/household. Perhaps this is not a necessary implication of the treatment of the family as a mediator but it is one which exists as an ever-present danger in this line of analysis.

For these reasons, I prefer the alternative formulation of the 'place' of the family in social space, not simply as lying between S and s but as being both of these at the same time. In short, the family is both societal and individual, both institutional and personal, both public and private. This understanding of the double-edged character of the family and household was probably easier to appreciate in societies somewhat simpler than our own where, say, to be head of the household was also to occupy a wider political status and where family and lineage were major or central mechanisms of social placement. However, if we have some difficulty in appreciating the two-edged character of family life in our own society, this is itself a fact of some importance, one which derives in no small measure from the particular social and historical circumstances in which we live. The same considerations apply whether there is a tendency (say among family therapists) to locate the family almost entirely in the personal or interpersonal sphere or (say among Marxists) whether there is an opposite tendency to locate the family almost entirely in the institutional sphere. In both cases the dialectic is lost. The processes by which this has come about are themselves open to historical investigation.

Thus an approach which sees the family as being both institutional and personal at the same time has a variety of advantages over alternative understandings. In the first place, it moves away from too stark an opposition between the two elements (indicated by S and s in my discussion) towards an approach which sees the two in constant interplay. In the second place, it tends to avoid a reification of the family since, in this discussion, it can be argued that the very terms which are used in the analysis – 'family', 'marriage', 'parenthood' – themselves have a history, a socially constructed character and that terms such as 'mother' and 'father', 'husband' and 'wife' are both at one and the same time institutional and individual. Finally, this formulation may help us to remove some of the sources of gender bias built into alternative formulations. Women, no less than men, have a societal as well as an individual or personal face even if, ideologically, this understanding may be obscured or denied in our society. For these reasons, therefore, I prefer this two-edged formulation of the location of the family in social space. However, it may be argued that this kind of argument would apply to a whole range of institutions, and not simply the family. Indeed, following Durkheim, we might argue that people themselves present this two-edged character. Whether or not there is something particular or peculiar about the family in this respect will be deferred until later.

(IV) A QUESTION OF TIME

I have, up to this point, sought to discuss the location of the family in social space. However, this discussion has sidestepped the complex issues of the temporal location of the family, the recognition that we are dealing with time as well as with space. Indeed, many of the terms which we have already used in discussing the place of the family in social space have a built-in time dimension to them. Questions of socialisation and reproduction are indeed meaningless if we fail to appreciate that we are talking about the continuity of individual, family and society over time.

The fact that the family has a built-in time dimension is one which is both obvious and ignored: 'many institutions exist over time, as do many social relations, but families are partly composed of relations *across* time' (Fitz and Hood-Williams, 1982, p. 72). The contrast may be highlighted by considering two other kinds of social situations, a friendship and a professional body. A friendship is something that persists over time, but is terminated by either the death of one of the parties or the break up of the relationship for some other reason. The relationship, although it lasts over a period of time, is not in our society transferable. A professional body is not only much larger but has an organisation that enables it to persist over time, in spite of the death of all the original members or in spite of a complex turnover of all the committee members. The chairs remain the same even if the individuals occupying them change at regular intervals.

The notion of an institution persisting across time is different from both of these two examples. It implies, firstly, that there are clear points of demarcation called 'generations' (such generations can only exist in a metaphorical sense in professional organisations) and various rules by which generations may be said to succeed each other. In other words, there are rules about the transmission of property, rights and duties, family names and so on across generations.

One particular way in which attempts have been made to capture the temporal dimension involved in the family is through various notions of the family life cycle (see, e.g. Cuisenier, 1977). We have come across this idea at various points in the previous discussion in, for example, the account of the work of the Rapoports and in the chapter on historical approaches where the life cycle approach was contrasted with the life course approach. There is considerable variation within the 'life cycle' approach in, for example, the number of stages which are adopted for different models.

There are several points to be noted about these models. In the first place, the focus is usually upon the household, rather than the family, or to be precise and somewhat clumsier, 'the elementary family as the basis for a household'. Secondly, the cycle is made up of a combination of factors. These include:

1 Classical 'life crises' around marriage, birth and death.
2 Biological ageing (of both parents and children).
3 Turning points, related to outside agencies. Here this is chiefly schooling, although other models might also include something to do with retirement age.

Thirdly, it will be apparent that, complex though these models are, they represent a considerable simplification of reality. Even ignoring the increasing possibility of divorce and separation which gives rise to a variety of domestic trajectories, the models presented here and elsewhere represent a considerable smoothing of the family processes. Thus, in practice, there will be considerable overlapping of some of the stages, particularly in relation to children where small children will overlap with school-age children and school-age children may overlap with post-parental phases in relation to at least one other child. It may also be seen that various possibly important turning points are missing from the models. Many such models fail to take account of starting work or retirement and some fail to incorporate the death of one of the spouses in the final stages of a cycle.

Whether such models take us much beyond Shakespeare is doubtful. What they all have in common is that they are theoretical models constructed by the analyst for a variety of purposes. Whether or not they accord with the way in which family life is actually experienced is open to question. These models provide a quasi-naturalistic model of family processes; since some of the events so recorded are key events in the lives of most individuals in the lives of most societies, it is easy to suppose that what we have here is some natural growth and decay model rather than a social construction or, as Goode notes, a 'narrative device' (in Cuisenier (ed.), 1977, p. 61).

In any event, family life cycles only represent part of the story and this is where the 'life course' approach represents an exciting set of potentialities. In the first place we can concentrate on the individual in a life career from birth to death. In other words we are dealing (in industrial society) with a bundle of careers based upon family, occupation and work and education with age as a thread around which all these (and possibly other) careers are woven. In the second place we have the life cycle of the elementary family beginning with marriage and ending either with the death of both spouses or with divorce and separation. And finally we have the household life cycle, which is based upon the residential unit. This last one is the most complex, although potentially fascinating, and is rarely used, although it is to some extent compounded with the elementary family life cycle.

What we have up to now is a model of time and process based upon one particular unit, whether that unit is an individual, a family or a household. We have not yet captured the sense of relationships across time, referred to earlier. Here, as we stated, the basic unit is the generation and the central concern is the overlap of generations, both within the same household and outside and between different households. We are concerned with a whole range of features in these relationships between generations: transmission of property and wealth; the passing on of the family name; the passing on of family themes and stories; and the more unconscious psychoanalytical processes analysed by Freud and others. We are here concerned also with questions of reproduction and socialisation. At this point we begin to see the links between individual life careers, family and household life cycles and history and social change.

At this point we are dealing with a complex process of overlap between two senses of the term 'generation'. In the first sense, the term is used in an egocentric way, that is it is based upon a particular individual and that individual's relationships to generations before and after. Seen as life careers and family life cycles these necessarily overlap with other individual's generations. In the second sense, we have something which is more akin to cohort and refers to links across and between families as much as to links within families. Indeed, members of the same generation in the first sense may be members of different generations in a cohort sense. Generations in this second sense are never naturally bounded and are shaped by particular historical experiences (Shils, 1981, p. 35). In some cases, these generations may have names such as 'the post-war generation', 'flower-power generation' and so on. They necessarily refer to constructed and worked and reworked versions of history that are shared by persons across families but, as experiences, are transmitted through families over generations in the first, familial sense of the word. In this way, in relatively stable sectors of society or communities, class cultures are kept alive and social identities are reproduced. In more complex or fluid societies the work must also be done by specialised institutions such as schools or the media, although here too, these are often filtered through familial settings. In Shils's words:

> The first link in the chain which binds past and present and future into the structure of a society is reforged every time an infant is born and survives. (Shils, 1981, p. 169)

We see now the particular theoretical importance of the family. Not only does the family exist at the interface between the individual and society but it also establishes links over time, not simply links between and across family generations, but also links that constitute the continuity of society itself. Time is built into the nature of the family just as it is built into the notion of society itself, and the important question is the way in which societies handle the inter-relationships between the two.

Themes

In passing, we may note one possible deep reason for the concern over the rising divorce rate discussed in an earlier chapter. A stable society, of the kind elaborated in the utopian models of functionalists and which may have existed in other times and at other places, has a relatively orderly relationship between the generations in the two senses of the word, that is between family life cycles and historical experience. Values, skills and experiences may be transmitted in a relatively orderly way. In a society where divorce and marital breakdown is becoming part of the common experience and where (unlike other societies characterised by high divorce rates) there are not any clearly established rules for reordering generational relationships following divorce, this apparently unproblematic relationship between generations in the two senses of the word is shattered. This is not to say that divorce is itself and alone the cause of these sets of problems. Divorce rates are but part of a whole range of other problems to do with social continuity and discontinuity such as war, technological change and social and geographical mobility. Divorce may indeed be a potent symbol of this concern about discontinuity rather than its cause.

(A note on *events*. Speculation as to what are the basic units of society have continued since the beginnings of sociology and have revolved around a choice between the individual or the collectivity, however these entities are understood. One possible further candidate for consideration as a basic unit is 'the event', here chosen because unlike the others it has an explicitly built-in time factor. We need to take into account the way in which the family constructs events and, in so doing, constructs itself. Family events are, therefore, a major feature of family themes. The scope for classification is immense; here is just a preliminary listing:

1 Anthropological life crises (births, marriages and deaths).
2 Regular events which are ceremonialised (birthday, anniversaries).
3 Other regular or near regular events (holidays).
4 Turning points in the careers of individual family members (first day at school, graduation, retirement).
5 National or religious ceremonies which have, in part at least, a family base (Christmas, Thanksgiving)
6 Events perceived as crises (sudden illness or accidents; affairs, desertions; trouble with the police) and so on.

Conclusion

The stuff of family life, and of life elsewhere for that matter, is made up of events and it would be well to consider them as possible candidates as the building blocks of family and society, combining as they do groupings larger than the single individual and based upon a temporal and a phenomenological dimension.)

(V) PECULIARITIES OF THE FAMILY

Any discussion around the so-called 'functions of the family' quickly comes up against the question of functional alternatives. Thus to what extent are any of the assumed functions of the family necessarily linked to that particular institution, or how far is it possible that they might be performed by other institutions? In other words, how far are we confronted with a confusion between functions which may be necessary for individuals or societies and a particular institution which might be conveniently placed to perform these functions but which is not of itself a necessity? (See Morgan, 1975, pp. 17–59 for further discussion.) In talking about the family at the interface between individual and society and the family as a key link in temporal sequences, how far am I committing the same error, of elevating what happens to be the case into what must be so?

Traditionally, the question has been resolved by the assertion that the family is in some ways a basic institution, one which is found in all kinds of societies and historical periods and one which is fundamental for society. Such assertions are by no means absent in more recent times; Berger and Berger, for example, maintain that the family is 'the leading candidate for the status of basic institution in human society' (Berger and Berger, 1983, p. 3). To many this is bound up with the idea of child-care and socialisation

> Socialisation and child care, then, are not only important functions which the family performs, they must be considered as the *definitive* elements of the family. (V. Gecas in Nye et al., 1976, p. 33)

And certainly, contemporary socialists and feminists need to ask, and are beginning to ask, why it is that individuals continue to be so attached both to their particular families and to the idea of the family. We are surely dealing with something a little more fundamental than ideological indoctrination, even if we take this in its widest possible sense (Barrett and McIntosh, 1982, pp. 100–1).

Berger and Berger, although they argue for the basic character of the family, would not argue thus on the simple grounds of biology. They, like most other sociological writers on the family, would argue for its socially constructed nature as against any naturalistic interpretation. When we claim that the family is socially constructed we are in fact presenting a variety of inter-related arguments. It is being claimed that the particular way in which questions of child care, socialisation and sexuality are handled vary between societies and are related to the history, culture and economy of the society under consideration. It is being claimed that the boundaries of the family, what constitutes a family and who are to count as family members, are not given but are the product of the work of individuals operating within a particular social and cultural context. And it is being claimed that the particular meanings, cognitive, emotive and evaluative, that are attached to the words 'family', 'marriage' and 'parent' themselves have identifiable histories and are, like the familial boundaries, sustained by on-going activities of the 'family members'. To argue thus is to in some way commit oneself to a phenomenological project, although one which is informed by historical and structural analysis and which has critical consequences. To speak of the family as being socially constructed is not to trivialise it nor is it to minimise its importance either to society or to individuals.

It is in the full recognition of the socially constructed nature of the family and all the overlapping implications that this formulation has that I argue for the peculiar importance of the family in both the area of relating society and the individual and in dealing with society in its temporal dimension. In the first case, I argued that I preferred to see the family as showing both sides, the individual and the societal rather than treating it as a mediator between two hypothesised entities, the individual and the society. Clearly it is both possible and necessary to say the same of most other social institutions with which we may be concerned: schools, factories, churches, etc. In this case, how-ever, the family (as socially constructed) does have certain peculiar features. In the first place, and after making all the necessary qualifications, it is the family which is particularly concerned with socialisation and reproduction. In other words it does have a particular concern about the relationships between individuals and the particular social formation in which these individuals are born which cannot be said to the same degree of other institutions.

One necessary qualification that does need spelling out is that by family in this context and in this society I imply, to a very large extent, women. This leads to the second crucial feature of the family as an institution with a two-faced character. The family is a central institution for the regulation of the gender order in society and for the articulation of that order with other features of the social structure, such as social stratification. Again, we may point to all other institutions where this is true as well – labour markets and educational institutions – but the difference is both one of degree and of intensity of focus.

Thirdly, the family has a feature which renders it particularly distinctive in our society and that is in terms of the intensity of its interaction between members, particularly between parent (mother) and child but also often between adults. In earlier chapters I argued how the idea of the relationship in the strong sense of the word is itself something socially constructed with its own history and which is especially, if not exclusively, mapped upon the institutions of marriage and the family. This intensity of family interaction gives rise to the importance of family themes and family-based projects in the lives of individuals, and contributes to the reproduction not only of society but also of the institution of the family itself and the particular gender order which is shaped around it. It is here that it is important to consider the contributions made by family and marital therapists, by persons with psychological and psycho-analytic backgrounds and by some systems theorists. All these have an appreciation of the richness, the intensity and the complexity of family themes, processes and interaction even if they often stop at the walls of the house and do not show the way in which these themes are woven out of material from the wider society as well as from the on-going dramas within the household.

This intensity is, of course, something that has its reverberations over time and here too the psychoanalytic and systems perspectives, particularly those that take a multi-generational perspective, have much to offer a sociological account. Here I repeat the distinction between interactions over time and inter-actions across time. Most institutions persist over time; indeed, that is part of the definition of an institution. But the family is particularly and almost uniquely, concerned with interactions and relationships across time, whether we are dealing in the realm of the unconscious or whether we are dealing with more tangible concerns of property and wealth and inequality. Thus it would seem that in a variety of crucial respects the family does have a peculiar part to play in society at the point of intersection between the individual and society and over time. It does not do this alone or 'naturally', although the identification of the family with nature and hence with particularly unique social and psychological functions is the work of ideology.

(VI) QUESTIONS OF IDEOLOGY

I have argued that people's attachment to both their own families and, more generally, to the idea of the family was more than being simply a matter of ideological indoctrination. In this last section I attempted to show what this something 'more' might be. In general it can be argued that in the case of the family, ideology has particularly amenable raw material with which to work. While the family itself is not 'natural', it is to 'do' with nature and things natural in a way that is true for few other institutions. It is not simply a fact that so many of the events and processes with which the family has to deal are so clearly points where biology meets culture – childbirth, nuturing, sexuality, ageing and death. All these events can and have been handled in institutions other than those we conven-tionally understand by the term 'family'. It is more to do with the way in which these biological events are so woven in with social and cultural events, biological parenthood with social parenthood, and with social parenthood the effective linking of the family with questions of time and continuity. The families' particular location at the frontier between the individual and society means that the family appears at one and the same time so universal and yet also so intensely personal.

So, what is meant when it is stated that the family should be 'the focal point of all analyses of ideology' (Collier, 1977, p. 172)? Let us take an example. Humphreys's study of casual sexual encounters between men in public toilets *Tearoom Trade*, shows how many of the participants in these encounters are married. The author argues that these participants prefer quick, impersonal sexual encounters as reflecting a desire to protect family relationships. Often, these men are involved in segregated conjugal role-relationships (Humphreys, 1976, pp. 105–6). What is happening here? Clearly, there is a lot to do with the desire to maintain the appearance of respectability, to avoid degradation both for oneself and for those to whom one is related and perhaps, as Humphreys does not argue, a fear of losing a source of unpaid labour and emotional support. Yet, if we wish to consider how it is that married family life has come to be seen as a token of respectability, or more, a sign of fully paid-up membership of society, we have to look at the work of ideology and the way in which ideology cooperates with the particularly favourable raw material with which it has to deal.

What ideology does, in effect, is to select from the range of possible ways in which a society might handle the relationships between the biological and the cultural, particularly in the sphere of childbirth and parenthood, and to proclaim the method so selected as *the* method, as natural and inevitable. Thus ideology endorses particular domestic arrangements, particular ways of bounding and defining the family, pronounces these ways as not only inevitable and natural but also desirable, cutting off or marginalising possible alternatives and, finally but most importantly, obscuring the fact that these arrangements work to the benefit of particular social orders – patriarchy and capitalism and to particular sets of persons within these orders.

Having got so far it is important to note several difficulties with this, and with most, accounts of ideology.

(a) The implied contrast between ideology and science. Whatever the terms that are used, the assumption is that ideology is in some way a flawed, slanted, less comprehensive form of knowledge than some other forms of knowledge. In some versions (positivist, Marxist) these other forms of knowledge may be labelled as scientific. In other versions (feminist) these other forms of knowledge may be more to do with experience, particularly the experiences of women and of other oppressed groups in society. Of the two versions, I think that the second one is to be preferred since it does not necessarily lay claim to the heavily charged label of 'scientific' (a term which itself might be defined as ideological) with all the connotations of possessing some superior kind of insight that is denied to the majority of the population. Here, the alternative understandings of family (or whatever) are often known or understood experientially but these forms of knowledge are effectively denied legitimacy in the society as a whole. Ideology is to be understood as a form of struggle between competing versions, rather than a simple and once and for all accomplishment.

(b) The implied functionalism which states that these ideological constructions of the family serve the interests of particular social formations, and of particular groups or sets of persons within these formations. We are clearly dealing with complex social processes, and insofar as it is being argued that societies in some sort of way can be said to have a degree of coherence, to hang together, then some sort of functionalism is indeed implied. However, such functional coherence is clearly seen as having certain definable historical roots and is not perceived as being necessary or eternal. Moreover, there is a lack of equivalence between the two main sets of beneficiaries, capitalists and men. It can be argued that the relationship between a particular family form and capitalism is in many respects accidental, or at least not as strong as more functionally inclined Marxists would like. The real strength of the family lies in the way in which it supports the gender order, an order which is linked to capitalism in many ways but which maintains its own autonomy. Since the gender order, or patriarchy, is older than capitalism, the apparently eternal or naturally rooted character seems that much more assured and hence the family is much more amenable to its deployment by capitalism.

There is one final issue to do with ideology. The family is not simply something that is ideologically constructed; it is also itself the conveyer of ideology. Paradoxically, as Collier has noted, the family is able to do this because it appears to be other than ideological, indeed, because it appears to be located in the field of the natural and the universal (Collier, 1977, p. 172).

While there are a variety of particular ideological themes that the family is able to mediate – themes to do with values of hierarchy, the gender order and the class system – it perhaps operates at a more profound level than any of these. The family may, following Althusser, be seen as the main site in which individual subjects are constructed, subjects in the dual sense of being both subjects of a particular regime and subjects in the sense of being the locus of identity, the 'I'. The notion of self or the individual has, of course, a particular burden in capitalist society where it is linked with other values to do with private property and free enterprise. The family, as an ideological apparatus therefore, simultaneously does both the work of constructing and shaping individual subjects and also, in the same moment, itself as the authentic and natural agency for this task.

Any theory that deals with ideology must have some kind of explanation as to how that ideology comes to be challenged, to be seen through or substituted. Many of the more sweeping, all-embracing accounts of ideology fail to do so. One answer, already suggested, that ideology must always, at some point run counter to experience, that there must always be a tension between the two, especially amongst those who have the least stake in the system. This may be true, under certain special circumstances, for women or for the working class. Another answer lies in the fact that ideologies are often contradictory and that certain historical circumstances may show up these contradictions and, at the same time, show these ideologies for what they are, as ideologies. Thus, there are contradictions between the formal rhetoric of capitalism and individualism (which is formally gender free) and the abiding patriarchal values which at times work hand-in-hand with capitalist values but which at other times come into contradiction with it. And finally, following from some of these points, it may be argued that ideologies function on behalf of dominant groups in society and while these groups may attempt to present these particular ideologies as universal, they are always open to challenge from subordinate groups.

(VII) DEFINITIONS AGAIN

We may see now the extent to which Weber was right when he stated that definitions should come towards the end of an enquiry. I have constantly slipped into using the term 'family' in order to avoid any more complex circumnavigation around the term such as 'that which is commonly regarded as the family in our society'. To elaborate upon some distinctions made by Barrett and McIntosh we may distinguish a variety of levels. At the first level there is the family as conventionally understood. In fact these conventional understandings are often more complex than is sometimes supposed, as in the phrase 'I'm having the family over for Bank Holiday'. Nevertheless, we are dealing here with the terms that are conventionally understood and which members use to refer to their own sets of relationships which are based upon birth or marriage. In the second place there is what Barrett and McIntosh call 'familism' which refers to a positive and overt attachment to the idea of the family, especially insofar as this idea is enshrined in one's own family relationships. At a popular level these ideas are expressed in popular phrases such as 'family hold back' or more overt expressions of family loyalty among wealthier sectors of society. Finally, there is familialism, the extension of family terms into everyday life or as popular images. Here we have the brothers and sisters of trade unions or religious orders and the family grocers and family-sized packets of crisps. Thus there are currently available sets of images about the family (ones which often run counter, as has frequently been noted, to actual household compositions) which serve to shape and inform our own understandings of our own families. Or rather there is a dialectic between the two levels.

Definitions of the family, therefore, are ideological constructions, shapings around certain key areas of life and experience. To seek to enquire into the processes by which families are defined, to research into the uses made of terms to do with the family and family processes is to seek to understand the working of ideology. In using the terms family and marriage, one is to some extent reinforcing dominant ideological concerns.

It might be possible to find alternative terms, or to scatter the page with quotation marks or to qualify the words every time they are used, although all these devices are clumsy and never thoroughly effective. Perhaps it is better to seek to deconstruct the word wherever possible, to highlight contradictions and ambiguities in its uses. Thus we have the fairly widespread understanding that the talk of 'family care' (in relation to the elderly or the disabled) in practice means women; this is one example of a process of deconstruction in action.

In the course of this book I have attempted to show that theory is a practical activity, that, as Keynes noted long ago, the activities of women and men in dealing with practical matters are shaped by theories both latent and manifest and also that these practical activities are the proper subject of critical examination by people who might call themselves theorists. In the case of the family, and doubtless of other areas and institutions as well, in theorising we are engaged in a complex and often contradictory activity. We seek to speak of historical circumstances, of structural constraints and of ideological constructions while preserving some sense of human agency, of individual experience and the ability to reflect upon, to use and to work that experience. We seek to call into question the very labels which we use – 'family', 'household' and 'marriage' – while recognising that these terms do have a meaning, or a range of meanings, for persons engaged in their day-to-day lives, and that both these labels and these everyday understandings and experiences have their historical origins. We seek to recognise the special character of family themes and family processes without reification, reductionism or essentialism. The task of theory, as I see it, is to render mysterious without mystifying.

In my previous book, *Social Theory and the Family*, I sought to some extent to show how current social and sociological theories might contribute to our understanding of the family. *To some extent*, I should like here to suggest the opposite orientation, namely, to suggest that understandings of the family may inform the wider processes of sociological theorising. Coward has noted how the study of family and kinship loomed large in nineteenth-century social thought (Coward, 1983, p. 48) and, of course, family metaphors and understandings informed earlier political thought (Schochet, 1975). In more recent years, however, sociological theory has tended to say very little about the family and family theorising has tended to become something of a backwater. Suggestions for the development of a new discipline of 'Famology' may take such discussions even further from the mainstream of social theoretical concerns.

This would be a pity for it is high time that the study of the family, with all the qualifications and hesitations that may surround the use of that term, regained a place at the centre of sociological theorising. This is not because in any obvious or natural sense the family is a 'basic unit' in society or even, although this is of greater significance, that it is widely considered to be a unit of this kind. It is rather because a consideration of some of the issues subsumed under the study of the family takes us to the heart of some of the key issues in sociological theorising. In studying the family we are inevitably confronted with the question of the relationships between levels of analysis, with all the relationships imperfectly captured by the opposition of 'individual' and 'society' or any of the other oppositions considered earlier in this chapter. In such a study we are also inevitably confronted with issues of continuity, of process and of time, issues to do with the relationships across time, between generations and of the reproduction of social formations. In exploring these issues I have encountered a variety of approaches, all of which I have found useful to some degree although this is not to say that any easy synthesis is either possible or to be desired. I am, however, convinced that issues raised by considering two or more contrasting perspectives in juxtaposition can raise questions central, not only to the study of the family, but also to the business of theorising itself.

Notes

CHAPTER 7   SYSTEMS THEORISING

1 I derive the term and notion of a 'running outcome' from my colleague, Isabel Emmett and from our discussions, over a long period of time, about understanding workshop behaviour.
2 The echo here, of Sennett's *Families Against the City*, 1970 is intentional. Sennett's study of middle-class families in Chicago may be seen as a case study in the development of privatisation in the face of a particularly turbulent environment.

CHAPTER 8   FAMILY HISTORY

1 The strength of the belief that, in the past, there was something called an 'extended family' persists to this day as anyone who has taught undergraduate or extra-mural courses on the family will bear witness.
2 Some historians themselves may fail to tackle this problem. Thus most of the papers in the collection edited by Demos and Boocock (1978) stress the family household distinction and underline the processes by which various age categories and cycles are socially constructed, but tend to take the definition of the 'family' itself as a matter for granted.
3 I say 'textbook versions' because I am not convinced that these are correct readings of the original texts or authors.

CHAPTER 9   PHENOMENOLOGICAL APPROACHES

1 It should be noted that the choice of 'family members' to be invited into the studio for discussion is not usually treated as a problematic matter by the producers of the programme; neither is it so treated by Cuff in his use of this material.
2 The symbolic implications of the hard/soft distinction in characterising different research styles has not been lost on some feminist critics (see Roberts, 1981, p. 22).

3 I am indebted to Joel Richman for this felicitous adaption of Lévi-Strauss.

CHAPTER 10 CRITICAL PERSPECTIVES

1 It may be argued that the development of family therapy and systems orientations have made considerable strides in the reconciliation of the individualistic and the holistic at the level of the family.
2 In some senses, biologists, recognising a continuum of sexual characteristics with considerable overlaps and shades of variation are potentially more 'radical' than most sociologists who persist in using everyday cultural categories of 'men' and 'women'.

CHAPTER 11 CONCLUSION

1 This difficulty in interpreting some of the major currents in recent domestic history, when sociological and documentary evidence is in such abundance, may give us reason to pause a little when reading more confident pronouncements about the sentiments that characterised earlier historical periods.
2 We get into deeper water when we move from straightforward physical descriptions to different sets of meanings; it is arguable, for example, as to whether in this deeper sense, the Palace of Westminster is the same thing to a suffragette, a member of Parliament or a policeman guarding the building and its members.
3 I am grateful to Janet Finch for pointing out this usage to me.
4 Societies also exist in and over time; I take account of this troublesome fact later in this chapter.

Bibliography

ABRAMS, P. and McCULLOCH, A., 1976, *Communes, Sociology and Society,* Cambridge University Press.

ACKERMAN, N.W., 1966, *Treating the Troubled Family*, New York, Basic Books.

ACKERMAN, N.W. (ed.), 1970, *Family Process*, New York, Basic Books.

ALTHUSSER, L., 1971, *Lenin and Philosophy and Other Essays*, London, New Left Books.

ANDERSON, M., 1980, *Approaches to the History of the Western Family*, London, Macmillan.

ANDERSON, M. (ed.), 1980, *Sociology of the Family* (2nd edn), Harmondsworth, Penguin.

ANDOLFI, M., 1979, *Family Therapy: An Interactional Approach*, New York, Plenum.

ANGYAL, A., 1941, 'A logic of systems', reprinted in Emery (ed.), 1969, pp. 17–29.

APONTE, H.J. and VAN DEUSEN, J.M., 1981, 'Structural family therapy', in Gurman and Kniskern (eds), pp. 310–60.

ARIÈS, P., 1972, *Centuries of Childhood*, London, Cape.

ARMISTEAD, N. (ed.), 1974, *Reconstructing Social Psychology*, Harmondsworth, Penguin.

ASKHAM, J., 1982, 'Telling stories', *Sociological Review*, 30(4), pp. 555–73.

BACKETT, K.C., 1982, *Mothers and Fathers*, London, Macmillan.

BANNISTER, K. and PINCUS, L., 1971, *Shared Phantasy in Marital Problems*, London, Tavistock.

BANTON, M. (ed.), 1966, *The Social Anthropology of Complex Societies*, London, Tavistock.

BARRETT, M., 1980, *Women's Oppression Today*, London, Verso.

BARRETT, M. and McINTOSH, M., 1979, 'Christine Delphy: towards a materialist feminism?', *Feminist Review*, 1, pp. 95–106.

BARRETT, M. and McINTOSH, M., 1982, *The Anti-Social Family*, London, Verso.

303

Bibliography

BATESON, G., 1973, *Steps to an Ecology of Mind*, London, Paladin.

BELL, C. and NEWBY, H., 1976, 'Husbands and wives: dynamics of the deferential dialectic', in Barker and Allen (eds), *Dependence and Exploitation in Work and Marriage*, London, Longmans, pp. 152–68.

BELL, N.M., 1970, 'Extended family relations of disturbed and well families', in Ackerman (ed.), pp. 204–22.

BELL, R.E., 1975, *Family Therapy*, New York, Jason Aronson.

BENSON, D. and HUGHES, J.A., 1983, *The Perspective of Ethnomethodology*, London, Longmans.

BERARDO, F.M. (ed.), 1980, 'Decade review', *Journal of Marriage and the Family*, 42(4).

BERGER, B. and BERGER, P.L., 1983, *The War Over the Family*, London, Hutchinson.

BERGER, P.L. and KELLNER, H., 1964, 'Marriage and the construction of reality', *Diogenes*, pp. 1–23, reprinted in Anderson (ed.), 1980, pp. 302–24.

BERNARD, J., 1973, *The Future of Marriage*, New York, Souvenir Press.

BERNSTEIN, B., 1971, *Class, Codes and Control*, vol. 1, London, Routledge & Kegan Paul.

BODIN, A.M., 1981, 'The interactional view: family therapy approaches of the mental research institute', in Gurman and Kniskern (eds), pp. 267–309.

BOTTOMLEY, P., 1979, *Options for Family Policy*, London, Family Welfare Association.

BOURDIEU, P., 1976, 'Marriage strategies as strategies of social reproduction', in Foster and Ranum (eds), *Family and Society*, Baltimore, Johns Hopkins University Press, pp. 117–44.

BRADNEY, A., 1980, 'The family in family law', *Family Law*, 9(8)., pp. 244–8.

BRANNEN, J. and COLLARD, 1982, *Marriages in Trouble*, London, Tavistock.

BRODERICK, C.B. and SCHRADER, S.S., 1981, 'The history of professional marriage and family therapy', in Gurman and Kniskern (eds), pp. 5–35.

BROWN, M. and MADGE, N., 1982, *Despite the Welfare State*, London, Heinemann.

BURMAN, S. (ed.), 1979, *Fit Work for Women*, London, Croom Helm.

BURR, W.R., 1973, *Theory Construction and the Sociology of the Family*, New York, John Wiley.

BURR, W.R., HILL, R., NYE, L. and REISS, I. (eds), 1979, *Contemporary Theories about the Family* (vols I and II), Glencoe, Ill, The Free Press.

BURR, W.R. and LEIGH, G.K., 1983, 'Famology: a new discipline', *Journal of Marriage and the Family*, 45(3), pp. 467–80.

CAMBRIDGE WOMEN'S STUDY GROUP, 1981, *Women in Society*, London, Virago.

CARR, E.H., 1964, *What is History?*, Harmondsworth, Penguin.

CARTER, E.A. and McGOLDRICK. M. (eds), 1980, *The Family Life Cycle: A Framework for Family Therapy*, New York, Gardner Press.

CHODOROW, N., 1978, *The Reproduction of Mothering*, University of California Press.

COLLIER, A., 1977, *R.D. Laing: The Philosophy and Politics of Psychotherapy*, Sussex, The Harvester Press.

CONNERTON, P. (ed.), 1976, *Critical Sociology*, Harmondsworth, Penguin.

COURTENAY, M., 1968, *Sexual Discord in Marriage*, London, Tavistock.

COUSSINS, J. and COOTE, A., March 1981, *The Family in the Firing Line*, Poverty Pamphlet No. 51, London, National Council for Civil Liberties and Child Poverty Action Group.

COWARD, R., 1983, *Patriarchal Precedents*, London, Routledge & Kegan Paul.

CRAIB, I., 1984, *Modern Social Theory*, Brighton, Wheatsheaf.

CRAVEN, E., RIMMER, L. and WICKS, M., 1982, *Family Issues and Public Policy*, London, Study Commission on the Family.

CROMWELL, R. and OLSON, D.H. (eds), 1975, *Power in Families*, Beverly Hills, Sage.

CUFF, E.C., 1980, *Some Issues in Studying the Problems of Versions in Everyday Situations*, University of Manchester, Department of Sociology, Occasional Paper No. 3.

CUISENIER, J. (ed.), 1977, *The Family Life Cycle in European Societies*, The Hague, Mouton.

CUNNINGHAM-BURLEY, S.J., 1983, *The Meaning and Significance of Grandparenthood*, University of Aberdeen, Department of Sociology, unpublished doctoral thesis.

CUNNISON, S., 1983, 'Participation in local union organisation: school meals staff: a case study', in Gamarnikow *et al.*, 1983a, *Gender, Class and Work*, pp. 77–95.

DALLEY, G., 1983, 'Ideologies of care: a feminist contribution to the debate', *Critical Social Policy*, 8 3(2), pp. 72–82.

DAVID, M., 1983, 'The New Right in the USA and Britain: a new anti-feminist moral economy', *Critical Social Policy*, 2(3), pp. 31–45.

DAVIDOFF, L. and HALL, C., Sept. 1982, 'Home sweet home', *New Statesman*.

DEEM, R., 1982, 'Women, leisure and inequality', *Leisure Studies*, 1(1), pp. 29–46.

DELPHY, C., 1977, *The Main Enemy*, London, Women's Research and Resources Centre.

DEMAUSE, L. (ed.), 1976, *The History of Childhood*, New York, Souveneir Press.

DEMOS, J. and BOOCOCK, S.S. (eds), 1978, *Turning Points: Historical and Sociological Essays on the Family*, University of Chicago Press.

DONZELOT, J., 1980, *The Policing of Families*, London, Hutchinson.

DUHL, B.S. and DUHL, F.J., 1981, 'Integrative family therapy', in Gurman and Kniskern (eds), pp. 483–513.

Bibliography

EASLEA, B., 1981, *Science and Sexual Oppression*, London, Weidenfeld & Nicholson.

EDGELL, S., 1980, *Middle-Class Couples*, London, Allen & Unwin.

EDHOLM, F., HARRIS, O. and YOUNG, K., 1977, 'Conceptualising women', *Critique of Anthropology*, 3 (9/10), pp. 101–30.

EDWARDS, S.M., 1981, *Female Sexuality and the Law*, Oxford, Martin Robertson.

EDWARDS, S.M., 1984, *Women on Trial*, Manchester University Press.

EGAN, G., 1975, *The Skilled Helper*, Monterey, Brooks/Cole Publishing House.

EICHLER, M., 1979, *The Double Standard: A Feminist Critique of the Social Sciences*, London, Croom Helm.

EISENSTEIN, Z.R. (ed.), 1979, *Capitalist Patriarchy and the Case for Socialist Feminism*, New York, Monthly Review Press.

ELDER, G.H. Jnr, 1978a, 'Family history and the life course', in Hareven (ed.), pp. 17–64.

ELDER, G.H., Jnr, 1978b, 'Approaches to social change and the family', in Demos and Boocock (eds), pp. 1 39.

ELSHTAIN, J.B., 1981, *Public Man, Private Woman*, Oxford, Martin Robertson.

ELSHTAIN, J.B., (ed.), 1982, *The Family in Political Thought*, Brighton, Harvester.

ELSON, D. and PEARSON, R., 1981, 'The subordination of women and the internationalisation of factory production', in Young *et al.* (eds), pp. 144–66.

EMERY, F.E. (ed.), 1969, *Systems Thinking*, Harmondsworth, Penguin.

EMERY, F.E. and TRIST, E.L., 1960, 'Socio-technical systems', in Emery (ed.), 1969, pp. 281–96.

EMERY, F.E. and TRIST, E.L., 1972, *Towards a Social Ecology*, London, Plenum Press.

EMMETT, I., 1983, *Is Social Reality Merely a Social Construct?*, University of Manchester, Department of Sociology, Occasional Paper No. 10.

ENGLISH, C.S. and PEARSON, G.H.J., 1947 (3rd edn, 1963), *Emotional Problems of Living*, London, Allen & Unwin.

EPSTEIN, B. and ELLIS, K., 1983, 'The pro-family left in the United States: two comments', *Feminist Review*, 14, pp. 35–50.

EPSTEIN, N.B. and BISHOP, D.S., 1981, 'Problem-centred systems therapy of the family', in Gurman and Kniskern (eds), pp. 444–82.

FAMILY WELFARE ASSOCIATION, 1974, *Family Therapy in Social Work*, London, Family Welfare Association.

FIELD, F., 1980, *Fair Shares for Families*, London, Study Commission on the Family, Occasional Paper No. 3.

FINCH, J., 1983, *Married to the Job*, London, Allen & Unwin.

FINCH, J., 1984, 'Community care: developing non-sexist alternatives', *Critical Social Policy*, 9, pp. 6–18.

FINCH, J., 1984a, 'It's good to have someone to talk to: the ethics and politics of interviewing women', in Bell and Roberts (eds), *Social Researching*, London, Routledge & Kegan Paul.

FITZ, J. and HOOD-WILLIAMS, J., 1982, 'The generation game', in Robbins *et al.* (eds), *Rethinking Social Inequality*, Aldershot, Gower.

FLANDRIN, J.-L., 1979, *Families in Former Times*, Cambridge University Press.

FLETCHER, C., 1976, 'The relevance of domestic property to sociological understanding', *Sociology*, 10(3), pp. 451–68.

FOUCAULT, ML., 1979, *History of Sexuality*, London, Allen Lane.

FRAMO, J.L., 1981, 'The integration of marital therapy with sessions with family of origin', in Gurman and Kniskern (eds), pp. 133–58.

FRANKFURT INSTITUTE FOR SOCIAL RESEARCH, 1973 (1956), *Aspects of Sociology*, London, Heinemann Educational Books.

FRANKLIN, A.W. (ed.), 1983, *Family Matters (Perspectives on the Family and Social Policy)*, Oxford, Pergamon.

FREEMAN, M.D.A., 1979, 'Dealing with domestic violence', *Family Law*, 9, pp. 110–18.

FRIEDAN, B., 1965 (1st pub. 1963), *The Feminine Mystique*, Harmondsworth, Penguin.

FRIEDAN, B., 1981, *The Second Stage*, New York, Summit Books.

FRIEDMAN, A.S., 1970, 'Family therapy as conducted in the home', in Ackerman (ed.), pp. 102–10.

FRIEDMAN, A.S. and SARAH, E. (eds), 1982, *On the Problem of Men*, London, The Women's Press.

FULLMER, D. and BERNARD, H.W., 1968, *Family Consultation*, Boston, Houghton Mifflin.

GAMARNIKOW, E., MORGAN, D., PURVIS, J. and TAYLORSON, D. (eds), 1983a, *Class, Gender and Work*, London, Heinemann.

GAMARNIKOW, E. *et al.*, 1983b, *The Public and the Private*, London, Heinemann.

GIDDENS, A., 1979, *Central Problems in Social Theory*, London, Macmillan.

GILLESPIE, D., 1971, 'Who has the power? The marital struggle', *Journal of Marriage and the Family*, 33, pp. 445–58.

GITTINS, D., 1982, *Fair Sex*, London, Hutchinson.

GLENNON, L.M., 1979, *Women and Dualism (A Sociology of Knowledge Analysis)*, London, Longmans.

GOLDING, P. and MIDDLETON, S., 1982, *Images of Welfare*, Oxford, Martin Robertson.

GOLDTHORPE, J.H. (with C. Llewellyn and C. Payne), 1980, *Social Mobility and Class Structure in Modern Britain*, Oxford, Clarendon Press.

GONIN, C., 1984, 'Work and marriage', *Marriage Guidance*.

GOODE, W.J., 1956, *After Divorce*, Glencoe, Ill., The Free Press.

GOODE, W.J., 1982, 'Why men resist', in Thorne and Yalom (eds), pp. 131–50.

GOODMAN, I.F., 1983, 'Television's role in family interaction: a

Bibliography

family systems perspective', *Journal of Family Issues*, 4(2), pp. 405–24.

GOODY, J., 1983, *The Development of Family and Marriage in Europe*, Cambridge University Press.

GRAHAM, H., 1983, 'Do her answers fit his questions? Women and the survey method', in Gamarnikow *et al.*, 1983b, pp. 132–46.

GREENGROSS, W., 1976, *Entitled to Love*, London, National Marriage Guidance Council.

GURMAN, A.S., 1973, 'Marital therapy: emerging trends in research and practice', *Family Process*, 12(1), pp. 45–54.

GURMAN, A.S. and KNISKERN, D.P. (eds), 1981, *Handbook of Family Therapy*, New York, Brunner/Mazel.

GUSFIELD, J.R., 1963, *Symbolic Crusade,* Urbana, University of Illinois Press.

GUTHRIE, L. and MATTINSON, J., 1971, *Brief Casework with a Marital Problem*, London, Tavistock.

HALEY, J., 1979, *Problem Solving Therapy*, New York, Jossey Bass.

HALL, C.M., 1979, 'Family systems: a developing trend in family theory', in Harris *et al.* (eds), *The Sociology of the Family: New Directions for Britain*, Keele, Sociological Review Monographs, No. 28, pp. 19–31.

HALMOS, P., 1978 (2nd edn), *The Faith of the Counsellors*, London, Constable.

HALSEY, A.H. *et al.,* 1980, *Origins and Destinations*, Oxford, Clarendon Press.

HARBURY, C.D. and HITCHENS, D., 1979, *Inheritance and Wealth Inequality in Britain*, London, Allen & Unwin.

HARE-MUSTIN, R.T., 1978, 'A feminist approach to family therapy', *Family Process*, 17(2), pp. 181–94.

HAREVEN, T.K., 1978, 'The dynamics of kin in an industrial community', in Demos and Boocock (eds), pp. 151–82.

HAREVEN, T.K. (ed.), 1978, *Transitions: The Family Life Course in Historical Perspective*, New York, Academic Press.

HARRIS, B., 1977, 'The value of a wife', *Family Law*, 7, pp. 5–10.

HARRIS, C.C., 1983, *The Family and Industrial Society*, London, Allen & Unwin.

HARRIS, O., 1981, 'Households as natural units', in Young *et al.* (eds), pp. 49–68.

HART, N., 1976, *When Marriage Ends*, London, Tavistock.

HAYES, M., 1978, 'Evicting a spouse from the matrimonial home', *Family Law*, 8, pp. 4–7.

HEPWORTH, M. and TURNER, B., 1982, *Confession*, London, Routledge & Kegan Paul.

HESS, R.D. and HANDEL, G., 1950, *Family Worlds*, Chicago University Press.

HINCHCLIFFE, M.K., HOOPER, D. and ROBERTS, F.J., 1978, *The Melancholy Marriage*, London, John Wiley.

HOLMAN, T.B. and BURR, W.R., 1980, 'Beyond the beyond: the

growth of family theories', in *Journal of Marriage and the Family*, 42(4), 1970, pp. 729–42.

HUMPHREYS, L., 1976, *Tearoom Trade*, (2nd edn), London, Duckworth.

HUNT, P., 1980, *Gender and Class Consciousness*, London, Macmillan.

ILLICII, I., 1983, *Gender*, London, Boyers.

JACOBY, R., 1975, *Social Amnesia*, Boston, Beacon Press.

JEWSON, N.D., 1976, 'The disappearance of the sick-man from medical cosmology', *Sociology*, 10(1), pp. 225–44.

JORDAN, W., 1972, *The Social Worker in Family Situations*, London, Routledge & Kegan Paul.

JORDAN, B., 1982, 'Families and personal social services', in Rapoport, Fogarty and Rapoport (eds), pp. 447–58.

JORDANOVA, L.J., 1981, 'The history of the family', in Cambridge Women's Study Group, pp. 41–54.

JOURNAL OF MARRIAGE AND THE FAMILY, August 1971, Special Issue on 'Sexism in family studies', Vol. 33(3).

KANTER, R.M., 1978, 'Families, family processes and economic life: towards systematic analysis of social historical research', in Demos and Boocock (eds), pp. 316–39.

KANTOR, D. and LEHR, W., 1973, *Inside the Family*, San Francisco, Jossey Bass Inc.

KAPLAN, H.S., 1974, *The New Sex Therapy*, London, Ballière Tindall.

KASLOW, F.W., 1981, *Divorce and Divorce Therapy*, in Gurman and Kniskern (eds), pp. 662–96.

KATZ, D. and KAHN, R.L., 1966, 'Common characteristics of open systems', reprinted in Emery (ed.), 1969, pp. 86–104.

KELLY-GADOL, J., 1976, 'The social relations of the sexes: methodological implications of women's history', *Signs*, 1(4), pp. 809–23.

KEOHANE, N.A., ROSALDO, M.Z. and GELPI, B.C. (eds), 1982, *Feminist Theory: A Critique of Ideology*, Brighton, Harvester.

KESSLER, S.J. and McKENNA, W.,1978, *Gender: An Ethnomethodological Approach*, New York, John Wiley.

KING, M., 1974, 'Maternal love – fact or myth?', *Family Law*, pp. 61–4.

KING, R. and NUGENT, N. (eds), 1979, *Respectable Rebels: Middle Class Campaigns in Britain in the 1970s*, London, Hodder & Stoughton.

KINGSTON, P., 1982, 'Power and influence in the environment of family therapy', *Journal of Family Therapy*, 4, pp. 211–27.

KLEIN, M. and RIVIERE, J., 1962, *Love, Hate, and Reparation*, London, The Hogarth Press.

KOMAROVSKY, M., 1962, *Blue Collar Marriage*, New York, Random House.

KOVEL, M., 1978, *A Complete Guide to Therapy*, Harmondsworth, Penguin.

Bibliography

LAND, H., 1975, 'The myth of the male breadwinner', *New Society*, Oct. pp. 71–3.

LAND, H., 1980, 'The family wage', *Feminist Review*, 6, pp. 55–78.

LAND, H., 1983, 'Who still cares for the family? Recent developments in income maintenance, taxation and family law', in Lewis (ed.), pp. 64–85.

LASCH, C., 1977, *Haven in a Heartless World*, New York, Basic Books.

LASLETT, B., 1980, 'Beyond methodology: the place of theory in quantitative historical research', *American Sociological Review*, 45, pp. 214–28.

LATEY, W., 1970, *The Tide of Divorce*, London, Longmans.

LEE, J., 1984, 'Innocent victims and evil-doers', *Women's Studies International Forum*, 7(1), pp. 69–74.

LEONARD, D., 1980, *Sex and Generation*, London, Tavistock.

LEONARD BARKER, D.,1978, 'A proper wedding', in Corbin (ed.), *The Couple*, Harmondsworth, Penguin, pp. 56–78.

LEWIS, J. (ed.), 1983, *Women's Welfare, Women's Rights*, London, Croom Helm.

LEWIS, J., 1983, 'Dealing with dependency: states' practices and social realities', in Lewis (ed.), pp. 17–37.

LEWIS, L.S. and BOISSETT, D., 1967–8, 'Sex as work: a study of a vocational counselling', *Social Problems*, 15, pp. 8–18.

LIEBERMAN, S., 1979, *Transgenerational Family Therapy*, London, Croom Helm.

LOFTHOUSE, W.F., 1912, *Ethics and the Family*, London, Hodder & Stoughton.

LOWE, G.R., 1972, *The Growth of Personality*, Harmondsworth, Penguin.

LOWN, J., 1983, 'Not so much a factory, more a form of patriarchy: gender and class during industrialisation', in Gamarnikow *et al.*, (eds), 1983a, pp. 28–45.

LUKES, S., 1968, 'Methodological individualism reconsidered', *British Journal of Sociology*, 19, pp. 119–29.

MACGREGOR, R., 1970, 'Multiple-impact psychotherapy with families', in Ackerman (ed.), pp. 33–47.

MACKINTOSH, M.M., 1979, 'Domestic labour and the household', in Burman (ed.), pp. 173–91.

MACTINTOSH, M.M., 1981, 'The sexual division of labour and the subordination of women', in Young *et al.* (eds), pp. 1–15.

MARRIAGE MATTERS, 1980, *Proceedings of Day Conference*.

MATTHEWS, S.H., 1982, 'Rethinking sociology through a feminist perspective', *American Sociologist*, 17, pp. 29–35.

McINTOSH, M., 1979, 'The welfare state and the needs of the dependent family', in Burman (ed.), pp. 153–72.

McKEE, L. and O'BRIEN, M., 1983, 'Interviewing men: taking gender seriously', in Gamarnikow *et al.*, 1983b, pp. 147–61.

McLAIN, R. and WEIGERT, A.,1979, 'Toward a phenomenological sociology of the family: a programmatic essay', in Burr *et al.* (eds), pp. 160–205.

MERTON, R.K., 1957, *Social Theory and Social Structure* (2nd edn), Glencoe Ill., The Free Press.

MILLER, S.E., 1980, 'Review: Journal of Marriage and the Family', *Journal of Marriage and the Family*, 42(2), pp. 1032–4.

MILLS, C.W., 1959, *The Sociological Imagination*, New York, Oxford University Press.

MITCHELL, J.C. (ed.), 1969, *Social Networks in Urban Situations*, Manchester University Press.

MITCHELL, J., 1971, *Women's Estate*, Harmondsworth, Penguin.

MITCHELL, J., 1975, *Psychoanalysis and Feminism*, Harmondsworth, Penguin.

MITTERAUER, M. and SIEDER, R., 1982, *The European Family*, Oxford, Blackwell.

MONGER, M., 1971, *Husband, Wife and Caseworker*, London, Butterworths.

MORGAN, D.H.J., 1969, *Theoretical and Conceptual Problems in the Study of Social Relations at Work: An Analysis of Differing Definitions of Women's Roles in a Northern Factory*, University of Manchester, unpublished doctoral thesis.

MORGAN, D.H.J., 1975, *Social Theory and the Family*, London, Routledge & Kegan Paul.

MORGAN, D.H.J., 1979, 'New directions in family research and theory', in Harris *et al.* (eds), *The Sociology of the Family*, Keele, Sociological Review Monograph No. 28, pp. 3–18.

MORGAN, D.H.J., 1981, 'Men, masculinity and the process of sociological enquiry', in Roberts (ed.), *Doing Feminist Research*, London, Routledge & Kegan Paul.

MORGAN, D.H.J., 1982, *Berger and Kellner's Construction of the Family*, University of Manchester, Department of Sociology, Occasional Paper No. 7.

MORGAN, D.H.J., 1984, *Gender*, London, Longmans.

MORGAN, D.H.J., 1985, 'Gender: when is a key variable not a key variable?', in Burgess (ed.), *Key Variables in Social Research*.

MOSS, P. and FONDA, N. (eds), 1980, *Work and Family*, London, Temple Smith.

MOUNT, F., 1982, *The Subversive Family*, London, Jonathan Cape.

NAVARRO, V., 1982, 'The crisis of the international capitalist order and its implication for the welfare state', *Critical Social Policy*, 2(1), pp. 43–62.

NORTH, M., 1972, *The Secular Priests*, London, Allen & Unwin.

NYE, F. Ivan *et al.*, 1976, *Role Structure and Analysis of the Family*, Beverly Hills, Sage.

OAKLEY, A., 1974, *The Sociology of Housework*, Oxford, Martin Robertson.

OAKLEY, A., 1976, 'Wisewoman and medicine man: changes in the management of childbirth', in Mitchell and Oakley (eds), *The Rights and Wrongs of Women*, Harmondsworth, Penguin, pp. 17–58.

Bibliography

OAKLEY, A., 1981, *Subject Women*, Oxford, Martin Robertson.
OAKLEY, A., 1983, 'Women and health policy', in Lewis (ed.), pp. 103–29.
O'BRIEN, M., 1982, 'Feminist theory and dialectical logic', in Keohane *et al.* (eds), pp. 99–112.
OSMOND, M.W., 1980, 'Cross-societal family research: a macro-sociological overview of the seventies', *Journal of Marriage and the Family*, 42(2), pp. 995–1016.
PAHL, J. and PAHL, R., 1971, *Managers and their Wives*, Harmondsworth, Penguin.
PARR, J., 1980, *Labouring Children*, London, Croom Helm.
PEARSON, G., 1974, 'Prisoners of love: the reification of the family in family therapy', in Armistead (ed.), pp. 137–56.
PHILLIPSON, C., 1983, *Capitalism and the Construction of Old Age*, London, Macmillan.
PINCUS, L., 1976, *Death and the Family*, London, Faber.
PINCUS, L. *et al.* (eds), 1960, *Marriage: Studies in Emotional Conflict and Growth*, London, Methuen.
PLUMMER, K., 1978, 'Men in love: observation on male homosexual couples', in Corbin (ed.), *The Couple*, Harmondsworth, Penguin, pp. 173–200.
POLAK, L.A., 1975, '"Common Law" wife protected by Rent Acts', *Family Law*, 5, pp. 206–7.
POLLERT, A., 1981, *Girls, Wives, Factory Lives*, London Macmillan.
POLLERT, A., 1983, 'Women, gender relations and wage labour', in Gamarnikow *et al.* (eds), 1983a, pp. 94–114.
PORTER, M., 1983, *Home, Work and Class Consciousness*, Manchester University Press.
POSTER, M., 1978, *Critical Theory and the Family*, New York, The Seabury Press.
POULTER, S., 1982, 'Child custody – recent developments', *Family Law*, 12(1), pp. 5–12.
PRINGLE, M.K., 1974, *The Needs of Children*, London, Hutchinson.
PURCELL, K., 1982, 'Female manual workers, fatalism and the reinforcement of inequalities', in Robbins *et al.* (eds), *Rethinking Social Inequality*, Aldershot, Gower.
RANDALL, V., 1982, *Women and Politics*, London, Macmillan.
RAPOPORT, R., RAPOPORT, R.N. with STRELITZ, Z., 1975, *Leisure and the Family Life Cycle*, London, Routledge & Kegan Paul.
RAPOPORT, R. and RAPOPORT, R.N., 1976, *Dual-Career Families Re-examined* (2nd edn), Oxford, Martin Robertson.
RAPOPORT, R., RAPOPORT, R.N. and STRELITZ, Z.,1977, *Fathers, Mothers and Others*, London, Routledge & Kegan Paul.
RAPOPORT, R. and RAPOPORT, R.N., 1980, 'The impact of work on the family', in Moss and Fonda (eds), *Work and Family*, London, Maurice Temple-Smith.
RAPOPORT, R.N., 1960, *Community as Doctor*, London, Tavistock.
RAPOPORT, R.N., FOGARTY, M.P. and RAPOPORT, R. (eds), 1982, *Families in Britain*, London, Routledge & Kegan Paul.

RAPOPORT, R.N., RAPOPORT, R. with BUMSTEAD, J. (eds), 1978, *Working Couples*, London, Routledge & Kegan Paul.

RAPOPORT, R.N. and RAPOPORT, R., 1982, 'British families in transition', in Rapoport, Fogarty and Rapoport (eds), pp. 475–99.

RAPP, R., 1982, 'Family and class in contemporary America: notes towards an understanding of ideology', in Thorne and Yalom (eds), pp. 168–87.

RAYNER, E.,1971, *Human Development*, London, Allen & Unwin.

REICHE, R., 1970, *Sexuality and Class Struggle*, London, New Left Books.

REIGER, J.F.T., 1981, 'Family therapy's missing question: why the plight of the modern family?', *Journal of Family Therapy*, 3, pp. 293–308.

REITER, R.R. (ed.), 1975, *Toward an Anthropology of Women*, New York, Monthly Review Press.

ROBERTS, H. (ed.), 1981, *Doing Feminist Research*, London, Routledge & Kegan Paul.

ROBERTSON, R., 1969, *The Sociological Interpretation of Religion*, Oxford, Blackwell.

ROSALDO, M.Z. and LAMPHERE, L. (eds), 1974, *Women, Culture and Society*, Stanford University Press.

ROSE, J., 1983, 'Femininity and its discontents', *Feminist Review*, 14, pp. 5–21.

ROSSI, A.S., KAGAN, J. and HAREVEN, T.K. (eds), 1978, *The Family*, New York, W.W. Norton & Co.

RUBIN, G.,1975, 'The traffic in women: notes on the "political economy of sex"', in Reiter (ed.), pp. 157–210.

RUDDICK, S., 1982, 'Maternal thinking', in Thorne and Yalom, pp. 76–94.

RUSHTON, P., 1979, 'Marxism, domestic labour and the capitalist economy: a note on recent discussions' in Harris (ed.), *The Sociology of the Family*, Keele, Sociological Review Monograph No. 28, pp. 32–48.

SAMUELS, A., 1976, 'The Children's Act, 1975', *Family Law*, 6, pp. 5–8.

SAMUELS, A., 1976a, 'The mistress and the law', *Family Law*, 6, pp. 152–8.

SANDAY, P.R., 1981, *Female Power and Male Dominance (On the Origins of Sexual Inequality)*, Cambridge University Press.

SARGENT, L. (ed.), 1981, *The Unhappy Marriage of Marxism and Feminism,* London, Pluto Press.

SATIR, V., 1967 (revised edn), *Conjoint Family Therapy*, Palo Alto, Science and Behavior Books, Inc.

SAYERS, J., 1982, 'Psychoanalysis and personal politics: a response to Elizabeth Wilson', *Feminist Review*, 10, pp. 91–5.

SCANZONI, J. and FOX, G.L., 1980, 'Sex roles, family and society: the seventies and beyond', *Journal of Marriage and the Family*, 42(2), pp. 743–58.

Bibliography

SCHOCHET, G.J., 1975, *Patriarchalism in Political Thought,* Oxford, Blackwell.

SCOTT, J., 1982, *The Upper Classes,* London, Macmillan.

SCRUTON, R., 1980, *The Meaning of Conservatism,* Harmondsworth, Penguin.

SEDGWICK, P., 1982, *PsychoPolitics,* London, Pluto Press.

SEGAL, L., 1983, *What is to be Done About the Family?,* Harmondsworth, Penguin.

SEGAL, L., 1983, '"Smash the family"? Recalling the 1960s', in Segal (ed.), pp. 25–64.

SHILS, E., 1981, *Tradition,* London, Faber.

SINGER, I., 1973, *The Goals of Human Sexuality,* London, Wildwood House.

SKYNNER, A.C.R., 1976, *One Flesh: Separate Persons,* London, Constable.

SKYNNER, A.C.R., 1981, 'An Open Systems, group-analytic approach to family therapy, in Gurman and Kniskern (eds), pp. 39–84.

SMITH, D.E., 1974, 'Woman's perspective as a radical critique of sociology', *Sociological Inquiry,* 44(1), pp. 7–13.

SMITH, D.E., 1978, 'K is mentally ill', *Sociology,* 12, pp. 23–53.

SMITH, D.E., 1978a, 'A peculiar eclipsing: women's exclusion from man's culture', *Women Studies International Quarterly 1,* pp. 281–96.

SPECK, R.V. and REUVENI, V., 1970, 'Network therapy – a developing concept', in Ackerman (ed.), pp. 92–101.

SPIEGEL, D., 1982, 'Mothering, fathering and mental illness', in Thorne and Yalom (eds), pp. 95–110.

SPREY, J., 1979, 'Conflict theory and the study of marriage and the family', in Burr *et al.* (eds), vol. II, pp. 130–59.

STACEY, M., 1981, 'The division of labour revisited or overcoming the two Adams', in Abrams *et al.* (eds), *Practice and Progress: British Sociology, 1950–1980,* London, Allen & Unwin.

STANLEY, L. and WISE, S., 1983, *Breaking Out: Feminist Consciousness and Feminist Research,* London, Routledge & Kegan Paul.

STEDMAN-JONES, G., 1976, 'From historical sociology to theoretical history', *British Journal of Sociology,* 27, pp. 295–305.

STONE, L., 1977, *The Family, Sex and Marriage in England, 1500–1800,* London, Weidenfeld & Nicholson.

STORR, A., 1983, 'A psychotherapist looks at depression', *British Journal of Psychiatry,* 143, pp. 431–5.

STUDY COMMISSION ON THE FAMILY, 1983, *Families in the Future,* London, Study Commission on the Family.

SUSSMAN, M.B., 1970, 'Adaptive, directive and integrative behaviour of today's families', in Ackerman (ed.), pp. 223–34.

TAYLORSON, D., 1980, *Highly Educated Women: A Sociological Study of Women,* Ph.D. Candidates, University of Manchester, unpublished doctoral thesis.

THORNE, B., 1982, 'Feminist rethinking of the family: an overview', in Thorne and Yalom (eds), pp. 1–24.

THORNE, B. and YALOM, M. (eds), 1982, *Rethinking the Family: Some Feminist Questions*, New York, Longmans.

THORNES, B. and COLLARD, J., 1979, *Who Divorces?*, London, Routledge & Kegan Paul.

TOWNSEND, P., 1979, *Poverty in the United Kingdom*, Harmondsworth, Penguin.

TRACEY, M. and MORRISON, D., 1979, *Whitehouse*, London, Macmillan.

VOYSEY, M., 1975, *A Constant Burden*, London, Routledge & Kegan Paul.

WADEL, C., 1979, 'The hidden work of everyday life', in Wallman (ed.), *Social Anthropology of Work*, London, Academic Press.

WALBY, S., 1983, 'Patriarchal structures: the case of unemployment', in Gamarnikow *et al.* (eds), 1983a, pp. 149–66.

WALROND-SKINNER, S., 1976, *Family Therapy: The Treatment of Natural Systems*, London, Routledge & Kegan Paul.

WHITAKER, C.A. and KEITH, D.V., 1981, 'Symbolic-experiential family therapy', in Gurman and Kniskern (eds), pp. 187–225.

WHITEHEAD, A., 1981, 'I'm hungry, Mum: the politics of domestic budgeting', in Young *et al.* (eds), pp. 88–111.

WICKS, M., 1982, 'A family cause? Voluntary bodies, pressure groups and politics', in Rapoport, Fogarty and Rapoport (eds), pp. 459–72.

WILLIAMS, R., 1980, *Problems in Materialism and Culture*, London, Verso.

WILLIAMS, R., 1983, *Keywords* (2nd edn), London, Fontana.

WOOLF, V., 1943, *Three Guineas*, London, The Hogarth Press.

WORKING PARTY ON MARRIAGE GUIDANCE, 1979, *Marriage Matters*, London, HMSO.

WRIGHT, E.O. and PERRONE, L., 1977, 'Marxist class categories and income inequality', *American Sociological Review*, 42, pp. 32–55.

WRIGHT, E.O. *et al.*, 1982, 'The American class structure', *American Sociological Review*, 47, pp. 607–26.

YOUNG, K. *et al.* (eds), 1981, *Of Marriage and the Market*, London, CSE Books.

YOUNG, M. and WILLMOTT, P. L., 1975 (1st pub. 1973), *The Symmetrical Family*, Harmondsworth, Penguin.

ZARETSKY, E., 1982, 'The place of the family in the origins of the welfare state', in Thorne and Yalom (eds), pp. 188–224.

Name index

Subject index

Subject index